# WORLD PANORAMA

## 1918–1933

*International News Photos.*

LLOYD GEORGE, CLEMENCEAU AND PRESIDENT WILSON WALKING THROUGH THE GARDENS AT VERSAILLES

# WORLD PANORAMA

## 1918–1933

GEORGE SELDES

WITH ILLUSTRATIONS

LITTLE, BROWN, AND COMPANY

BOSTON 1933

Published June, 1933

PRINTED IN THE UNITED STATES OF AMERICA

*For Helen and her generation*

# CONTENTS

## PART ONE: A WORLD WELL LOST



## PART TWO: TOWARDS A NEW WORLD



## PART THREE: THE AGE OF REASON



## PART FOUR: OUR TERRIBLE THIRTIES

## ILLUSTRATIONS

# PART ONE: A WORLD WELL LOST

## Prelude to Peace

*Point 1:* Open covenants of peace, openly arrived at.
*Point 2:* Freedom of the seas, in Peace and War.
Booze is everybody's worst enemy. KILL IT.
Build to KILL.

Hang the Kaiser! Berlin by Christmas! Your King and Country Need You! Avanti Savoia! Food will win the war! (Recruiting station, 14th Street): Join the Navy and see the World. (Same poster, training field, France): Join the Air Force and see the Next. Food will win the war! Give till it hurts!

Booze is the worst nonessential. Stop it.

St. Mihiel: First All-American Victory.

"If you believe in my leadership," President Wilson told the voters of America, "and wish me to continue as your unembarrassed spokesman in affairs at home and abroad, I earnestly beg that you will express yourself unmistakably to that effect by returning a Democratic majority to both Senate and the House of Representatives."

"The hours are long,
The pay is small,
So take your time
And buck them all,"

sang the boys of the I.W.W. in the West, and Big Bill Haywood handed out revolvers from his Chicago desk.

The price of whisky is advancing.
American troops advance in Argonne.

"Send the word, send the word, over there
That the Yanks are coming
The Yanks are coming."

*Point 3:* Equality of trade conditions.

*Point 4:* Reductions of armaments.

"THE ISSUE IS LEADERSHIP" (Page advertisement). "Whose leadership do you prefer, that of Senator Lodge, Senator Penrose and Colonel Roosevelt, who would block the President, or the leadership of Woodrow Wilson?

"Back up the President who is recognized everywhere as the true spokesman of Liberals and Progressives throughout the world.

"Now that the hour of triumph of President Wilson's program for the LIBERATION OF THE WORLD is at hand, shall our President be politically discredited?

"Do not embarrass the President.

"Hold up his hand.

"Elect Democratic Senators and Representatives."

Election Day, 1918. Republicans sweep the Nation. Republican landslide. The country has spoken. It is through with Wilsonian liberal and progressive programs. The Fourteen Points have been dulled and bent. The President is repudiated by the People.

*Point 5:* Adjustment of colonial claims according to the wishes of the governed.

*Point 6:* Evacuation of all Russian territory.

*Point 7:* Evacuation and restoration of Belgium.

"You needn't waste your films, boys, taking this sort of picture," said the Intelligence Officer; "so far as America is concerned, there are no dead in this war."

Prussian militarism has degraded even art, music and literature. We must never again listen to their music or read their books. We must continue to hate the Germans even when we obtain victory.

The Germans built a crude but loving memorial to Lieutenant Quentin Roosevelt and placed a wooden cross and the wreck of his plane on the mound, and surrounded the spot where the aviator fell with a quadrangle of stones. The American troops, advancing, found it. Too late to counteract reports of German atrocities.

Lieutenant Luke, his pals said, was a coward. "That yellow bastard, he is always leaving a flight; says he has engine trouble. He's plain yellow." So Luke got up early one September morning and showed them. Ace of aces — and dead behind the German lines, within the month.

"Booze" is the greatest cause of crime in America. (Page advertisement.)

*Point 8:* Evacuation of France. Restoration of Alsace-Lorraine.

*Point 9:* Readjustment of Italy's frontiers according to nationality.

*Point 10:* Autonomous development of the Austro-Hungarian peoples.

American troops capture Grande Pré. The Yanks are coming.

"*Aushalten,*" commanded Ludendorff.

"*Ils ne passeront pas.*"

> "Keep your head down, Allemand.
> Keep your head down, Allemand.
> Last night, in the cold moonlight
> We saw you, we saw you.
> You were mending your broken wire
> When we opened a rapid fire.
> If you want to see your father,
> In the Fatherland,
> Keep your head down, Allemand."

"Gentlemen," said General Pershing, in a secret meeting with the war correspondents, "the enemy has placed his last two reserve divisions on the American Front. You may draw your own conclusions."

Peach kernels will win the war.

Irvin Cobb met a Negro soldier, a walking case, slightly wounded. "Congratulations, Rastus; you've done your bit, you've been at the Front, you've been in action, you've gone over the top; I'm proud of you. . . ."

"Boss," replied Rastus, "what you all talkin' about? Cap'n says, go here, an' I goes here; Cap'n says go there, and I goes there — and suddenly a perfeckly strange gentl'man come up and shot me."

Caruso sang the "Star Spangled Banner" at the National Motion-picture Exposition.

Lost Battalion released in American Advance.

*Point 11:* Independence of Rumania, Servia and Montenegro.

"Booze" is everybody's worst enemy. KILL IT.

"But back of all the shouts of 'Liberty and Freedom'," said the *American Economist,* "is the bare cold fact that this is an economic war."

"We will never forget our hate
We have all but a single hate
We love as one, we hate as one
We have one foe and one alone
ENGLAND"

"And when you get the bayonet in," said the drill sergeant, "be sure to give it a twist — like this — otherwise it'll stick in the damn Hun's guts — you won't be able to get it out — and some other Hun'll get you; see?"

American troops on road to Sedan!

"And we won't come back till it's over, over there."

A girl who jilts her sweetheart who is in the trenches for a slacker at home is the same as a Hun spy.

Jobs will be kept open for all our soldier boys until they return from France victoriously.

"Mother take down your service flag,
Your son's in the S.O.S.
He's S.O.L., but what the hell,
He's surely suffered less;
His face is pale, from drinking ale,
Or else I miss my guess,
So, mother, take down your service flag,
Your son's in the S.O.S,"

the boys from up front sang to the Service of Supply men in the rear and a riot followed.

*Point 12:* Relinquishment of Turkish control of non-Turkish populations.

*Point 13:* Creation of an independent Poland with free and secure access to the sea.

Alcohol is not a food, not a medicine, not a tonic, not a stimulant.

Armistice terms sent Germans.

Bolshevism is threatening the world. Bolshevism is dead and there is no one to bury it.

One million cases of influenza, seventy-six thousand deaths in November.

"Under Orders", a most novel war play, "the triumph of virtuosity." "Up in Mabel's Room" was the popular bedroom farce. Rabbi Wise denounced "lingerie drama, annexes to the brothel"; the stage is immoral; it will be terrible for the clean boys when they return from France. Henry Arthur Jones thought: "The English drama has never been in so degraded a condition." The Reverend William Burgess said: "The modern stage is set for hell . . . a fleshy debauch more repulsively lewd than nudity itself."

"There is no such thing as personal liberty," stated William H. Anderson of the Anti-Saloon League, "unless a man is the sole inhabitant of a wilderness. Every man gives up what he calls his personal liberty in return for the benefits he derives from society."

Bolshevism is the new menace to world peace.

Now is the time to stop the hat-check evil. Now is the time to get through a law abolishing child labor. Now is the time to pass an amendment to the constitution prohibiting alcohol.

November 5. Clemenceau, mounting the tribune of the Chamber of Deputies, was hailed "Father of Victory." The Superior Council had sent its armistice terms to President Wilson for approval.

"We will now leave Germany to Foch. *Vive Père-le-Victoire!*"

November 6. The House of Commons heard that a German military and naval delegation with a white flag had crossed the Allied line.

London: The Hun is on the Run.

Paris: *On les aura!*

The "false alarm" armistice.

Berlin: Kaiser ordered to abdicate by Socialists.

Bavaria proclaims Republic.

Sailors raise red flag at Kiel.

Revolution breaks out in Germany.

With the American Expeditionary Force in France: The Rainbow Division has entered Sedan!

November 10. Orders to the American Army:

1. You are informed that hostilities will cease along the whole front at 11 o'clock, A.M., November 11, 1918, Paris time.

2. All communication with the enemy, both before and after the termination of hostilities, is absolutely forbidden.

3. Every emphasis will be laid on the fact that THE ARRANGEMENT IS AN ARMISTICE ONLY AND NOT A PEACE.

4. There must not be the slightest relaxation of vigilance. Troops must be prepared at any moment for further operations.

*Point 14:* A League of Nations to guarantee independence and territorial integrity to great and small States alike.

*Le jour de gloire est arrivé!*

## CHAPTER ONE

### Twenty Million Farewells to Arms

Sound, sound the clarion, fill the fife,
To all the sensual world proclaim,
One crowded hour of glorious life,
Is worth an age without a name.

— MAJOR MORDAUNT

NEVER in history were so many millions of men proud and certain they had lived through time's greatest days.

An age, an old world, had died on the battlefield and they had been present at the birth of the new. The Great Years of Peace would come out of the Great War. Nothing like this had ever happened before. What, compared to our struggle and our Armistice, were the Biblical Flood, the Fall of Troy, the March of Cæsar, the Burning of Rome, Marathon, Waterloo, the Crusades? Myths, legends, facts, dead history, things found in books, all very stale and never important. We had been at Armageddon and we had come through.

The Fourteen Points are "the charter of liberation of the world." Revolution, midwife of history, is already delivering baby republics in all corners of Europe. A leader has arisen whose great words are valued next only to those of the Man who was crucified.

The phrase "to make the world safe for democracy" is not yet sour or ridiculously dead, but a living ideal for which blood is still wet on the battlefields of many nations; and the brotherhood of man is no longer cold convention from Sunday pulpits or impassioned soap boxes, but a divine revelation about to be grasped from the skies, which to-day smile in unaccustomed silence. All the dispossessed and unhappy peoples, friends and foes alike, feel that the last great war has been fought and not in vain, because the great peace which is to last forever was worth the sacrifice of all the youth and all the treasure of the generation. (To-morrow the commanding generals, frightened by all this brotherhood-of-man and democracy nonsense, will enforce the order which proclaimed the "arrangement" an armistice and not a peace, and the soldiers will in time be driven back into the fetters of unthinking discipline.) To-day we live in the golden age when men need no longer kill and die, and hate and death need never return. . . .

"Look, we have come through," a British officer exclaimed in amazement. Every one who possibly could got drunk and said it was great to be alive. A few minutes after the Armistice an American soldier pronounced his farewell to arms. "I wouldn't take a million dollars for my experience," he said; "and I would give a million rather than go through it again."

Before the night was over, lit with joyous explosions of shot and shell, thousands of our men repeated the thought and it went from our army to the French, the British, even to the Germans and the Austrians and the Italians. It resounded in Europe. Twenty million soldiers joined in this valedictory to the World War.

No one then questioned the military stupidity of the American attack Armistice morning. We had put over a tremendous barrage at eight o'clock, as if the killing and wounding of another few hundreds would better round off the casualty totals of thirty-four million. In bewilderment the enemy was compelled to reply, and the slaughter continued until the clock struck eleven, and even beyond that. At one minute of the hour most of the firing ceased and the choked rumble and deafening crashes which had continued day and night for almost five years were followed by an amazing silence. Then there was a spasm of explosions when artillerymen prolonged the war for the honor of saying back home they had fired its last shot. Then came the miracle of long silence.

A cheer was heard. Thousands of men cheered. Great outbursts of sound, no definite words, with the mouths wide open. Then thousands of men stood up, their heads above the trenches, the rims of their shell-hole craters; they leaped from the fox holes dug the days before when the throbbing, universal commotion in the air was filled with danger and death; they rushed out of torn woods and broken houses.

A man could stand up! Only the millions who had ever crouched under fire, the millions who had kept their heads down in fear, day after day, year after year, can be gripped by that phrase, a stroke of genius by which Ford Madox Ford enlightens that day. A man could stand up — and live to tell.

From the English Channel to the mountains of Switzerland men stood up unafraid. Every one suddenly shouted. In a few minutes the terror of death was gone. In a few minutes millions of men became reconciled to millions of men whom they would have murdered cold-bloodedly and without afterthought the dawn of that same day. Hate disappeared. The shouting was not the cry of victory. Neither the American, Canadian, British, or French soldiers for a moment regarded themselves as winners of a world war. (That was left for the civilians back home.) They yelled merely because they were alive and the war was over. No one celebrated victory at the Front.

The terror was gone out of the landscape too. Earth, Mother Earth, had been the greatest friend, the mother protector; unto her men had returned always to safety, but never had nature been so sinister. A tree, a shrub, a little rise, a little gully, the sun and the moon and the stars, were things of fear and death. The sky had pulsated with engines of destruction. Now one could take a walk among the innocent, blasted trees which had looked like men with bayonets. One could bury the pieces of missing men.

As the German soldiers, shyly, awkwardly, still frightened,

met the American soldiers in No Man's Land, the latter in that great spirit which characterized the nation, offered, first of all, food for the hungry.

A great trade in souvenirs sprang up. There was an old joke, — French fought for glory, the British for sportsmanship and the Americans for souvenirs, and it seemed justified that gay, gray morning. Thousands of American soldiers began speaking the language of their fathers, the language of the enemy, to the consternation or delight of friend and foe.

Sometime that afternoon the American command's order against fraternization was enforced. But at night the Germans lit bonfires. Rockets and signal lights, green and gold and scarlet and blood-red, lights used to direct raids and snipers and to catch the enemy patrols so they could be cut down by crossed machine-gun fire, Very lights, parachutes with the once cruel calcium white flares, bright as daylight, were fired into the air with wasteful happiness. Their signal for killing was no longer real. The night before you had to "freeze" when the white light went up, play dead and perhaps be dead a second later; to-night they curdled no blood in soldiers' hearts but caused an ecstasy at being alive.

On a large part of the British Front it drizzled. Tommy Atkins was not mad with victory. Nor, for that matter, were the veteran French. They took it much more calmly than the Americans, but they too fraternized with the Germans, and they too could hear and be thrilled by the singing of birds in No Man's Land. Occasionally they heard also the droning of German airplanes flying over to surrender. Once in a while there was a boom of a German hand grenade fired off in fun, and at night along the whole Front the great blasts and terrific detonations were the German munitions depots being sprung by German soldiers who were shouting "*Nie wieder Krieg.*"

"*Nie wieder Krieg,*" shouted the Germans.

"*Jamais plus de guerre,*" echoed the French.

"Never again," cried the British and American soldiers.

Solemnly many men shook hands and vowed that "This must not happen again."

"This shall not happen again," said four American war correspondents who had for a year been writing nothing but glory and heroism and victory, who had not dared to write a word of horror and suffering and death. If the Angel of the Lord had appeared to them that morning on the battlefield from which the dead had not yet been hastened away, and said to each one, Would you die to prevent another such war? all four would gladly have gone out and died. A month later, under the friendly guidance of high officers, they were writing passionately in favor of another war, a war against the new great enemy of mankind, the menace descending upon Germany from Russia.

In London the army "virtually disbanded itself." Nothing in all the million reports on the Armistice tells the story so well. The war was over. For that day the army disbanded itself in the streets of London.

There was a comradeship which had never been seen or felt before, probably would not be experienced again in the memory and knowledge of generations.

Private soldiers drilled officers; there were mock quadrilles; the spirit of war was burlesqued in Trafalgar Square and the police did nothing.

"The British," explained a Briton, "are a good-tempered race, never much envenomed, save in the worst days of the war, the time of air raids." That, too, was civilian embitterment, whipped up daily by the Northcliffe press, at a time when Allied airplanes were doing their best to bomb enemy civilian cities. Despite Northcliffe's pride in helping bring Britain into the war, despite the lies about crucifixion of Canadian soldiers and the boiling down of human bodies for axle grease, the British masses almost forgot all their hate that day. "What other people," rightly exclaimed the London *Nation*, "could have daily imbibed the poison of its popular press and yet unconsciously supplied the antidote from its own simplicity of heart?"

In the streets of London the brotherhood of man was celebrating Armistice Day.

"It is the most wonderful victory for liberty in the history of the world," said Lloyd George. "Let us thank God," and "Thank God it's over," said all the French people when they read the official proclamation:

"Blood ceases to flow. Our dead can sleep in peace. *Le jour de gloire est arrivé. Vive la France.*"

General Pershing came to Paris to see Marshal Foch. They shook hands and were speechless a moment, then embraced in the French way, kissing each other on both cheeks. The American commander in chief was "rather overcome with emotion" but he pulled himself together shortly and decorated Foch with the Distinguished Service Medal. But then, Foch was an exception. The other French commanders, Petain, Gouraud, Weygand, Mangin "the Butcher", never turned aside their eyes or felt a quiver on their lips. Foch was the greatest of them all, but his emotions were at times embarrassingly human. There was no kissing, no overcoming emotion, no pulling oneself sharply into military frigidity when the two great Anglo-Saxon leaders met: Pershing decorated Marshal Haig, the Scottish bagpipes played, the march past "completed a memorable event."

Witness again the effect of the Armistice on the Latin. When Pershing came to Clemenceau the Tiger, "we fell into each other's arms, choked up, and had to wipe our eyes." If only the million doughboys in France had caught Pershing at it! What would have happened to his reputation which won him the sobriquet "Black Jack"?

Yes, it took this miraculous event to melt the blood and iron in the militarized souls of hitherto fearless and tearless generals. On the twelfth, the second day of celebration in Paris, returning from his visit to Foch, Pershing in his memoirs describes the capital looking "as though the whole population had gone entirely out of their minds. The city was turned into pandemonium. The streets and boulevards were packed with people singing and dancing and wearing all sorts of odd costumes. The crowds were doing the most clownish things. One could not hear himself think, it was such a bedlam."

It took him two hours to cross the Place de la Concorde, "the crowd was so dense and riotous. It happened that I was recognized before we had gone very far, and the French men and women boarded the car, climbed on top of it and got inside, and no amount of persuasion would prevail upon them to let me pass."

But he was rescued by a group of American soldiers, and he concludes his impressions of the Armistice by saying that "if all the ridiculous things done during those two or three days by dignified American and French men and women were recorded, the reader would scarcely believe them. But they were in Paris and the war was over."

Farthest away from the slaughter, kept almost completely ignorant of the facts of war by the censorship and propaganda, America, which had struck the decisive blow although she had really only just begun to fight — and to suffer thousands of deaths on some days — indulged in not one but two armistice celebrations.

It is a fact that orders to cease firing had been given on that mad seventh of November. On the Chimay-Guise road, from eight to ten that night, there was no shooting because a German delegation was coming through; somehow this temporary cessation of hostilities on one road became known both at the Front and behind it. Roy Howard, head of the United Press, dining with Admiral Wilson, commander of our fleet in French waters, was told about an armistice and cabled from Brest:

> Unipress New York Paris Armistice Allies Signed Eleven Morning Hostilities Ceased Two Afternoon Sedan Taken Morning By Americans Howard Simms.

"Unipress" is the United Press of America and "Howard Simms" are Howard, and William Philip Simms, Paris correspondent. The cable should have been held up by the censorship bureau. But it somehow passed. Messrs. Howard and Simms had also sent the following qualifying cables:

> Paris Urgent Brest Admiral Wilson Who Announced Brest Newspapers 16 Oclock Armistice Been Signed Later Notified Unconfirmable Meanwhile Brest Riotously Celebrating.

And:

> Brest Urgent Armistice Bulletin Based Local Announced By Admiral Wilson Admiral Supposing Official Was Filed With Approval Local Newspapers Bulletined Brest Celebrated Nightlong.

But the war censorship which accidentally let the first glorious cable escape, stupidly retained the two explanatory bulletins. The "flash" therefore remained hanging in the air like the creation of a magician, and America went mad.

The State Department in due time issued its denial, but the hysteria was beyond control. One of the memories that will live with the generation is the tearing up and trampling underfoot of armfuls of late-edition newspapers which denied the false armistice and which in turn was in this manner denied by the populace.

At 2.56 the morning of November eleventh the State Department announced "The Armistice has been signed." It went into effect at eleven that morning, Paris time, while America was still asleep or sleepy. Could a nation go mad twice in four days? It could. On the second or True Armistice, believe the press or not, six thousand Kaisers were hanged or coffined in New York City alone. It was a day of parades and prayers and universal joy. The madness of the false armistice was repeated. The "can't-do-it-twice" prophets were defeated. On the doors of closed shops appeared signs "Closed because of thankfulness" and "Too happy to work, come back to-morrow." Confetti, ticker tape and torn-up telephone directories came down in white deluge. No one believed the celebration would ever be equalled or surpassed in future history.

At 3.20 A.M. the Statue of Liberty was set blazing. At 4 A.M. Mr. Wilson was awakened; he said "That's interesting" and fell asleep again. But, later on, he got up and wrote his forty-word proclamation:

"My fellow countrymen: The Armistice was signed this morning. Everything for which America fought has been accomplished. It will now be our fortunate duty to assist by example, by sober, friendly counsel and by material aid in the establishment of just democracy throughout the world."

In somewhat more hysterical and less elegant ways the editorial writers and the advertising men also took up their pens and machinery. Editorials proclaimed that "white and black, yellow and red" races had united, that "Jew and Gentile, Protestant and Catholic" had become as one religious sect, that America was "the melting pot of universal brotherhood"; that the "blood-bought visitation of the brotherhood of mankind" had been won. . . .

"No armies ever entered battle with higher ideals and nobler conceptions of sacrifices they were to make than those of the United States. . . . They do more than make war for democracy. They fight for civilization and peace and justice against medieval tyranny, against wrongs deeply entrenched and against cruelties almost unbelievable. There is no doubt in their minds that this is the war to end wars."

The advertising men simply let go. One of them began with:

"Time's greatest, highest hour has struck. . . .

"The mightiest victory in the whole history of this little planet . . .

"Now for the New America. . . ."

Concluding with:

"Last year we sent overseas 155,945,000 sticks of chewing gum."

The ecstatic writer for Brill Brothers declared that "Allied and American heroism, with the help of Almighty God, and with the Holy Spirit . . . had conquered. The Prussian Beast and his whelp lie dead or caged. . . . Henceforth Freedom reigns. . . . May God's mercy be on our own and the Allied dead. . . . Overcoats and suits, priced for this occasion only, at $31.00."

On the ninth of November, coincident with Admiral Wilson's announcement, "The statement of the United Press relative to the signing of the Armistice was made public from my office on the basis of what appeared to be official and authoritative information", there was real grand news in the press of the world. Foch had sent couriers with the Allied terms, there were mutinies of German soldiers and sailors, American business leaders had declared there would be no economic "war after the war", and seats for women and for organized labor were urged for the Peace Conference table. The next morning Prince Max announced that "The Kaiser and King has decided to renounce the throne." Armistice morning brought not only the report of Pershing's advance on a seventy-one-mile front with the capture of Stenay, but officially from Berlin that the revolution had resulted in victory "almost without the effusion of blood"; a general strike had been declared; a regiment of Nuremburg chasseurs had "passed over to the people" and the Alexander Regiment, "after hearing a declaration of Deputy Wells, had gone over to the revolution." Joyfully the saddle-maker Ebert announced to his republic:

"Fellow Citizens: This day the people's deliverance has been fulfilled. The Social Democratic Party has undertaken to form a government. It has invited the Independent Socialist Party to enter the government with equal rights."

President Wilson read the terms of the Armistice. "Thus the war comes to an end. . . . The object of the war is attained. . . . Armed imperialism is at an end, its illicit ambitions engulfed in black disaster. . . . Peace . . . will satisfy the longing of the whole world for disinterested justice."

Because he could trust no one, because he was a lonely man and afraid of all men, Woodrow Wilson decided to go to Paris and force through the peace of justice which he feared the Allied statesmen might not fulfill. He permitted this rumor to circulate and watched the reaction. He then proclaimed the historic Thanksgiving. "God has in His good pleasure given us peace . . . the confident promise of a new day as well, in which justice shall replace force and jealous intrigue among the nations."

In Winston-Salem, unfortunately, the Armistice, which had abolished all color and race and class prejudices, was set aside for a day, and a girl spectator, a fireman, and three Negroes were killed in a race riot. On the nineteenth Marshal Petain entered Metz and the streamer of black crêpe which had hung on the statue in the Place de la Concorde since 1870 was torn off at last. Alsace and Lorraine were restored to the Motherland. British cavalry on the twenty-first galloped over Waterloo field on its way to Germany. Over the North Sea the German fleet rode solemnly into a British harbor and surrendered. Retribution and justice had come. In the Senate, Wilson's peace plan was attacked by Republicans, especially those vague League of Nations and freedom of the seas points which were against American tradition and policy. Scandal broke out over wooden ships. The International Association of Machinists threatened a nation-wide strike to save Tom Mooney, whose execution was set for December thirteenth by the State of California.

On December second Wilson informed Congress he must go abroad. It was his duty to safeguard the peace of justice and liberty the army had won.

"We turn to the task of peace again.

"I am the servant of the nation.

"I shall be in close touch with you . . . and you will know all I do."

Congress looked at Wilson with its cold, professional, sceptic eyes and did not applaud. Some suggested the office of President be declared vacant, others wanted a delegation of eight of the loudest-speaking Senators to accompany the quiet-spoken Chief Executive. Estrangement was evident.

The London *Times* came out squarely against the freedom of the seas.

Squarely and unashamedly Okuma of Japan said his nation would help the Allies seize parts of China, Africa and the Pacific Islands if Japan were allowed to seize other parts for herself.

On the fourth of December, in the steamer *George Washington,* fitted with a wireless telephone on which experiments in two-way conversation would be made, the President sailed for Europe. Hamilton Fyfe addressed him:

> "Now God be thanked that in the dreadful hour
> Of the world's madness, He raised up a man
> To speak in wisdom's tone and wield the power
> That only noble mind and honour can. . . ."

Less poetic souls, such, for example, as Stephen Pichon, Minister of Foreign Affairs of France, engaging in parliamentary debate whether or not the Peace Conference should be secret, announced that League of Nations or no, France would fix her own frontiers and that intervention in Russia was considered by the Allies as inevitable.

"The war is beginning anew," shouted some one from the Left benches.

As Wilson sailed, the war was beginning in new forms. The victors were already fighting each other diplomatically for the spoils, and plans were being drawn up by Maréchal Foch for the invasion of Bolshevik Russia. The economic question could not be suppressed. The German mercantile fleet was to be divided. What were the resources of the various German colonies? Who was going to get which? How was trade to be restored? Was America to succeed in holding the markets she had taken from Britain during the war? What about tariff? Industries must be protected. Tariffs must be made against foreigners. Would there be a tariff war against America?

The President heard nothing of these rumblings of war. He was not interested in the pocketbook, he was thinking about the heart of the world. As he landed in France, the heart of Europe's masses turned towards him. Reverently the world hailed him as The Prince of Peace.

## Interlude 1918

Individual Murder a welcome relief; the date: November 28; the place, Page 1. At last the world was becoming sane. And the next day: the black bear Mollie, one year old, weighing a hundred pounds, ran loose in Central Park, chased joyfully by thousands, from cave to tree, into rejoicing hearts of millions weary of the war.

In December, war plays closed with a bang. Editors advised writers to lay off.

"Bloodless heroes who had never seen France" returned on ships from out at sea for grand ovations. Congress received Mr. Wilson's message without applause.

Advertisements announced whisky, case $28.50; gin $21; domestic ports and sherries 65 to 90 cents a bottle. "The new dry law goes into effect July 1. Prices are now lower than they can possibly be in the future. Need we say more?"

Ty Cobb of chemical warfare came home.

Strachey published "Eminent Victorians", a "brutal" book; the author "A Literary Prussian." Eugene O'Neill had "In the Zone" on Broadway. "Lightnin' " was the hit.

Paderewski claimed the presidency of Poland because he represented four million Poles in the United States. Hindenburg was reported dead for the fourth time in six months; four times in sanitariums, three times in insane asylums. Lenin was assassinated for the third, but not last, time.

> "We've paid our debt to Lafayette,
> Now where the hell do we go,"

sang soldiers marching toward the Rhine. A little dog led the First Division across the Coblenz bridge and showed his contempt of Germany at the first telegraph pole.

Mayor Hylan forbade the red flag in New York City and all unauthorized foregatherings in the streets. "I'm off charity for life," said Henry Ford. Mr. Wilson saved Mooney's life.

Germany cabled Wilson, "Send us food; distress is urgent." America could not understand. War profits for 1917 were reported as five billion dollars; 1918 probably more. America's accomplishment in round numbers: army of five million men authorized; two million transported to France; war chest of fifty-seven billion dollars; loans to Allies nine billion dollars; navy of one thousand fighting ships; eighteen million tons of food shipped abroad.

"It must be a people's peace," said President Wilson.

"President Wilson," said James J. Montague, "is aboard the liner *George Washington,* making 20 May-I-knots an hour."

SCENE: French Hospital.

*Doctor:* "I'm sorry, my boy, that you lost your arm."

*American Soldier:* "No, no, doctor, I did not lose it. I gave it to France . . . MY France."

Let "We will never use German toys again" be our motto, urged a woman's club. A famous statesman thought the Ukraine was a musical instrument.

The Emir Feisul's claims are supported by a British officer, Colonel Thomas E. Lawrence, described as "a small man, five feet three inches in height, blond, beardless, easily passing for a woman in Arab dress." Palestine will be awarded to the Zionists, whose president, Professor Chaim Weizman, invented T. N. T. "Bolsheviki near end in Russia; Peasants Revolt."

"There is not a single fat woman in Germany," cables first journalist to arrive.

Wall Street only blue spot in America Armistice week. Now is a good time to kill the hat-check evil.

Food profiteers exposed. Meat packers exposed. Clothing makers exposed. They ran riot in price-raising, unchecked by government board. Dear milk plot exposed. Coal profiteers are pushing up prices. Senator Knox, Republican, leads attack on President. At a costume ball in Berlin, the first prize is a pound of butter, the second ten eggs.

America has been purified by the war. "Frills and expensive dresses are no longer being worn by our women; sex allurements are gone."

## CHAPTER TWO

### THE PRINCE OF PEACE

MR. WOODROW WILSON came to Paris to complete the regeneration of mankind; M. Saionji wanted only a small slice of China and Signor Orlando came to get a piece of Yugoslavia. As for M. Clemenceau . . .

At lunch with George Adam, the "father of victory" was asked by the journalist what he thought of the Fourteen Points. The reply will bear repeating. "*Le bon Dieu,*" said M. Clemenceau; "the good God had only Ten."

That was Georges Clemenceau's attitude, which made the Treaty of Versailles and "broke the heart of the world." As a young man he had been a socialist, had given himself to this just cause and that, had fought for Dreyfus, suffered ostracism, loss of public life. In due time he became a realist, dropped his ideals, turned into the fiercest patriot France had ever had. He was not angered by Mr. Wilson's idealism. He looked upon the American President as a little child.

When Woodrow Wilson sailed for France on December 4th, not quite a month after the Armistice made on his terms, a war ended by an enemy which had had a revolution because it believed everything he said, he was hailed around the world as the greatest man of our time. Some people called him the greatest man of all time, some compared him to the Man who had become God. In Italy he was soon to be worshiped as the Prince of Peace — for a few weeks at least.

In recorded history there had never been an instance of one statesman speaking for the people of the world as Woodrow Wilson spoke in those days. The greatest religious leaders at the greatest day of their lives had never appealed to so many and diverse nations and races. At that moment he could have given the signal in all lands, he could have said to millions and millions, "Arise and follow me to Utopian times, shake off the tyrants, destroy the oppressors, down the politicians, the feudal land-barons, the exploiters." He could have achieved some sort of Wilsonian revolution, saved humanity academically by merely uttering a few words.

He did, in fact, try to utter those words. But too late. From the first day of the Peace Conference, when he let M. Clemenceau fool him into agreeing that sessions should be secret, until that day in April when he ordered steam up in his private liner as a threat to return to America, he had so deeply compromised himself that the faith of the world in him was shaken, and his followers were fighting among themselves. M. Saionji was now trading a strip of mainland for a fort and an island, Signor Orlando was drawing lines around Fiume, and M. Clemenceau, being told that Ignace Paderewski, the greatest pianist in the world, was now premier of Poland, remarked laughingly, "What a fall!" M. Clemenceau had much to laugh about in the spring and summer of 1919.

On the second of the three days in which the American Army clanked across the Rhine bridge, magnificently alarming the military Germans, the President of the United States arrived in Paris, where he was described as "the King of Humanity." The night of December 13 saw greater rejoicing than the night of the Armistice, if one believes certain enthusiastic reports. Certainly the Place de la Concorde equaled the madness of the month before. It was one vast illuminated dance hall with no room to dance but enough for embraces and close confetti throwing. The memory of bloodshed was now a bit dimmed. The people of France too joined the people of Germany in the hope and belief that the tall, thin, ascetic messiah had come to announce the new great age.

To M. Poincaré, the President promised a permanent peace

and punishment of the guilty. To the socialists he said that from now on the world must coöperate through the instrumentality of a league of nations.

Two days later the victorious French Government refused the socialists and labor unions a permit to march by Mr. Wilson's home. The President remained at his window, waiting to salute the workingmen of France. He did not know of the governmental action. MM. Poincaré and Clemenceau had not told him. They sent the police and the military to frighten and subdue the "pacifists." There was no parade, although several thousand, unorganized, straggled through the cordons. The next morning the victorious French press denounced the workmen of France for bowing to Wilson "like supplicants at the passage of a King."

British labor too held a meeting and announced simply, "We are behind the President." The reactionary Northcliffe press was duly alarmed. British and French journals of the Right agreed that Mr. Wilson, whenever he chose, could upset the premiers of both governments by merely expressing a wish for more liberal régimes.

Meanwhile the President was seeing the Italians Orlando and Sonnino, asking them to reduce their exaggerated claims for more territory in Europe. At the Sorbonne he received a degree and said, "My conception of the League of Nations is just this — that it shall operate as the organized moral force of men throughout the world."

All the oppressed nations sent kings, princes, premiers and delegations to Mr. Wilson and called him the sole arbiter of the New World. President Masaryk came with thanks for the new nation of Czechoslovakia. The Poles did the same. In colorful robes the Sherif of Mecca touched his head and his heart and bowed to the ground. General Skoropadski, hetman of the Ukraine, presented his claims. For anti-Bolshevik Russia, Professor Paul Miliukoff gave advice. From America came word of the lifting of the food ban, of "open hostility to liquidating loans to France", of resentment of the soldiers in having no say in the making of peace and their "hostility to a bone-dry law passed without the soldier vote."

For Christmas morning Mr. Wilson cabled that "the certainty of lasting peace is our Christmas gift."

The President spent the day with the army. "It must be a people's peace," he said.

Very faintly the sniping of Messrs. Roosevelt, Knox and Lodge began to be heard in Europe; very faintly European politicians began asking whether or not the American people were behind their representative, or only his own party, or that party divided.

Accompanied by several hundred journalists, Mr. and Mrs. Woodrow Wilson crossed the Channel escorted by three British destroyers, starboard and larboard, which cut patterns in the quiet waters. In London the President received "the greatest welcome given a foreigner in British history, a people's welcome." King George himself provided the visitors with ration cards for butter, sugar, jam, oleomargarine, lard, meat. A neat gesture! While the heads of the English-speaking nations dined in Buckingham Palace, the press was given a banquet in the Savoy. Sir George (now Lord) Riddell presided. Anglo-American friendship was cemented in oratory. A Virginia editor, fortified by port and champagne, made the following speech:

"Gent'men: Before the war I used to think the British were a g— d— lot of s— of b—, but now . . ."

He was dragged down, and the next day's big event, the luncheon by Lord Northcliffe, was divided into two parts, many of the cementers of international bonds eating at a second table, about a mile away.

Nineteen-eighteen came to an end. Mr. Wilson returned to Paris to fall out with M. Clemenceau before continuing his Mohammedlike hegira to Rome. M. Clemenceau openly declared himself for old diplomacy, the balance of power. . . . "If such a balance had preceded the war, if England, the United States, France and Italy had agreed, say, that whoever attacked one of them attacked the whole world, the war could not have occurred. The system of alliances, which I do not renounce, will be my guiding thought at the peace conference. . . ."

Mr. Wilson did not take this seriously. "If the future had nothing for us but a new attempt to keep the world at the right poise by a balance of power, the United States would take no interest in it," he said and believed all he would have to do was to explain to his brother idealist and all would be well.

He went to Rome to receive the homage due to a messiah. He paid no attention to the news that an American attack on the Archangel Front "with light casualties" had resulted in Bolshevik villages and blockhouses being captured, that France had issued her claim for Armenia, Lebanon, Syria — the word "protectorate" dared not be used and the word "mandatory" had not yet been suggested. The American Army of Occupation had ordered the burgomasters to refrain from celebrating the New Year with customary noise, with conventional firecrackers, and all enemy citizens had to be indoors by eleven o'clock. American soldiers, previously ordered to refrain from talking to German citizens, were additionally warned "not to fraternize with German children." The press viewed with its daily alarm Italy's seizure of territory along the Adriatic. France now claimed more purely German territory beyond Alsace and Lorraine, and poor little outraged Belgium proposed the annexation of Luxembourg and pieces of Holland, while "Poland is threatening and perhaps actually has occupied Danzig, a German city, with a mere sprinkling of Poles, thus to cut off East Prussia and West Prussia." It was unjust, alarming, said the Allied press; it was a new *casus belli* with which to open the Peace Year.

The "most powerful figure in the history of the world" arrived in Rome. Pope Benedict sent a New Year's message to the American people "as the champions of these same principles which have been proclaimed by both President Wilson and the Holy See, insuring the world justice, peace and Christian love." The President visited the King and the Pope. The Pope presented him with a mosaic judged to be worth forty thousand dollars. It was placed in the trunk with the gifts of King George, King Victor Emmanuel, and the presents in gold and silver and precious stones from lesser and greater men.

Long, long afterwards, Mr. Wilson learned the truth about this visit to Italy. To a committee of notable citizens which included a prince and many officers decorated for heroism, he said he had chosen Rome for his great appeal to all the peoples of Europe to join the American people in a friendship which would never again be broken by dissensions and wars. He did not know that this committee was repudiated as "Red" and that the government had sent regiments of soldiers to threaten and club the one hundred thousand Romans who had come to the Palazzo Venezia Square. President Wilson was not allowed to talk to the European public. The monarchy was scared.

In Genoa batteries from the hills thundered welcome and workingmen knelt behind the lines of soldiers and prayed to Wilson as to their favorite saints.

In Milan he said, "The social structure rests upon the great working classes of the world; these working classes in several countries of the world have by their consciousness of community of interest, by their consciousness of community of spirit, done perhaps more than any other influence to establish a world which is not a nation, which is not a continent, but is the opinion, one might say, of mankind."

The socialists and the labor unions dominated the celebrations. They were joined by the Liberal Party, the Catholic Party, the Union of Reformed Socialists and the Republican Party. For one day the government's censorship was lifted from press, speech and thought. The people of Milan were free — for one day. They called upon Wilson to smash imperialism, the enemy's and also their own. Forty socialist mayors carrying red flags, appealed to him to help Italy in the appalling industrial situation.

He replied that the League of Nations would surely do something. The government was angry.

A certain Milanese editor, whose name was later to cause a shiver throughout the Continent, wrote a headline: "Welcome to President Wilson in the name of the traditional ties of democracy." A typographical error crept in. It read "traditional lies of democracy." It was a portent. The writer of the headline was Benito Mussolini.

Mr. Wilson returned to Paris and the serious business of saving the world. He read with some concern the speech of Senator Lewis saying that "a conspiracy existed of Republican senators, for political purposes, to belittle the President and make his mission for world peace a failure."

On the 12th of January, 1919, the Peace Conference opened informally in Paris; on the 18th formally in Versailles. Just halfway between these dates it became apparent that it had already failed in one of its main points. Mr. Wilson's proclamation of a peace of the people, not of governments, a peace made with pitiless publicity, was completely negatived by the announcement that the Supreme Council of the Associated Nations would meet in secret and that a bulletin of accomplished facts only would be published. The world was thus banished from advising, debating, criticizing, participating, in the peace.

M. Clemenceau had urged secrecy. He had won. The battle for publicity was in reality the battle for a just peace. It was waged by the American Government and the American press. It failed. After the American protest to President Wilson, the British press protested to Lloyd George. What had become of "open covenants openly arrived at"? There was no answer.

To-day the reason for this black diplomacy is only too apparent. It is not the "sharp and not diminishing discords" among the premiers, as officially announced by Reuters, but the fear these premiers had that the workingmen, the peasants and the soldiers back home would destroy them when they learned the truth about what was happening in Paris.

On Saturday afternoon, January 18, at three o'clock, the Peace Conference opened under the presidency of Premier Clemenceau. Fanfares of trumpets greeted the delegations. Mr. Wilson additionally was cheered. A ruffle of drums announced M. Poincaré. M. Clemenceau declared that the first subject to be discussed was the proposal of a league of nations. Not a king was present, not a prince, and every man there had a beard or was bald, except the American representative, the only clean-shaven diplomat. There were no women present.

To the arsenal which M. Clemenceau had prepared for fighting Mr. Wilson there was added at that last moment a report from his jurists that the Kaiser could be punished for the war. The report quoted Wilhelm as having written to the Emperor of Austria:

> My soul is torn asunder, but everything must be put to fire and blood.
>
> The throats of men and women, children and the aged, must be cut, and not a tree left standing.
>
> With such methods of terror, which alone can strike so degenerate a people as the French, the war will finish before two months, while if I use humanitarian methods, it may prolong for years. Despite all my repugnance, I have had to choose the first system.

M. Clemenceau kept his hand on the report, ready to answer any wild Wilsonian claim for leniency with the Germans. Interpreting Lloyd George's speech, Lieutenant Mantoux referred to M. Clemenceau as "a grand youth."

"No, no," interrupted the British Prime Minister; "I said 'grand young man'; that's different."

The congress laughed. It was the only note of humor in a grave afternoon.

The victory in placing the League first on the agenda was followed in Versailles by another victory for President Wilson. Russia would be recognized. All factions, Bolshevik and anti-Bolshevik and monarchist and emigré, would be invited to a truce conference on the island of Prinkipo, where Mr. Wilson would help them form a true government of all the people. "They [the Associated Powers]," read the official announcement, "recognize the absolute right of the Russian people to direct their own affairs without reservation. . . ."

Bolshevik Russia at first was willing. But Serghei Sazonoff, the Tsarist Minister who was later disclosed as not having stopped the mobilization of Russia when the Tsar himself was willing to postpone the war, speaking for his people, informed the congress that "I refuse to sit at the table with assassins." Other Russian factions did likewise. The plan was forgotten.

Mr. Wilson proposed to sink all submarines and to forbid building new ones. That little plan too was soon forgotten.

On the 25th of January the League of Nations was unanimously adopted. Three days later President Wilson could report another victory; all annexation of colonies was dropped by the winning nations. Instead, the League would own them and would distribute mandates, here and there. Mr. Wilson was having victories all along the front. Soon he proposed that the blockade against Germany be lifted so food could be sold. But the French objected, saying the Germans might spend money on eating which they should save up to pay war reparations. The French won.

The French won, the Japanese won, the British won, the Poles won, everybody won; and Mr. Wilson either did not realize his defeats or, as the majority of his critics now agree, hoped to win everything back through his League of Nations. What Mr. Wilson did not realize was that the people of Europe had begun by backing him, would have backed him, had he fought through the conference without a single compromise, and that their faith in him was going, was gone; it was now too late to regain their confidence with his high words.

The vicious Continental European press was again in power. One who saw clearly, Mr. Wilson's delegate to the impossible Prinkipo conference, William Allen White, did tell the American people what was happening. He noted that Wilson was being attacked by the reactionary press of the world, that he was no longer in February of that fatal year, the "Christ come again" of January, whom Italian peasants worshiped. Now only the social democrats of the world were in unflinching support. The labor unions were sympathetic but already suspicious. In Italy the scandal caused the monarchy by the Wilson visit was being stilled by the monarchist newspapers. In Paris the press made constant attacks on the President: he was personally ambitious, an egotist, a seeker of power, and he was of course pro-German. M. Clemenceau deliberately used his venal press to poison Franco-American relations. The only nation permitted to receive uncensored reports of the negotiations was the United States, but the French censor tore up the best part of the two American newspapers printed in Paris. The Army Edition of the Chicago *Tribune* and the Paris Edition of the New York *Herald*, for example, tried to report the plan to remove the Peace Conference to a neutral country and they had reported the desperation of the American delegation in the face of the continued propaganda attacks from the French press.

*Le Figaro, La Liberté, Le Journal des Debats,* then turned on the press in America, even to accusing the New York *Times* and the New York *World* of being pro-German and the several hundred correspondents at the conference of carrying on German propaganda. They deplored the fact that American news was not censored. As usual, one of those "better Americans", those expatriates who are always apologizing for their own dear country, was given an opportunity to speak. Thus the pro-French bunkum of Walter Berry, president of the Chamber of Commerce in Paris was headlined, "Boche propaganda is inexhaustible" in *La Liberté's* attack on the newspapers of America.

The day came when President Wilson read the covenant establishing a league of nations. February 15th was gray and misty outside. Mr. Wilson's voice was as gray and misty as the day. He droned. He read without accent, color, human feeling, in a tired, middle-aged voice. Once or twice he exchanged small smiles with his wife.

The gentlemen of the press were the first to realize that some great event was taking place behind these tired words, that some new Magna Charta was being announced, some new declaration of independence of all the nations of the world.

There was no applause. A dull translation into French followed.

The next morning it was hailed throughout the world as marking a new stage in the social and political progress of mankind!

Mr. Wilson cabled every member of the House and Senate Foreign Affairs Committees to wait silently until he returned. He sailed for home. Most Senators, regardless of party, were of the opinion he had violated the Monroe Doctrine. He was soon to learn how true were the angry words of former President Roosevelt, who had addressed the nations of Europe a fortnight after the Armistice: "Wilson has no authority whatever to speak for the American people at this time. His leadership has been emphatically repudiated by them."

The German national assembly in Weimar listened "in agonized silence" to Matthias Erzberger, delegate to the new armistice conference in Trier, giving General Foch's new terms. Erzberger had protested. General Foch, he said, replied that "These are purely military measures in accordance with Wilson's Fourteen Points." They were nothing of the sort. Foch, said Erzberger, had told him that the terms had "the unqualified approval of President Wilson." Mr. Wilson was on his ship and could not be questioned.

Kurt Eisner, Red Premier of Bavaria, was assassinated by Count Arco-Valley.

An anarchist named Emile Cottin fired seven times at M. Clemenceau, wounding the premier slightly.

"Why did I do it?" he replied to the police. "Because Clemenceau is the greatest enemy of humanity.

"I wished the man who is preparing for another war to disappear.

"I am a friend of man, not excepting the Germans, a friend of humanity, of fraternity. This is my red-letter day."

Aged Clemenceau, agile despite his eighty years, a little man with a very large head, round and bald, a man with sad blue eyes, lay in bed fighting for his life. He had been fighting for the life of France. He must not be misunderstood. For him there was nothing in the world but France, no league of nations, no brotherhood of man, nothing but his own people, his own land; and this conference was the turning point in the history of his nation, and he would die rather than have it turn the wrong way. To Italy, for instance, which was demanding the domination of Southern Europe, which wanted to replace Austro-Hungary as dictator of Balkan destinies. To England, for instance, who wanted her old privilege maintained, domination of the Seven Seas for at least another century and arbiter of Continental balances.

Landing in Boston, Mr. Wilson said, "No nation now suspects the motives of the United States." He addressed Governor Calvin Coolidge and the American people. "I have fighting blood in me and it is sometimes a delight to let it have scope, but if it is a challenge on this occasion, it will be an indulgence." And more of like rhetoric.

M. Clemenceau recovered, Mr. Lloyd George waged Mr. Wilson's battle until his return. The French thesis that Germany must starve and keep its money for reparations was nullified when the British premier read a telegram from General Plumer, commanding the Army of Occupation, saying "The British soldier would revolt rather than continue to be compelled to see starving children and women on the streets of the German towns." The Allies sent a communication to Weimar offering food until August — also insisting the German merchant fleet be delivered at once.

President Wilson returned to France and to secret conferences, where his Allies continued to destroy the Fourteen Points, leaving him only the League. The traditional spoils of war were being divided traditionally. One day the President revolted. He would make no more concessions. At last his American eyes had been opened. All his principles were involved. He ordered steam up in the *George Washington*, which was to come to Brest and take him away from France forever.

Wily Lloyd George called in the editor of *Le Matin* and gave him a long interview denying there was "divergence among the negotiators." *Not a word appeared in the French press of Mr. Wilson's threatened withdrawal; for three days, from the seventh to the tenth of April, the crisis was suppressed in the newspapers in Paris.* Meanwhile Wilson was pacified. The Monroe Doctrine was written into the League. Negotiations proceeded. On the twentieth of April there was a crisis in Italy's claim for Fiume. Italy produced her secret treaty, the infamous corpse of secret diplomacy which the Bolsheviki had exposed in November, 1917. The treaty had been printed everywhere and every one in the world but Mr. Wilson knew about it. Italy had sold her support to the Allies for a definite price. Paragraph Number IV gave her "Trentino, the whole of Southern Tyrol, as far as its natural and geographical frontiers, the Brenner"; Paragraph Number V gave her Dalmatia; Paragraph Number VII gave her "the right to conduct the foreign relations of Albania", etc. On the twenty-first Italy bolted. President Wilson, the "New Saviour of democratic Italy", had become the abomination of nationalistic Italy in just fifteen weeks.

Then Japan struck. While Messrs. Clemenceau and Lloyd George were begging Wilson's concessions for Italy to restore the conference, the Japanese decided to ruin it completely unless their secret desire to seize parts of China were publicly gratified. With the world falling down, the Allies surrendered to Japan. Japan received more in Kiaochow and Shantung than Germany had ever had. The Chinese delegation cabled home, "We have failed in our mission to the peace conference. Shall we stay?"

But they did not leave. Then a conciliatory note, with terms about Fiume kept secret, was despatched to Italy, and on May 7:

In the main hall of the Trianon Palace Hotel at Versailles, at tables which almost formed a square, the most drastic peace terms ever imposed upon a great nation were given to Germany in the solemn French hope that Germany was forever crushed.

The Chasseur Alpin guard of honor had blown fanfares at the arrival of all the notables. It was withdrawn just before the Germans rolled up slowly in French military limousines, noteworthy "prisoners of war." Instead of a military salute, they faced a rattle of camera shutters.

M. Clemenceau sat at the center of the head table with President Wilson at his right, Lloyd George at his left. When the German delegation filed in, there was the tension which a notable journalist, Herbert B. Swope, described as "the same feeling as in court when the judge pronounces sentence of death on a murderer."

M. Clemenceau said:

"Gentlemen, Plenipotentiaries of the German Empire:

"It is neither the time nor the place for superfluous words. . . . The time has come when we must settle our account.

"You have asked for peace. We are ready to give you peace. . . .

"We must say at the same time that this second Treaty of Versailles has cost us too much not to take on our side all the necessary precautions and guarantees that the peace shall be a lasting one. . . ."

All present noted that M. Clemenceau addressed the losers as representatives of the German Empire, not Republic. It was deliberate. France had no faith in the change of government reported from Weimar and Berlin. For the coming four or five years it was to show no belief in republican sincerity. M. Clemenceau continued for a few minutes. He had sentenced the criminal to death. A secretary tiptoed across the hollow square and laid a copy of the treaty in front of Count von Brockdorff-Rantzau. It was as simple as all that.

To the anger of M. Clemenceau and the surprise of the diplomats of the world, the German delegate asked to be heard. There followed an incident unequaled in the history of the century. Count Brockdorff-Rantzau did not rise. He had been so ill he could hardly walk into the hotel. Starving Germany could not have sent a better picture to the Allies. To give himself Dutch courage, Count Brockdorff-Rantzau had also taken several small drinks of brandy. Not only did he not rise but he did not ask permission to sit while speaking. He spoke:

"Gentlemen: We are deeply impressed with the sublime task which has brought us here to give a durable peace to the world. We are under no illusion as to the extent of our defeat and the degree of our want of power. We know that the power of the German army is broken. We know the power of the hatred which we encounter here. . . .

"It is demanded of us that we shall confess ourselves to be the only ones guilty of the war. Such a confession in my mouth would be a lie. . . . We energetically deny that Germany and its people, who were convinced that they were making a war of defense, were alone guilty. . . .

"In the past fifty years the imperialism of all European States has chronically poisoned the international situation . . . the disregard of the rights of peoples to determine their own destiny contributed to the illness of Europe, which saw its crisis in the World War. . . .

"Crimes in war may not be excusable. . . . The hundreds of thousands of noncombatants who have perished since November 11 by reason of the [food] blockade were killed with cold deliberation after our adversaries had conquered and victory had been assured to them. Think of that when you speak of guilt and of punishment."

As Count Brockdorff spoke, those who understood him looked at M. Clemenceau. When the interpreters began translating, the Tiger squirmed, frowned; it was feared he would forget himself and let his anger silence his enemy. But he merely kept on repeating "Louder, louder" in a pained, angry, exasperated voice. He leaned over to President Wilson, kept whispering during the translation, then subsided into his chair as if bored by such useless talk.

The delegates were shocked, electrified, knocked breathless. They could not believe their ears; their eyes were reserved for M. Clemenceau, the father of victory. And when the German in conclusion accused the Allies of murdering hundreds of thousands of innocent people by the food blockade, dignified diplomats gasped heavily.

The next morning the French press tore its hair in anger. What! The Germans had dared ask for Justice instead of Clemency! Unheard-of arrogance! The French and the Allies had been insulted. Not once, but three times. As Count Brockdorff was being helped up the steps of the hotel "he threw a cigarette among the Allied officers"; moreover, sitting at the conference table, "he broke a paper cutter placed before him"; moreover, "he showed no respect for the treaty because he placed his gloves on it."

Impotent rage could go no further. One may well wonder to-day whether the recorders of this insolence and arrogance might not smile a little over their own brave words. Perhaps they might also admit that old Count Brockdorff that day was just as heroic a figure as those machine-gunners who had chained themselves voluntarily to their guns to hold up the enemy while their brothers retreated in safety.

On the twenty-eighth of June — the French chose that day because it was the anniversary of the shot that started the World

War — in the Hall of Mirrors of the Palace of Versailles — the French chose that place because the Germans in their foolish pride had used it to proclaim their Reich — the treaty of peace was signed without any noteworthy incident.

The Prince of Peace returned to a land which knew him no more.

## Interlude 1919

Light travels in a curve, and not in a straight line as we have always believed. The sun went into total eclipse. A British expedition proved that light from the stars bent or was deflected in passing the sun. "The most important event in the history of science . . . the Swiss author of the theory of relativity, Albert Einstein, vindicated." Swiss? The Armistice was less than a year old.

Staggering spectacle at Scapa Flow. Orderly rows of ships reeling and rocking and swaying. Plunging, head over heels, with shots of steam, a tumult of spray, one down by the stern, one down by the bow . . . the perfidious Germans had sunk their fleet.

An American tourist not only kissed but bit off a piece of the Blarney Stone. Lady Astor was elected the first woman to Parliament. What about Countess Markiewicz of Dublin? But she is a rebel. . . . "Don't think for a moment that I am ashamed of my Virginia blood," said Nancy Langhorne Astor . . . "one section of the Labor Party, the young intellectuals, are red-hot Bolshevik cranks; half of them never fought in the war."

The outstanding features of the Ford-Chicago *Tribune* libel suit were: Ford still considers wars of aggression as murder and professional soldiers as murderers; his reiteration that to him history was so much bunk . . . but he did not consider himself an "ignorant idealist"!

"What is an idealist?" asked the judge.

"One who helps another fellow to make a profit," replied Henry Ford.

Sixteenth of September the Hoover boom was born at a banquet of the American Institute of Mining and Metallurgical

Engineers. "Is he not fitted to handle the ship of state?" — "Who, who, who, Hoover." Both Democrats and Republicans "continue to speculate regarding Herbert C. Hoover, whose political sympathies are unknown. Both sides claim him." Three years ago he voted for Wilson. "In making a composite picture of the next President, from the six leading possibilities of each party, we have used Mr. Hoover's photograph in each set."

American doughboys sent home photographs of themselves sitting on the Kaiser's throne.

Five arrested for violating dry law July Fourth; the *R. 34* reaches Nova Scotia; Dempsey wins in the third; Lloyd George announces the Kaiser's trial soon; Soviets rule Italian cities; Northcliffe tries to curb anti-American bias of British press; one hundred and forty American soldiers ask permission to marry German girls; labor unrest in France; high cost of living rules American cities, almighty dollar held in contempt.

Lieutenant Commander Albert C. Read and crew of the *NC–4* left Rockaway on May 8, reached Newfoundland the sixteenth, the Azores the seventeenth, Lisbon the twenty-seventh, — first men to fly across the Atlantic, — and there was not much hurrah. Politics had displaced war; aviation displaced politics. June 14–15, Jack Alcock and Arthur Whitten Brown, Britons, landed at Clifden on the Irish coast, having flown from St. Johns, Newfoundland, in sixteen hours twelve minutes, the first non-stop flight across the Atlantic. Alcock dazed, Brown deafened. "Our journey was terrible. We scarcely saw the sun, moon or stars. The fog was dense. Sleet chewed bits out of our faces. The wonder is we are here at all." In London there was an outpouring in the streets. "No man flying the ocean will ever again get much of an ovation."

Admiral Kolchak, leader of the anti-Bolshevists, to march on Moscow soon.

American troops cross the Rio Grande and beat Villa.

Germans offer five billion dollars cash, twenty-four billions, total.

The Prince of Wales, visiting Coblenz, blushed, amazed and indignant when majors "cut in", taking actresses and nurses out of his hands. He wore a captain's uniform and was outranked. Sixty-four girls wrote home about it.

The British delegation in Paris provided detectives to keep its stenographers from rouging or flirting.

Mr. Hearst paid tribute to Mr. Wilson: ". . . a prejudiced policy in the interests of England, a vacillating frame of mind, . . . a reversal of attitude, . . . an abandonment of principle, . . . a treacherous betrayal of the interests of the American people, . . . a shameless repudiation of previous pledges. . . ." Senator Boies Penrose accused the President of receiving "several million dollars' worth of presents" while abroad. President Paderewski denied his government had condoned pogroms.

"Via Fiume" replaced "Via Wilson" in twelve Italian cities.

The Spanish influenza had claimed half a million dead in America; it was five times as virulent in military camps as among civilians.

The big harvests, Europe's need of commodities and the government financing of industry have made financiers certain that the readjustment from a war to a peace basis will be accomplished in the United States without any great disturbance. On the 19th of November, Congress defeated the peace treaty and three days later (1) the Harding boom was born and (2) Lenin, announcing Kolchak had been crushed, called it a "miracle."

Christmas, 1919: "Orgy of wanton extravagance and wild expenditure." "Unparalleled prosperity." Henry Morgenthau reported five million would die of starvation in Europe within the winter.

Reviewing the first year of the Armistice, Lord Robert Cecil declared that hatred of the enemy had waned, but hatred of war remained; therefore the world could hope for the best of all blessings, PEACE.

# CHAPTER THREE

## Lands Fit for Heroes

Although Wilson suffered defeat at home, his magnificent phrases did not cease to echo throughout the world. Slick gentlemen like Lloyd George, Poincaré, Clemenceau, Mussolini; idealists like Masaryk and Pilsudski, De Valera and Griffith; bombastic D'Annunzios, crafty Feisuls, humanitarians, patriots, and crooks were repeating noble promises to the people and coining new ones.

The two elements that were to contribute most to the making of the new age, which might even establish a poetic parliament of man, a federation of the world, were the men in uniform, some fifty or sixty millions, and the laboring masses. It was not forgotten that the Russian revolution had been started by workers and soldiers, committees later called soviets, and that the German revolution was the act of the sailors, soldiers and workingmen who had organized their Arbeiter-und-Soldatenrat. The leaders of all nations promised:

A new world. (Do not be content, said Lloyd George addressing labor, with anything less than a new world.)

A land fit for heroes.

Freedom and justice for labor (Resolution of the Pan-American Labor Conference meeting in Laredo, Gompers presiding, in 1918).

End of conflict between capital and labor; workingmen's coöperation in industry (promises of Schwab, Giolitti and others).

Land for the returned soldiers (in America, Britain, Italy, Bulgaria, etc).

A new deal for everybody. (Lloyd George)

Industrial Democracy. (Wilson)

The problem that faced the world of peace was the returned soldier, the workman, and the soldier turned workman again. In America every Sunday the newspapers and every month the magazines blazed forth with beautiful and inspiring stories of the new freedom and the great result of the war: friendship, coöperation between capital and labor. "Partners in the Future of America." — "We have entered upon a social era," predicted Mr. Schwab, "in which the aristocracy of the future will be men who have done something for humanity and their nations. There will be no rich and no poor."

When New Year's Day, 1919, dawned it was believed in Anglo-Saxon lands and in the new republics of Europe that the voice of Labor would dominate the peace conference, which, having arranged the political problems to the satisfaction of every one, would provide a decent standard of living throughout the world. Gompers came to Paris not merely to advise the President, but to organize the International Labor Federation, which would supersede the Second Internationale, the Third Internationale, a score of national labor organizations, and work with kings and premiers in organizing the promised world coöperation of capital and labor which would approach a Utopia. In January, Mr. Gompers had the blessings of America.

But in February, or March, or April? As the Versailles meeting turned into a conspiracy for national ambitions, the hopelessness of international action became apparent. The labor movement in every country was denounced in the same press which was encouraging the politicians to more land and commerce grabbing, as radicals, Reds, socialists, Bolsheviki. Even the mild support of Mr. Gompers to certain unionizing attempts was termed an attack on the traditional individualism of America.

As for capital, it was well represented by Judge Gary. Judge Gary was willing to place one billion dollars, or half the value

*Underwood and Underwood*

MARSHAL JOSEF PILSUDSKI, WAR MINISTER AND DICTATOR OF POLAND

of the United States Steel Corporation, into the fight to l
union labor out of Pittsburgh. Judge Gary said it was
principle of the thing he was fighting. Judge Gary won.

Labor everywhere thought: now is the time for brotherhood; the Judge Garys in America, the coal-mine owners in Britain, the Stinneses and the Hugenbergs in Germany, the Loucheurs and the Schneiders in France, thought, now is the time to give labor the death blow.

The cost of living went up but wages were not increased. In Budapest workers and soldiers roved the streets crying, "Give us food." In Germany the Stinnes group announced proudly that it was paying wages higher than the official demand of the labor unions. By selling coal and iron abroad for gold, keeping that gold abroad, it was able to do so, yet profiteer enormously because the mark went down every day. Strikes and revolts marked the year 1919. In Italy workmen occupied the factories of Dalmine (prelude to the general occupation of Turin, Genoa and Milan the next year). Said Mussolini:

"We are so little kindly disposed towards the bourgeoisie that we have placed at the head of our program: expropriation of riches, confiscation of the superprofits of the war, a heavy levy on capital. We will accept no dictatorship."

In America the year 1919 was marked by new strikes almost every day. The headlines for the 14th of August, for example, read from left to right:

Actors Strike in New York
Painters Strike For 5–Day Week
Ford Gets Six Cents Damage in Tribune Suit
New Haven Shopmen Go on Strike
Petlura Moving on Kieff
Warning to Carranza to Stop Killing Americans
Interborough on Strike

and on the 25th the police of Boston began to unionize and create, incidentally, a new national hero.

Last to withstand the American Federation of Labor had been the newspaper writers, the police and the actors. Now the actors had come in and in several cities even the police were joining. The actors had had their Equity; it affiliated with the American Federation of Labor on the second of August. First to walk out was the Chu Chin Chow company, which was trying to beat the London record of five years continuous. Marie Dressler organized the chorus girls. David Belasco declared he would quit producing plays if the actors won. Marie said she would retire from the stage if they lost, "and," she added, "no one will miss either of us." The press called Equity a Soviet, but found much to laugh about in the excitement along Broadway.

There was no humor however in the attempt of a newcomer named William Z. Foster to get the entire Pittsburgh district out. Union labor had been destroyed with considerable bloodshed by Frick, and the open shop remains there to this day. The strikers appealed to President Wilson to mediate but Judge Gary refused.

That same September saw the railroad strike in England. It was to be followed a year later by the coal strike, two comparatively quiet preludes to the great general strike in the spring of 1926, the long-delayed "revolution" which Britain had feared when its soldiers returned in 1919 to find the land fit for heroes.

In October, General Wood led a thousand regular troops into Gary, Indiana, and declared martial law. Judge Albert B. Anderson in Indianapolis ordered the United Mine Workers to cancel their order for a soft-coal strike. There was a whisper that the court had violated the Constitution of the United States. The Department of Justice offered the sympathetic press proof of its headline contention, "Reds planning to overthrow American Government", a "manifesto" by the "Federation of Russian Workers", whoever they might be; in New York alone a thousand men were arrested and great excitement prevailed, although there was almost no mention of the fact that nine hundred and sixty-three of them were released immediately. Mr. Gompers, who was trying to work with the government, protested now and then feebly. He did, however, call the Anderson anti-strike order "unparalleled injustice in the history of the United States."

At the end of 1919, Lloyd George, Poincaré, Noske in Berlin and even Woodrow Wilson, all of whom had promised everything to the soldiers and workingmen, were using military force to defeat labor movements. The President, who had cabled his message to Congress in May, urging repeal of the wartime prohibition law as it applied to wine and beer, return of the railroads, telephones and telegraphs, woman suffrage, land for the returned soldier and a new coöperative partnership between capital and labor, now, December, 1919, sent a message to Congress saying that labor unrest in America was "superficial rather than deep-seated." He now believed "the right of individuals to strike is inviolate . . . but there is a predominate right, the right of the Government to protect all of its people." He had opened the road to Daugherty and Harding.

France, turned chauvinistic by victory, kept a million men under arms to protect its spoils from its two enemies, the Germans who were daily exposed as planning new wars in revenge with the aid of Russia, and the liberal labor movement at home.

In May, 1920, there was a railroad strike. Almost immediately unhappy and disillusioned labor of all political colors joined in, and there was a general strike which for a moment had the aspect of the awaited revolution. Premier Millerand blamed it on certain individuals in correspondence with Moscow "who imagined they could see the birth of a revolution for which they were waiting, and which others, outside France, also expected." Soviets were found in Paris, Marseilles, Strasbourg, other cities. The Bolsheviki were blamed. But that was not just. The French people, like the people of other lands, had been deceived in the peace of the politicians, and this was their protest. M. Millerand ordered the troops to make ready. The strike was broken in a month.

While the British were using bombs from airplanes to kill the men who had revolted in Johannesburg, President Harding asked the governors of twenty-eight States to supply soldiers for the protection of strike-breakers at their mines. William Allen White was arrested for displaying a sign: "We are with the striking workers 50 per cent.; we believe in a living wage and fair working conditions." The climax came when, on the first of September, 1922, Daugherty obtained a blanket injunction against the railroad men, forbidding picketing or using union funds for the strike or holding meetings or issuing statements to the press, or directing the progress of the strike. It was "the most dramatic event in the history of labor in America." "Government by law has ended," stated Matthew Woll, Vice President of the Federation. "Government by injunction now rules the Republic . . . the Government has started the flame that breeds Bolshevism." In a message to Congress, December 8, 1922, Harding asked for a law which would prohibit strikes forever.

The world feared Bolshevism, but as for the rest of Mr. Woll's statement, the attitude of the American press and public, was — Well, what of it? Where now was Wilson's "genuine coöperation and partnership based upon a real community of interest and participation in control?" Industrial democracy receded into oblivion and the injunction triumphed.

The labor problem was met in all countries with suppression and bloodshed. The soldier problem proved easier in one land, harder in another. In Italy, as will be shown later, the capitalization of soldier discontent and the organization of jobless privates and officers gave one group of crafty farseeing industrialists control of a government and raised one man to unparalleled powers.

Soldiers throughout the world were disgusted, angry, disillusioned. The second Grenadiers, the first regiment to return to London, marched the streets to the tune "Hail the Conquering Hero Comes" from massed bands. Twelve men of one original battalion and not a single officer who went with it to France survived. The press reported that the men laughed and smiled. They did not. They marched in gloom and sadness. Other soldiers came back and found no work. Some went into the Strand and Piccadilly, selling their war medals. The politicians feared a bad time was coming.

In the spring of the first year of peace, numerous veterans' associations appeared in the United States, including one which was not only socialistic but almost openly communistic. To put an end to all individualistic movements, Lieutenant Colonel Theodore Roosevelt, Jr., in April issued a call for a convention in May in St. Louis for the purpose of organizing the American Legion.

The American soldier had not shown himself as articulate as the British, the German, the Italian. Nor had he yet found leadership. Most important still was the fact that the majority was civilian, despite the uniform, and civilians were the best haters in the world. On the day following the Armistice the march of socialists to celebrate the German republic was attacked by soldiers in New York. A crowd leaving a hall where speakers had said Mooney's trial had been unfair was assaulted by uniformed men who beat women to the ground, while policemen stood by, refusing to use their clubs on heads covered with military caps. In Utica, some time later, American Legion lads cut electric-light wires, leaving Fritz Kreisler to play forty minutes in the thrilling dark, but in New York City the Legion gave the same Austrian a testimonial. In Bogalusa, Louisiana, three were killed in a fight between the Legion and a miscellaneous mob. Soldiers led a crowd of good citizens of Washington County, Texas, which took Anton Pawlosku, whipped him in the public square, painted him yellow, and forced him to march through the streets carrying an American flag and shouting at each prod of the club, "To hell with the Kaiser" and "Hurrah for Uncle Sam" at the alternate prod. That was on November 12, 1918.

Hatred and intolerance had been organized better in America than anywhere in Europe. The rioting, the violence, the brutality blamed on soldiers just following the Armistice and for a long time afterwards was generally the exhibition of civilian emotion clad in khaki. Soldiers did not hate. At least, not until they had been absorbed in new movements, new hysterias.

When serious American war films were shown in Europe, soldiers frequently collapsed with laughter; when "Shoulder Arms" went the rounds of camps and troopships, there were sometimes tears. For such a contribution to patriotism as the Fox film, "The Prussian Cur", there could be nothing but disgust. The scene showing a soldier crucified by the Germans was "vouched for by a Baltimore clergyman who gives instances where four Canadians were crucified in one room."

Fifteen years of investigation have failed to find any proof of this or thousands of other reported German atrocities. The real soldiers did not need refutation. They knew that the war was made up of individual and mass murders and not atrocities. Such films were for civilians. It went on, up to the Armistice and after. Chancellor Day of Syracuse had decreed that "it is religious to hate the Kaiser" and the leader of the Chicago Ethical Culture Society in an article, "The Duty of Hatred", spoke of the time soon coming "when the wild beast has been caged so that he can no longer burn, poison, rape and destroy", and the press was printing letters from "A Soldier Boy's Mother", protesting, after the war, against the sending of food to the starving children of Vienna and Berlin, mentioning atrocities, adding, "I think the mother of every other American soldier boy will agree with me in saying that no mercy should be given to them."

The returning soldiers, not the first to come back and get the ovations, but the men who had been in the trenches, were amazed at this envenomed spectacle in America. Even the prize-winning ship-building poster with "Build to Kill" was a shock to many. Those who had suffered in the Villers-Cotterets drive, had seen the fields strewn with their own dead outside Thiaucourt, had gone through the Argonne hell, did not come back to join in the hysteria of hatred. Frequently the men in uniform preaching revenge for atrocities were none other than the heroes of battles with sardine cases and cartons of cigarettes of Brest, Bordeaux and St. Nazaire. A man like Whittlesey, intelligent and sensitive, was not listened to. He was the most celebrated individual at the time of the Armistice, but he was a failure in the unhappy peace which followed.

Long before the Armistice, Philip Gibbs had found that the Germans were human beings. He saw them frequently in the middle of a battle as the British line advanced. "Truth was on their lips when I met them, for men do not lie when they are still trembling with horror and when their life is a miracle of escape. . . . They cursed the war as an outrage against God and men."

At the beginning, in France, Gibbs had found that in this one European country there were no pacifists, no conscientious objectors, and all men said, "This is the war to end war. By our death we shall overthrow militarism and win peace for the world."

But as the bloody years dragged on without peace, Gibbs heard these same soldiers say "to the statesmen and diplomats, to the newspaper men and commercial men, to the jingoes and breeders of hate, and exploiters of world markets, and financiers of wealth produced by labor": "You also are guilty. We, who are going to die, accuse you also as our murderers. Your villainy, your stupidity, your poisonous philosophy, your betrayal of Christian ethics, and the old spell words of falsity which you put upon those who were ignorant as we were ignorant, have helped to bring about this beastliness. You are only a little less to blame than those Germans who were more efficient in the same evil use of power and in their hold over the minds of their people. We shall go on to the end, but after the end there will be a beginning, and a new democracy enlightened by the revelation of this war will sweep away the old frontiers of hatred, the old spell words, the old diplomacy, and arrange new relations between civilized peoples based upon mutual interests instead of fear and force."

The Russian soldiers had walked home from the Front in 1917. Before leaving the trenches they had fraternized with the Germans. It was not Bolshevism then, it was fraternization, the very same thing that had occurred the first Christmas of the World War on the Western Front when the British, French and Germans shook hands and traded food. The Russian soldiers had been betrayed by their Tsar, their generals, their munitions profiteers; they were driven in dumb herds to the front and their dead bodies covered fields two and three deep. There had been no slaughter like that in history. Those who at last walked away from the Eastern Front had spoken of peace and tyranny to their German friends. This is what Ludendorff calls the Bolshevik virus which ruined his army's morale.

These real soldiers were the men who came home hating the war.

The longer they were in it, the more certain they were. The battlefields of Rupert Brooke of the early days of fighting became the battlefields of Siegfried Sassoon of later time.

> "The place . . . rotten with dead; green clumsy legs
> High booted, sprawled and gravelled along the saps;
> And trunks, face downward, in the sucking mud,
> Wallowed like sandbags loosely filled;
> And naked sodden buttocks, mats of hair,
> Bulged, clotted heads slept in the plastering slime."

The soldiers, the real soldiers of Flanders and the Chemin des Dames and the Argonne and Verdun, were sick of the war and sick of the civilians who made the war, and sick of everything civilian, including civilian gloating in enemy suffering and enemy dead. Sassoon saw these hate-filled civilians in the London theater, watching one of the many war plays, heard some one say, "We're sure the Kaiser loves the dear old Tanks."

"I'd like to see a Tank come down the Stalls,
Lurching to rag-time tunes, or 'Home, sweet Home'
And there'd be no more jokes in Music-Halls
To mock the riddled corpses round Bapaume."

A French poet, Marcel Martinet, addresses "the civilians of unshrinking courage, around their writing desks, their dining tables", urges the soldiers to

"Come, come with outstretched hands,
You with burnt eyes, with eyes thrust out,
With noses gone, with stinking wounds,
You, hideous without lips, without jaws even;
Your faces are a terrible scar; approach,
And closing in, and pressing all around,
Stare at them with your dark and sightless sockets —
At these fine folk who don't believe in pity!
. . . The non-combatants who stand so firm. . . ."

Songs of hate were written by civilians in training camps, perhaps, or in Tin Pan Alley. They were heard only at home. Marching around the front the Americans once sang, "I didn't raise my boy to be a soldier" or sentimental ditties of peace years, while British Tommies had "Keep your head down, Allemand", a friendly advice on how to avoid a bullet in the head, or more often,

"Take me down to the sea,
Where the Allemand can't get at me;
Oh, my, I don't want to die,
I want to go home."

Which the British army did not find treasonable. Seeger and Kilmer wrote poems of the Rupert Brooke era, heroic and sentimental. After the Armistice, high dispute raged in the American ranks over the authorship of the army's newest and most popular ballad:

"Darling, I am coming back;
Silver threads among the black;
Now that peace is drawing near,
I'll be home in seven years.
When the next war comes around,
In the front ranks I'll be found,
I'll rush into war, pell mell,
Yes I will — like hell, like hell."

No, they would never go to war again, these Sassoons and Martinets who had seen the riddled corpses at Bapaume and the hideous faces of their comrades or the legs of their brothers sticking out of shallow graves. They would never go to war and they would never hate the Germans, who had turned out to be human beings and who probably never did cut off children's hands or turn soldiers' bodies into axle grease. Probably nothing but propaganda to all those stories. They were coming home to live in the lands fit for heroes. But if danger threatened those lands, if the Bolsheviki were destroying, burning, killing, raping — if, as the papers said, they were nationalizing women and property, destroying the church . . . reaching out into the labor unions in London, Lancashire, the coal mines of Pennsylvania — if they had already gained most of Germany and were preparing to invade France — if the Labor Party was already tainted and likewise the American Federation of Labor and the Confederation Generale du Travail, if — if —

Britain was only three per cent. illiterate, the United States six, France fourteen and Italy thirty-seven, but the wartime psychological examinations in American camps had revealed that forty-seven and three-tenths per cent. of the population had the mentality of children of twelve. (The motion-picture producers made their fortune through knowing this fact before it was scientifically established, and on June 26, 1919, it was capitalized by the *Illustrated Daily News,* as America's first tabloid journal called itself. The word "moron" was soon given universal currency and eventually weeklies were printed to cater to the sub-moron population. Mr. Mencken called it the

Booboisie.) Yet at the end of the war vast masses of boobs, morons, and uninspired millions, civilians and soldiers alike, had been stirred by noble words. In the first few months of 1919, the universal craving for a new world, political and industrial democracy, lands fit for heroes, and all that sort of idealistic ballyhoo was diverted into Red hysteria, lynchings, supernational adventures, patriotic intolerance, civil wars, bloodshed and violence throughout the world.

The same soldiers who swore "This must never happen again", the same shouters of "*Nie wieder Krieg*" and "*Jamais plus de guerre*" were marching in the Rhineland and the Ruhr, fighting in Archangel and Siberia, erupting into Vilna and Fiume, and where there was not bloody strife there was a moral crusade for the supremacy of the Nordic white, for the salvation of mankind by the prohibition of strong drink or books containing six bad words, or jazz music, or the teaching of mid-Victorian Darwinism, or anything, in fact, which the superior people felt it its duty to impose upon a 47.3 per cent. childlike world.

Hatred and intolerance were remobilized; redirected. Morally and militarily. The new crusades led into many lands and many continents of the universal emotions.

## Interlude 1920

On the first they gave wine away free and on the sixteenth we went dry forever. In the clock room of the Foreign Office the Société des Nations came into life with Leon Bourgeois as first chief; Clemenceau withdrew his candidacy for President of the French Republic when caucus showed defeat. "I had dreamed that if elected I would be a link between the government of yesterday and that of to-morrow." The French preferred Deschanel.

The Yankees bought Babe Ruth, who established a major league record last year with twenty-nine home runs, for more than one hundred thousand dollars, — the highest price ever paid. Grover Cleveland Bergdoll, millionaire draft dodger, escaped from America. "It is another American plot," declared the French press when Georges Carpentier married. Plot? Because a married prize fighter never wins.

Pittsburgh had found a new diversion, — wireless jazz. Music was being transmitted half a mile away by radiotelephony, and yet was sufficiently loud on reception for dancing. The experiment had been conducted by the Carnegie Institute of Technology. The Tech orchestra played and University students danced. Their halls are half a mile away. Professor Edwin R. Rath used a magnavox and two strings of electric wires. There was one disappointment: drums did not get over. Scores of radio students reported they had "listened in." The words were added to the language. The day was May 20. Harry Phillips Davis, Westinghouse Vice President, asked Frank Conrad, "who had been sending out phonograph records", to join him and in November they opened KDKA for popular entertainment.

Mr. Hoover killed the Hoover boom. "I am an independent progressive . . . I still object as much to the reactionary group in the Republican Party as I do to the radical group in the Democratic Party . . . I realize perfectly well that such a course does not lead to nomination to the Presidency. . . ."

Bryan declared he favored a "one standard of morality" amendment to the Constitution.

"You are the greatest Italian that ever lived," said an admirer to Mr. Ponzi, who was making millions by fraud through the mails. "Oh, no," he replied modestly; "there are Marconi and Christopher Columbus."

A train rushed at night from Paris to Montbrison with dignitaries for to-morrow's war memorial ceremonies. North of Montargis trackwalkers at a charcoal fire shortly after midnight saw it pass, then saw a ghost. It soon materialized. A slightly battered gentleman in a long nightgown, face scratched and stained with sand and blood, came to the trackwalkers. "Believe it nor not, Messieurs, I am the President of the French Republic." — "Or perhaps the Czar of Russia," replied a trackwalker, "and where are your pants?" — "But I am the President of France," insisted the ghost. The trackwalkers said, "Now, now," and offered the ghost a bite of ham sandwich, a drink of pinard, which was accepted. They then took the shivering, unclad stranger to the local prefect of police, and it *was* the President of the French Republic. M. Deschanel had opened a window. He had felt giddy. In due time he resigned; then died.

Jack Reed lay dead of typhus in Moscow. Born 1887 of wealthy bourgeois Portland, Oregon, parents; Harvard, 1910, with Villa at Torreon; "the world's greatest war correspondent"; German Front; French Front; Russian revolution. Trotsky offered him the consulate in New York. Dosch-Fleurot, fellow journalist in Petrograd, said, "You'll land in jail." Reed replied, "It may be the best thing I can do to advance the cause." — "You are a writer, not a propagandist," argued Dosch. Reed's enthusiasm grew. "When I am consul," he said, "I suppose I shall have to marry people. I shall simply say to them, 'Proletariat of the world, Unite'."

The socialist convention nominated convict Number 9653 for President, the speaker quoting Riley's:

> "There is 'Gene Debs, a man who stands
> And just holds out in both his hands
> As warm a heart as ever beat
> 'Twixt this and the judgment-seat."

Mildred Harris, suing Charles Chaplin for divorce, asked for half his fortune and called him a Bolshevik.

The Hoover boom waxed. "Sentiment is crystallizing among the Democrats," said the leading Democratic organ.

November, 1920: Italy and Yugoslavia sign a peace treaty; Judge Landis is made Tsar of baseball for seven years; a severe break in the stock market; unemployment grows; depression; pictures transmitted by wire telestereograph; First Assembly of League of Nations in Geneva; ouija board America's post-Armistice sport; General Wrangel, last to flee Sebastopol, first to arrive in Constantinople; League sends troops of four powers to Vilna.

There was starvation in Vienna; all classes joined as scavengers in the capital's garbage cans. Crops failed in Hungary. Famine in Russia. The world faced the high cost of living. The radio club of New York City had fifty-two members and one had spent twenty-eight hundred dollars for an adequate equipment. On December 19, stocks hit a new low in a record-breaking day of 1,800,000 shares and Christmas was declared the bleakest in American history.

## CHAPTER FOUR

### The "Lost or Found" Generation

THE papal encyclical of Christmas, 1922, dealt with moral laxity engendered by the war.

Two years earlier Pope Benedict XV had declared that "the world to-day is afflicted by five great plagues." He dealt with them in the following order:

Negation of authority.

Hatred among brothers.

Thirst for pleasure.

Disgust for work.

Forgetfulness of the supernatural objects of life.

In Anglo-Saxon countries the righteous citizens believed the war had opened the bottomless pit of immorality into which the youth of the world were leaping with thoughtless enthusiasm. All the forces of goodness, decency, cleanliness and morality stood on the brink, throwing about life preservers, or hying themselves to the seats of legislation in the belief that the universe could be reformed by a thousand prohibitory laws. Dancing, smoking, short skirts, petting, evolution, card-playing, Sunday baseball, extra-marital sex relationship, wine-bibbing, jazz and Freud were to be curbed or abolished, and books, the stage, movies, art and one's neighbor's views must be censored. A new moral crusade began in many lands the time of armistice.

Civilization, explained Professor Geddes of St. Andrews University, is high or low, according as women are at a premium or discount. Certainly it was true of that component part known as morals. In Europe it was estimated there were fifteen million women doomed to spinsterhood because of vagaries of the birth rate and the death of ten million young men; in Britain alone there were two million surplus women — and some of them, especially those who had had experience in war work in France, were determined they were not going to live an inhibited life, husband or no husband.

Thus England came upon what an anonymous critic, "The Gentleman with a Duster", so aptly called the drift age of morals. Society was going to the dogs and the "contagion of materialism" was destroying the world, the world of 1921. Everything held worth while before the war was gone, or going. "Fashion in degraded manners and morals has also degraded the happy playfulness of the human spirit. Life is no longer amusing. It is not vivacious but noisy. There is no zest, no richness, no sparkle, no color, no fire, no splendor. It is drab. It is dreary. There are crazes instead of stability. There is a rush for excitement, a taste for cocktails and cocaine, a constant winding-up of the brain to experience reactions. The one secret of happiness, quietness at the center, is lost. The one great reward of existence, a sense of growth, is forgotten."

Many other philosophers of this period also found how true was the German Nietzsche's phrase, "Not joy but joylessness is the mother of debauchery."

The "Gentleman" notes a new sort of woman, "The Woman Who Knocks About." She is not the "professional" bad woman of the streets, but a working woman or even upper class; all she wants is "a good time." — "They have ceased to feel the smallest respect for virtue." — "Love is a joke, one of the amusements, one of the sports, one of the recreations of society. To take it seriously is provincial." This anonymous writer was soon followed by Aldous Huxley, in several brilliant novels, leading up to "Point Counter Point", showing us just this sex-adventuring, reckless society.

The low state of national morality in England was emphasized legally, scandalously, in the case of Russell *vs.* Russell by the defendant's attorney: "During the war women mixed with men to an alarming extent. They did things which would have shocked our ancestors. The result is you have the new woman of independent or Bohemian habits." During the war women thought nothing of going out with officers, and they drank a lot; the men didn't care, for to-morrow they were going back, to the gas at Ypres, and probably to death. They married or they did not marry; it did not matter. They made love. That mattered, for the moment.

After the war, the Honorable John Hugo Russell was through with the "moral chaos" of the years just over; he wanted to go back to the moralities of his mother's time; but British conventions had been smashed on the fields of Flanders. The Honorable Mr. Russell could not restore them. He could only expose his wife, and Time's changes, and seek peace in divorced loneliness.

The word "sex" could now be used; the problems of sex could be discussed. In a public meeting, a debate at the London School of Economics, Miss Sheila Kaye-Smith, to the consternation of the old-timers, declared that "sex is one of the few surviving emotions in modern life that has not become civilized out of nature", and Miss Rebecca West approved; but the *Westminster Gazette* reminded both the next day that Stevenson, in "Treasure Island", and Sir Rider Haggard have shown "it is quite possible to write a novel without a single petticoat."

In Germany morality fluctuated directly with the *valuta*. When the rate of exchange was good for the foreigners, morals were bad among the natives, and vice versa. Immediately after the Armistice no one could bribe a German official; when the mark went to ten, thirty, three hundred, to the dollar, one could smuggle, betray, seduce, demoralize, cheat, steal and swindle with considerable immunity and help from well-bribed persons. After 1923, the gold mark back, the old Prussian moralities reasserted themselves.

In the terrible inflation years the streets of Berlin, notably the Friedrichstrasse and the Kurfürstendamm, were stranger than the reputed red-lit alleys of Port Said and Singapore. To the marching army of professional streetwalkers came thousands of volunteers, the jobless daughters of the hungry workmen, fighting for good corners and spots near the exists of the "nackt-cabarets."

Occasionally even innocent tourists would be approached after midnight with a sinister hiss "*zigaretten — zigaretten*" and for thousands of marks, the equivalent of a quarter of a dollar, find a little paper thrust into their hands which contained a surprising white powder. Cocaine and heroin by the pound were smuggled out of the Rhineland factories into the capital.

At the Hotel Adlon, the palace opened by the Kaiser, high-class "ladies of the evening" could be invited without persuasion to accompany the tourist anywhere at an enormous sum in thousands or millions of marks, worth actually a dollar or two. They were not the usual sort of professional lobby women of grand hotels, as witness the fact that the economic recovery of Germany two or three years later found at least two of them beaming in electric glory from motion-picture palaces in Berlin and later in America.

Most curious of all was the public appearance of types hitherto kept secret among nobility and the very elect of modern vice. No longer were the whispers of the Eulenburg scandal confined to the Hohenzollern court. On Unter den Linden, from the Friedrichstrasse to the Wilhelmstrasse, women dressed in men's clothes and men dressed in women's clothes offered new sensations to dubious visitors, causing no end of speculation among the uninitiated from normal lands.

They sent a quarter of a million strong young Americans into Germany and expected them to live for a year or so without as much as speaking to a German fräulein. No fraternization. That meant anything from holding hands to marrying. An American woman agent who gave delightful parties in her secret apartment, inviting officers to meet German girls, furnished the authorities with complete lists the next morning. Soldiers could not be kept from "trying to make the grade", as the popular expression of the time had it, and soon the hospitals referred to as the "cake and chocolate wards" were fully occupied. Apparently the starving German population had been deprived of good soap and all chocolate for many years, and a doughboy armed with these two commodities, cheap at the commissary, found great success among the susceptible ladies. Alas, they frequently rued. A strange and anomalous hypocrisy pervaded the army. The good folks back home had expected the two million soldier boys abroad to have nothing but platonic relations with the French and Germans. As for the Germans, it was a military crime even to talk to them, let alone platonize, and the good men of the Y.M.C.A. went through the army riveting as best they could all the pre-Freudian inhibitions about sex. Several thousand soldiers, believing it was better to marry than to burn, did so, and came home with whole families. Many times as many thousands merely "fraternized."

The noble Allies who divided the German colonies justified themselves with tales of Teutonic fury and barbarism which were either wholly untrue, or at worst less horrible than Japanese colonization methods in Korea, the Black and Tan war in Ireland, the Belgian atrocities in the Congo, the Amritsar massacre in India, the methods of Allied colonizers throughout the world.

In addition, a moral note was struck. It was found that in the Cameroons and elsewhere the wicked Germans had permitted Africans to go about without the well-known Mother Hubbard which American missionaries had forced upon Hawaiians and other beautiful island tribes. In Africa, the conquerors decreed not only a sheet-skirt for men and women to cover the whole body — the natives of course had been wearing "G-strings" for centuries — but specified how many yards of cloth constituted morality.

This moral reform was not the work of missionaries. It was the decree of civilized governments which had cotton cloth for sale. The traders asked for the law, the calico manufacturers of Europe forced it through parliaments, and for five francs, a shilling or half a yen per native, clean profit, Africa and the Pacific islands were saved. In some equatorial colonies the traders now forced the natives to wear more clothes than the ladies of Deauville, Brighton, and Cap d'Antibes. This proves how dictatorial government is best for the common people.

For certain reasons, which may here be left to students of politics and psychology, all dictators have decreed moral reforms. Not excluding the Bolsheviki. The Communist Party in Moscow still expels members for certain moral lapses. In Italy, Mussolini too furnishes an interesting case. Shortly after seizing office he began a purity crusade. In March, 1923, he banished a book called "La Garconne," whose author, Victor Margueritte, had already been excluded from the Legion of Honor. Mussolini then set the American customhouse officials a fine example by confiscating one of the classics, the "Memoirs of Giovanni Casanova." Young Fascists in Genoa ran around for a week, morally seizing young girls whose dresses were too near the knee and marking their stockings at a point near the ankle which they knew Mussolini would approve. Mussolini censored the stage.

All this was done in certain years when the Duce was desirous of making a settlement with the Vatican. Years in which *rapprochement* failed were marked with a completely opposite policy. Thus we have the Pope issuing a statement some time later that the Fascisti encourage immorality throughout the kingdom. The lesson is quite obvious. Moral revivals are frequently an instrument in the affairs of opportunistic politics.

In Spain the moral crusade burst with a scandal almost equaling Goya's painting of his mistress, the Duchess d'Alba, once naked and unashamed, in cold marmoreal beauty, the other time, to comply with the conventions, clothed in intriguing voluptuousness. (A century later, almost the first act of a liberal republican government was to place the Maja, the naked

Maja, of course, on its postage stamp, much to the dismay of one hundred and fifty-seven postmaster-generals of one hundred and fifty-seven moral nations.)

Father Francisco Marin Calasanz, a sort of John Roach Straton of the Catholic *noblesse* of Madrid, was the cause of a national upheaval. When his titled congregation arrived one Sunday it found, prominently displayed near the altar, magnificent new photographs of Queen Victoria, the Duchess de Frias, the Countess de Cleris, and other titled ladies. A pleasant surprise. Father Calasanz began preaching a sermon on women's dress. The congregation became nervous.

Pointing a bony finger at the picture of the Queen of Spain, the priest then uttered the words, "They are shockingly immoral." There was silence in the church. The tumult broke outside. It involved the press, the king and the queen, the nobility, the censorship, the indignant masses. The illustrated newspapers rushed editions with Father Calasanz' selection of décolleté beauty. King Alfonso immediately ordered the paper suppressed. The editors protested. The pictures had been used before in the social columns, had been printed in Europe and America as representing the flowering beauty of the ancient land. King Alfonso ordered the court photographer to destroy all negatives. He did not, however, before a complete set had been sold to Americans. The queen's décolleté became the topic for general European gossip. Her dresses were pictured. Britain complimented her on her little feet frankly more than peeping out of skirts not so short as the bold New Yorkers were wearing, but still revealing what the unanimous press called shapely ankles. Spain's Victoria was different from Queen Mary, whose dresses swept the ground and rose almost to her ears — and Spain had liked that. Now the whole court was running to cover.

There is no better commentary on the immediate post-Armistice era, known as a time of moral laxity and decay, than the arrival of the gigolo. The erudite will probably find evidence of him in Ur of the Chaldees, passages in the Bible, similar characters in Shakespeare.

The gigolo who concerns our time came into being in 1919 in Deauville and was usually a Russian prince who couldn't make a living otherwise. To starved, rich, Anglo-Saxon ladies he offered romance at a reasonable price, a platonic dancing partner, or a guide to Freudian release from inhibitions at standard rates. Frequently American chewing-gum heiresses, movie queens and enriched divorcées insisted on no relationship without legal marriage. The gigolos in desperation sometimes consented.

Their patrons came from all nations. In the case of His Royal Highness, Prince Zerdechenko, Emir of Kurdistan, sentenced to six months' imprisonment for unlawfully wearing the Legion of Honor ribbon and forging a passport, the Nice authorities gave the public an amazing diary which reflected rather bitterly on the fifty elderly women who had made the self-made prince quite prosperous. Some of the entries were:

Mrs. B———, fifty, American, widow, fat, ugly, crazy about titles, drinks heavily, dances horribly. Pays $40 a night.

Countess X———, sixty, Italian, married, soaked with perfume, almost squeezes me to death. Looking for adventure. $10.

Madame O———, forty-five, Greek, pretty, married and has mania for repeating, "Oh, if my husband should come here!" Inveterate gambler. Pays well when she has money. Tried to make a touch once.

Duchess Q———, fifty-five, Spanish, widow, passionate, apparently rich, insists on dancing until dawn, will marry any one with uniform or title. Has a charming daughter named Carmencita who dances divinely. Old lady pays $30. Sent flowers to Carmencita. Bill $30.

Madame Z———, sixty-five, Egyptian, rich, dances well, divorced, looking for amusement and adventure. Face twisted by beauty specialist and insists sitting dark corners. Hasn't gone out in daylight for twenty years. Pays $50.

Lady P———, fifty, English, divorced, magnificent jewels, possessed of what the French call "the Demon of Middle Age", the woman who has never had her share of affection and caresses. Easily flattered about age. Loves solitaire. Uses half nelson while dancing. Pays well.

The prince himself was disclosed as some sort of an Oriental named Bonson, really a pants-presser from Soho, but he had the bearing and the manners of nobility.

Of all the nations of the world, France alone went through no moral hysteria in these days. The war had caused neither degeneration, which the reformers so greedily found in other countries, nor hopes of magnificent regeneration which the idealists had pictured. Censorship was usually political and economic, not moral. The "La Garconne" case failed to stir the legal authorities. The suppressed verses of old Baudelaire were printed. Cocteau and Gide were permitted to defend their own specialized systems of pathological human behavior without Comstockian interference; such ladies as had been inspected by the police were still permitted to walk lackadaisically on the Grands Boulevards, and *jeunes filles* were still kept immaculate by doting mothers and dot-providing fathers for the economically sound young men of the inevitable bourgeoisie.

During the Peace Conference, Paris was dancing mad. The swagger restaurants charged a dollar for two eggs, five dollars for a game bird that had cost only one dollar in the market; the poor housewives, however, had to pay a dollar and a half for a pound of steak, fifteen cents for an egg, two dollars a pound for butter. Food was scarce; transportation was short; middlemen were cheating; commerce was disorganized. At the Hotel Crillon the management regretted it had to raise its price from two dollars to three dollars for simple meals for American employees of the missions, despite the fact that many foodstuffs came from the army canteen at comparatively ridiculously low prices. But every one danced. There was madness in spending. The soldiers threw money away. The Folies Bergeres became more naked than ever and sold drinks until ten o'clock, a full hour below the legal closing time. Public dancing had been forbidden.

But in discreet cellars the tango was being shown and in the conference delegation hotels the one-step and the fox trot were practiced openly. The congress danced — as it had done in Vienna in 1814.

At Maxim's the good old pre-war days were mourned by proprietors, waiters and *belles poules*. Times had changed, and for the worse. Before the war, Russian grand dukes would come every day, buy dinners for all the little girls, give flowers to passers-by, throw dollar cigars to the orchestra, spend five hundred to a thousand dollars a night; now there are only rich Americans, who take either water or five drinks, spend ten dollars and think they are ruined. Times have changed. Americans do not know how to be gay. That is why Paris is so quiet. French youth never wasted much time in Montmartre. Now boys and girls go in for sport, especially football, and vice doesn't pay as well as before. Moreover, dignitaries and soldiers returning to America had been spreading reports that sin was vanishing from Paris. The propaganda against the gay city was spreading. It might be true, all right, but it was deplorable. What would become of all that great investment in what the world called "entertainment." Something should be done about it. Some persons actually suggested that Ambassador Jusserand issue a pronunciamento to the American people, saying that there was still sin in Paris and a lot of fun for everybody.

The Jazz Age pleased Paris and Berlin too. A German critic honored the new music as the Hegelian synthesis — "it is not a putting together, it is a tearing apart . . . analysis gone mad . . . in jazzism you get careless of law . . . anarchism . . . the last word in *Kultur* . . . no amusement . . . work . . . therefore mankind's redemption . . . pfitt, pfatt!"

Jazz had been brought to Europe by Jim Europe. If it ruined a continent, you may blame it on the leader of the hundred negro players of the old Fifteenth Infantry. France was lost. England, austere and puritan, abandoned herself. Sergeant Eric Borchard and Private Hiler amazed Berlin. Eventually it reached

Moscow in a communist transformation. The cabarets of Constantinople reeked with jazz and Russian folk songs.

"If you don't like jazz you are out of tune with your time," the new boss of the temple of Euterpe, Mr. Irving Berlin, had officially decreed. But even the liberal preachers shook their heads. "Jazz spells inner degradation, by drink, drugs and sex abandonment; also extravagance, domestic destruction, suicide and fatal accident," opined the Reverend Percy Stickney Grant as late as 1922. "What is jazz then? A music of animal noises which makes you want to chatter and twist your tail around a tree. . . . Cubism and other extravagances are at least serious attempts to go forward. The 'Nude Descending a Staircase', although it reminds me of a lumber wagon discharging its load, after the horse has run away, does strive for a deeper analysis of material forms. But jazz goes back to the jungle. Dancing was primarily intended to help young people bear the burden of sex . . . the slight contact to a certain extent brought relief. It gave romantic outlet. But jazz changes relief to excitement. . . . Symbolism becomes sensuality. It is a gesture of the devil."

Likewise the Reverend John Haynes Holmes may smile to-day when he reads his declaration one decade old that "Jazz is an indescribable atrocity. Only a spiritual revival can remedy the state of affairs it has helped bring about." Rabbi Stephen S. Wise thought, "Jazz is a narcotic publicly and shamelessly indulged in . . . I lament the prostitution of music and the dance." Imagine then the thoughts of rock-bound puritanism. The good people were unanimous. Few sang with F. P. A.:

> "And music, heavenly maid, now has
> To rise above the slime of jazz."

The Public Morals Board of the Methodist Church, deploring one of the war's greatest moral tragedies, the use of cigarettes by our hitherto pure women, solemnly advised them that their unborn children are "drugged by tobacco in the blood of a smoking mother." Rouge was coming in "for girls so ailing they have to use it to present a counterfeit of health." The General Federation of Women's Clubs was asked in 1920 to stamp out all popular songs because Mrs. Oberndorfer thought ninety per cent. of them unspeakable. The bobbed hair of 1919 was credited by some to Irene Castle but others thought it the devilish plot of Emma Goldman to make all American women look like anarchists. The visit of the King and Queen of the Belgians caused two joyful scandals. Mrs. Mayor Hylan denied that when Her Royal Highness had said to her that being mayoress of a large city was a strenuous job, she had replied, "Queen, you said a mouthful." Mrs. Hylan should not have denied it; it is probably her only claim to American immortality. The other episode was Californian. The queen went bathing in a conventional Ostend one-piece costume. Should she be arrested for her bare legs, her uncovered royal toes? California proved more liberal than Atlantic City.

Armistice week, persons so inclined could spend evenings at motion-picture palaces, the Academy of Music in New York for one, where Theda Bara, the most popular vamp of her time, was advertised by William Fox as portraying "Salome, the Python of Palestine, sinuous, sleek, seductive — she twined herself about strong men and crushed them, heart, soul and body." Shortly afterwards "sex appeal" came to public attention. Mr. B. B. Hampton, president of four moral motion-picture corporations, exposed his colleagues who made films in which the heroine instead of being "a sad, sobby figure" is now "sex-appealing with all her might" and earning five thousand dollars instead of five hundred. In 1921 William Allen White, noting that the American novel had gone small town, found "Main Street", "Moon Calf", "Miss Lulu Bett" and Edgar Lee Masters' poems "having an earnestness of purpose and a common revulsion from the sex complex that has obsessed the world of letters in recent years." In Mr. White's time the crusade against the petting, the excitement, and the going to hell of the younger generation reached its climax. Clergymen representing fifteen denominations solemnly met in Philadelphia and designed a "moral gown." Ohio and Virginia legislatures debated bills forbidding décolletage. The Ohio measure provided that "no garment shall be sold which unduly displays or accentuates the lines of the female figure." Fifty-three editors of religious magazines reported an immorality wave of six months' duration, from the winter of 1920 to the spring of 1921. The Girl's Protective League met at the home of Mrs. Otto H. Kahn, where Miss Janet Richards led a discussion on the perils of the day, petting parties, cheek-dancing, midnight automobile rides and other modern developments, and the group asked, "Do boys need protecting from the vamping wiles of the modern girls?"

Women's dresses rose inch by inch, year by year, and almost always despite Paris. The smart débutantes of the first peace year wore clothes tight at the neck and at the ankles but wide at the hips, giving a rather obloid impression; in 1921 it was noted that short skirts had become a boon to mosquitoes and that owing to the disappearance of the righteous corset, the old-fashioned round garter had come back and could frequently be seen although still worn above the knee. In 1922, Paris, inspired by economically minded cloth manufacturers, dictated the abolition of the short skirt. During three years all limits had been reached, up and down. Not for the first time was Paris defied. American women refused to lower their dresses to the ground. Noted women writers coupled short dresses with the new freedom; Health Commissioner Copeland defied the crusaders by declaring short skirts were sanitary and healthful. Artists arose who said they were more beautiful. Other artists said they were more ugly. Paris ostracized New York as years behind the styles. America didn't care.

Were morals getting better or worse in 1922? A symposium of experts said worse. "There is such a thing as Bolshevism in the moral and spiritual spheres," replied the Reverend George W. Sandt, D.D., editor of the *Lutheran*. "We are suffering from its effects at the present time. A spirit of libertinism is abroad among our youth . . . bold and brazen defiance of decency and modesty in dress and speech and conduct. Women paint and powder and drink and smoke and become the easy prey of a certain class of well-groomed and well-fed high-livers whose chief business is 'to pluck the blush of innocency from off the cheek of maidenhood and put a blister there.' "

But while the preachers and reformers were occupied with the blush of innocency, the philosophers too were tasting the bitter banquet the war had provided. In Europe more than in America there was a pessimistic realization that a good age had died and that a bad age had come which might last forever. Sadly Sir Auckland Geddes viewed the world, where "a realization of the aimlessness of life lived to labor and to die, having achieved nothing but avoidance of starvation and the birth of children also doomed to the weary treadmill, has seized the minds of millions."

Between the pessimistic philosophers and the optimistic reformers there were also movements in which millions participated to end such conditions of life; from stark communism to diluted liberalism, to dictatorial egotism, came an attempt to create a present and promise a future in which futility of living, propagating, and dying would be succeeded by some idealism of beauty and hope.

This appeal to the masses was decried in Germany by Spengler, who before the war had begun his magnum opus, "Der Untergang des Abendlandes", which came to Anglo-American attention in the spring of 1922. Times were changing for the worse; there was no need for him to revise. He had already noted the direction of leading thought towards the general mob, the most characteristic feature of our time, and he called it intellectual prostitution in speech and writing. He had found Schopenhauer, Shaw's essays and even some of Nietzsche, nothing but journalism. Poets, priests, scholars had become journalists, and Ibsen and Shaw, he noted, had to be agitators too. The arts were already dying of senility. "What is pursued as art to-day is impudence and falsehood," meaning all music after Wagner, all painting after Manet. "Every form of modernism considers change as development." — "The Socialist, the dying Faust, is the man full of anxiety as to the future, which he feels presents to him his task and aim."

Within two hundred years, Spengler believed, Western civilization would come to its downfall. A rapid decline. We were at the end of all our spiritual resources. There was nothing but over-presumption, pride of intellect. Artists had lost their inspiration. The world, sophisticated, without faith, without religion or power to create, was slowing up to a final paralysis. There existed "boundlessly trivial optimism." Spengler urged the men of the new generation to turn "their attention to the technical instead of the lyrical, to the building and the sailing of ships instead of painting, to politics instead of the philosophy of perception."

It was a great time for the critic of America. Our morals, our money, our literature, our crime, our steam-heating, our jazz and our foreign policies were fit subjects for denigration now that we were a world power and conquering the markets of Europe, Asia, Africa and South America.

"America has got the gold of the world," Clare Sheridan quoted Kipling as saying to her at lunch one day, "but WE have saved our souls." What an international commotion followed! Borah rose to defend the American soul. Clemenceau and Josephus Daniels defended the American Constitution. Poor Kipling tried to repudiate the interview. Mrs. Sheridan insisted. There was a nice question of whether table talk in Sussex or Wessex was meant for the front pages of New York. But the question of purity of the American and British national souls continued to be discussed for a decade and more and came up in cartoons during all the reparations and war debts conferences year by year.

Mr. Einstein, home in Berlin after his first visit to America, was also trapped into criticism. "Women," he said, "dominate the entire life in America. Men think of nothing but work. They are the little play dogs of the women, who spend money in a reckless manner.

"Their excitement over a theory about which they understand nothing made a ridiculous impression on me. I found it comic.

"All people in America are so colossally bored. There is so little for them there. What poverty! What intellectual poverty!

"They do everything that is the fad of the passing moment — (the fad of the moment in New York was the ouija board) — In that way they threw themselves on the Einstein theory."

Little play dogs barked reply. Mr. Einstein was properly told off. It was easier with him than with Kipling; the year was 1921: Mr. Einstein was called a German!

## INTERLUDE 1921

"Every morning before you are fully awake and every evening as soon as you are in bed close your eyes and murmur twenty times in succession the phrase:

" 'Day by day, in every way, I grow better and better.'

"This phrase is a general one and the words 'in every way' are applicable to everything. It is well to be provided with a piece of string with twenty knots tied in it, so that the counting will be mechanical. Let the auto-suggestion be made with confidence and with faith. In case of pain use the phrase, 'It is going'." Thus Emile Coué, president of the Lorraine Society of Applied Psychology, in London. Six months later millions of Americans were tying knots.

Depression. Buyers strike. Fear. Gloom. Wage cuts. Millions unemployed. The five-cent loaf returned. America hoped nickel ice cream, fifty-cent neckties, quarter shaves, three-dollar shoes, the five-cent shine, the dollar shirt and nickel peanuts would also come back to relieve hard times.

March, 1921: "We are turning the corner."

September: Mellon gives boll weevil credit for upturn in business.

Harding Cabinet, including Fall, has Herbert Hoover as disinfectant. From the presidential inaugural address: "America has inherited a policy of non-involvement in Old World affairs." Washington reported "Bolshevik Government falls; Petrograd captured." The Chemical Warfare announced liquid poison, three drops, one death.

May 29: Two Italians will be tried for the killing of a paymaster April, 1920; Judge Thayer will preside. Eighty killed in race riot in Tulsa. The American Negro, said Mr. Dooley, is docile and easily lynched. Frank Vanderlip declared America economically illiterate. Doctor Frank Crane, "admittedly one of the greatest forces in the world to-day," joins "sell-yourself" or supersalesmanship and service bureau. Vitamins discovered at Johns Hopkins. Henry Hawker died in flames on Hendon Field. Washington announces, "Fall of the Soviets thought possible." American Legion, New Jersey convention, holds "Keep Debs in Prison" demonstration. Charlie Chaplin dined with Pola Negri in Berlin. Three hundred and three marks for a dollar. Germans flew in gliders; the world thought for three days that cheap wings had arrived.

Violin right hand, briar pipe left, Einstein arrived. "Mankind is suffering from too much nationalism." Alderman Falconer never heard of him. "Who is Einstein?" he asked Monday; replying Tuesday, "I have learned he is a German." He blocked Einstein's freedom of New York City. Professor Reuterdahl of St. Thomas' College approved with, "Einstein is the P. T. Barnum of the scientific world."

"The war is over," declared Postmaster General Hays, restoring privileges to the *Liberator*. Marcus Garvey became Harlem's Black Messiah and Urbain Ledoux sold jobless men on an auction block.

Monarchists assassinated German Catholic leader Erzberger.

The Rue de la Paix ordered American women to wear ankle-length gowns; American women rebelled.

Six thousand of them and eighty-four thousand sportsmen attended the "most memorable fight in all recorded history" for nine minutes and fifty-seven seconds, at Boyle's Thirty Acres, paying a million and a half for Carpentier's dance with Dempsey. The end, immortalized by Igoe: "They have been unable to staunch the blood from Carpentier's mouth and he walks about slowly, with a crimson streak down his chin. Dempsey is at him now, might and main. . . . Georges is floundering badly. . . . Dempsey scents victory. . . . His right crashes to the Frenchman's jaw and he goes down with a thud . . . the referee counts . . . then 'nine' and up jumps the Frenchman, a picture of defeat . . . a right to the jaw. . . . The idol of France is down again. . . . Ertle counts him out." Fifty to one on Carpentier, predicted Shaw. "Dempsey was morally knocked out," replied the Irishman to taunting cables.

Ireland's greatest love romance was recalled on the 15th of February, 1921, in the death of Kitty O'Shea, "handsome, wistful, winsome, vivacious and intelligent, with a brain as keen as Becky Sharp, yet as honest as Amelia." Captain O'Shea played cricket, got drunk, did not beat his wife, had no interest in Ireland. Kitty dropped a rose in Parnell's path; the uncrowned King of Ireland picked it up; it was found among his papers, buried with him. Captain O'Shea chose the day Home Rule was certain to accuse his wife. "I have in my hand a parliament for Ireland," Parnell shouted to the Galway mob; "if you destroy me, you destroy it." Everything was destroyed — except one romance. Kitty married her "tall gaunt figure, thin and badly pale", but he died soon, after ten years of reckless passion which cost him a fortune, a career, his life. Britain, Ireland, America now joined tribute to Kitty; her famous letter was found: "For ten years Mr. Gladstone had known of the intimacy of Mr. Parnell and myself. . . . In view of the fact Mr. Gladstone and his colleagues were so pained, surprised and properly shocked when Mr. Parnell was publicly arraigned as my lover, the frantic way in which they applied to me when they were unable to find him was afterwards a source of considerable amusement to us both."

Sir John Ellerman's daughter, Winifred Ellerman ("she is worth half a million pounds sterling") and Robert L. McAlmon, poet, Minnesota half back, were married and went to France with Hilda Doolittle, another poet, with whom Winifred had been touring America: the honeymoon provided reading matter for a year.

Banker Stillman, W. E. D. Stokes and John B. Watson were the divorce-court stars of the year.

Clara Smith Hamon, young, beautiful, was accused of murdering John Hamon, "one of the political powers responsible for the nomination of President Harding."

Full-page advertisements announced the Miami land boom.

In May, Michael Farbman reported a famine in Russia; instead of trying Kaiser Wilhelm, the German Supreme Court tried a sergeant named Heinen. The Kaiser's book, purchased for two hundred and fifty thousand dollars by Clinton Brainard, Albert Boni and Cyril Brown, over the bid of Herbert Swope and the present chronicler, was the decade's biggest flop.

Conan Doyle, lecturing on heaven, proclaimed there was marriage there "but on a higher plane" and no babies. He showed photographs!

WJZ Newark, July 2, announced baseball play by play. Broadcasting went commercial.

McDonald confessed he had given perjured testimony against Mooney.

Alsace and Lorraine seethed with grievances against the French.

President Harding commuted Debs' prison sentence and the New York *Times* editorially howled and whined, "Certainly the majority will not approve; a shallow, howling, whining minority had its way." Doctor Harding, father of the President, eloped secretly with Alice Severns. "It's no business of his," he replied, referring to Warren G. "I'm seventy-six; I'm old enough to know what I want; I was lonesome."

## CHAPTER FIVE

### Disillusion Armed with Rifles

While I have said that the war has been won, it would perhaps be more accurate to say, there is a lull in the storm.

— CLEMENCEAU (February 9, 1919)

THE people of Europe and Asia and Africa arose with rifles in their hands and fought for those liberties or those lands which the peacemakers at Versailles, St. Germain, Neuilly and the Trianon had denied them.

Mr. Wilson had aroused the greatest idealism in the history of the living generations; it was natural that his repudiation and fall should lead to such disillusion that bloodshed would follow.

Disillusion took up arms. The world hunger for a just peace was complicated by the closer emotion caused by empty stomachs. While American warehouses bulged with food, Europe starved. Bolshevism and patriotism paraded through the ill-fed, discontented masses. There were rifles enough for every one.

The first nation to disturb the Peace Conference was Poland. It was bursting its temporary frontiers, east and west. Christmas, 1918, the statesmen feared that troops "marching on Berlin" would not stop at Posen. D'Annunzio, tired of Paris indecision, captured Fiume. In Italy workingmen seized factories and land. In India new laws were enforced with a massacre that started a nationalist movement. Spartacists and later monarchists attempted to seize Berlin and overthrow the Republic. Black and Tans waged civil war in Ireland. A new leader arose to restore destroyed Turkey. Democracy gave way to communism in Hungary, communism to monarchy, monarchy to dictatorship. These were the most important events, the first series of wars and insurrections, which mark the lengthening armistice of 1918:

### FIUME OR DEATH

Least sanguinary, most operatic, was the little war D'Annunzio fought for the benefit of humanity and the exaltation of his own ego among the Adriatic islands and in Fiume. Our poet thought he would lead "a revolt against all the vileness of the world", he would raise a small banner in a small city, but all the weaponless peoples, all the victims of governments, the Irish and the Egyptians, the colored races, Mohammedans and Christians, all men with salt and iron in their veins, would rally around him in many ways and lands. He knew he was the last great crusader. He said so in an interview.

Appointing an unheard-of journalist, one B. Mussolini in Milan, his "consul general" to raise money and more men, Gabriele d'Annunzio and a lot of soldiers and officers and peasants and roustabout boys and socialists and adventurers, on the 12th of September, 1919, marched to Fiume. In old trucks.

General Pittaluge, commander of the seaport, met the poet at the gates.

"Thus you ruin Italy," he declared.

"It is you who ruin Italy by opposing Fiume's destiny," replied D'Annunzio.

"I must obey military orders," countered the general.

"What? You would fire upon your brothers?" cried the poet. "Then fire first upon me." With a noble gesture D'Annunzio tore open his military tunic, exposing his undershirt.

Pittaluge was overcome. "With you I cry '*Viva Fiume*'," he cried.

"*Evviva Pittaluge*," cried D'Annunzio.

So they embraced and crying together led the march into Fiume. The forty trucks started their motors. The general advanced very militarily. D'Annunzio did his best in a bow-legged way. The next morning he put on a field marshal's uniform.

Comic opera as this may seem to-day, the attack and its success led directly to the making of the Fascist movement and the advent of Mussolini in Rome. The poet had supplied the black shirts, the black fezzes, the slogans, the spirit of armed adventure, the ideal of force triumphant. A shrewder man knew how to employ them on a national scale.

Italy, the people of Italy, cheered the *coup d'état* as an act of justice. Mussolini editorially proclaimed that "the government of Italy is not in Rome but in Fiume. It is that government which we must obey," — a declaration of pure treason which Premier Nitti promptly denounced. He also saw with alarm that sedition for the first time had entered the Italian army.

Every evening the victorious poet made an oration and listened to the cheers of his men; several times a week he led parades and again listened to shouts, watched the waving of stilettos, the shaking of muskets, and found it all magnificent. Like a pirate chief he organized more expeditions, raided towns, boarded ships, seized cargoes of food and ammunition; to his palace he called in socialists and communists with whom he discussed the eventual march on Rome, the dissolution of the Italian parliament, the inevitable dictatorship of the patriots. He gave Fiume a charter full of romantic poetry . . . "to instil into the daily life a sense of that virtuous joy which ought to revive the spirits of a people liberated at last from the yoke of restraint and falsehood." He also created ten classes of men, in ten corporations, the ninth for seafaring men, the tenth for the intelligentsia. The corporations, circumcised of poetry, remain in the Fascist State.

To the people of Fiume the poet said, "I shall not leave here alive nor shall I leave here when I am dead, for I shall be buried here, to become one with the sacred soil."

He appointed Anton Grossich president of the Free State of Fiume; the latter called for a plebiscite after taking good care that five thousand malcontents, all of whom miraculously happened to be Yugoslavs, had been deported before the voting began. A victory was claimed of two or three hundred ballots.

When Giovanni Giolitti became premier he lived up to his nickname of "Old Fox." After asking D'Annunzio to depart peacefully and receiving a bombastic reply, he negotiated with the Yugoslavs and with Mussolini. The former resulted in a treaty, the latter in a secret. Alceste D'Ambris, co-conspirator with D'Annunzio and Prime Minister of Fiume, was kept journeying from Fiume to Milan and back many times as the first year of the occupation ended with Giolitti's and the King's loyal troops concentrating outside the seaport for a definite battle. D'Annunzio demanded the millions of lire which Mussolini had obtained mostly from American Italians, and the reserve troops. He got neither. Premier D'Ambris later wrote publicly that the Milan editor betrayed the poet in return for a promise from Giolitti that in the future the Mussolini Fascisti would be permitted to arm and fight the meddlesome socialists and the newly dangerous party organized by Don Sturzo from Catholic ranks and known as the Populari.

D'Annunzio remained alone in Fiume. General Caviglia surrounded the town in December, 1920, sent a friendly ultimatum, waited, began a decent bombardment Christmas Eve. D'Annunzio replied by declaring war on Italy — in a few well-chosen poetic words addressed to no one in particular. There was "national mourning" in many cities.

On the twenty-eighth of December, D'Annunzio was permitted to ride peacefully away from the city more quietly than he came. "Italy is not worth dying for," he said in valedictory.

Mussolini incorporated the Arditi with his black shirts.

### AMRITSAR

In 1919 an officer commanding a small detachment of troops gave an order to fire. It has come close to costing the British Empire the loss of India.

That year a British jurist touring that unfortunate country found, according to the first complete account which Charles

Merz, a well-known journalist, later brought to America, that there were twelve hundred "anarchists" among the forty-five million persons who swarm in the country of Bengal. It was the time of the great Red fear. The new threat had come out of Moscow, the proverbial enemy of Britain in India, and everything tinged with nationalism was believed anarchistic or Bolshevistic. Judge Rowlatt had a bill passed providing for the suspension of civil liberties in any part of India on the decision of executive authorities. The Indians called it the Black Cobra Bill. Later, the Hunter investigation said it was "largely if not mainly responsible" for all that followed.

In the town of Amritsar, where a certain unimportant agitator then unknown in the wide world, a certain Mr. Gandhi, had appealed for passive resistance, a crowd had gathered in the *bagh*. General Dyer led his troops there. The crowd, it was later testified, was not even asked to disperse. Within thirty seconds General Dyer ordered fire to be opened. A great roar went up from the crowd, struggling wildly to escape from the *bagh*. The firing was not in volleys but each trooper took his time and aim until they had shot down two thousand persons, — dead, dying and screaming wounded all huddled together in a small square.

At the inquiry, December, 1919, Mr. Justice Rankin said:

"Excuse me for putting it in this way, General, but was it not a form of frightfulness?"

General Dyer replied: "No, it was a horrible duty I had to perform. I think it was a merciful thing. I thought that I should shoot well and strong so that I or anybody else should not have to shoot again. . . . If I had the right to fire one shot, I had the right to fire a lot of rounds. . . . The one thing was force."

Never had colonial militarism spoken more honestly. Nothing like ounces of prevention. Nothing like nippings in the bud. Nothing like frightfulness with an inferior people. Nothing like terrorism to keep a civilian population in check. Nothing like bloodshed, violence, wars, to hold, gain, win and get. Done by everybody. Everywhere. Any intelligent military mind knew that the Germans could never hold Belgium without terrorizing the civilians, the Bolsheviki could never keep power against a majority without officially instituting terror, as the French had done a century before; and what about the American troops in the Philippines not so many years ago, or in Haiti to-day? What about Japanese military occupation of Korea? What about a hundred similar uses of force before and after the World War?

The military mind had not been able to comprehend anything but resistance. Meetings led to protests, protests led to revolutions. The British called Gandhi a Bolshevik. Mr. Gandhi replied he was not a Bolshevik, in fact had no great sympathy for their philosophy. "Bolshevism," he said, "is self-indulgence."

But in the December following the year of the Amritsar massacre, he declared war on England. "Life is impossible under this present government. We will have to stagger humanity even as South Africa and Ireland did, — with this exception, that we would rather spill our own blood and not that of our opponents." What did it all mean? It was a movement called "*swaraj*" explained Gandhi.

Then it was the world began asking, "Who is this man?" The world was told. He is a saint. He is a revolutionist. A fanatic. A patriot, an ascetic, an idealist, a dangerous man, a messiah. He had seventy-five million followers by the end of 1921, many of whom worshiped him and some of whom picked up the dust under his bare feet. When the Prince of Wales visited India and there was rioting, Mahatma Mohandas K. Gandhi, as he was now known, blaming himself for the troubles, would eat nothing, but lived on water until peace was restored. "I cannot describe the agony of those two days whose events stink in my nostrils," he said, as he started his career as the greatest hunger striker in English history.

He denounced the use of violence, force in any form. Western civilizations he termed "the worship of materialism, the worship of the brute in us."

*Underwood and Underwood*

GANDHI AT THE ROUND TABLE CONFERENCE, LONDON

In planning his war on England, he asked himself how could one hundred thousand men rule three hundred million. Force was not the complete answer, ". . . but more by securing our coöperation in a thousand ways and making us more and more helpless and dependent on them as time goes on." This view led to his declaration on the non-coöperation movement. It was adopted as a policy by the Indian National Congress of September, 1920. The boycott and the spinning wheel became Gandhi's program. He wanted every one to weave his own cloth. "Of all my plans and foibles, of all my weaknesses and fanaticisms, or whatever you like to call them, *khadi* (homespun) is my pet one. This is sacred cloth. If I can introduce the spinning wheel into every home in India, I shall be satisfied for this life; I could go on with my other schemes in my next life if it pleased God."

Many began to spin. Students spun and talked the passive revolution, and Gandhi asked that old songs be sung as every one spun, and that traveling singers go about India, teaching the people to sing at their work. In 1922 civil disobedience grew throughout India. On the tenth of March Gandhi was arrested for sedition and a few days later sentenced to six months' imprisonment without hard labor.

### HUNGER AND REVOLT IN GERMANY

"Hunger is the mother of anarchy," said Herbert Hoover, as he sailed for Europe on January 1, 1919; President Wilson tried his hand at a semi-official statement proposing relaxation of the food blockade of Germany, but Clemenceau opposed and the British Admiralty announced its ships would enforce strictly the French decree. Sentimental appeals for food found no sentimental echo. M. André Tardieu, later to be premier of France, wrote daily pieces for the world press, declaring that Germany was arming secretly, was not sincere, was not to be trusted and certainly not to be aided. Mr. Wilson's noble idea that food, not guns, would cure the world of Bolshevism, was ignored.

Nothing could convince the Allies that Germany was acting

in good faith. The propaganda of hatred continued just as successfully after the war as in the past four years. The German people felt they had been betrayed by President Wilson, on whose advice they had destroyed the Hohenzollern dynasty and made peace. The starvation which began in the fatal winter of 1917 became worse. Karl Radek and other communists preached the proletarian revolution. It came with the new year.

For two weeks there was fighting in Berlin. Finally the socialist government succeeded in seizing the Silesian railroad station and storming the trenches the Spartacus group had dug in the Tiergarten. Karl Liebknecht and Rosa Luxemburg were captured. On the night of the sixteenth they were killed. The government announced that Liebknecht had been shot "while trying to escape" and that Rosa Luxemburg was dragged by a mob from an automobile and lynched when her police guards were overpowered. Both statements were official falsehoods. But the communist uprising was over.

Gustav Noske, military governor of Berlin, was held responsible for creating two martyrs for communism in Germany. "It is regrettable," he admitted, "it will make a bad impression abroad." He did not then realize that his actions and his failures would lead soon to his demotion, and year by year in the building up of the second largest Communist Party in the world.

The elections showed complete republican victory. The Majority Socialists had more than one hundred and sixty seats in the Reichstag, the Catholics ninety-one, Democrats seventy-five, the Nationalists only twenty-eight, the much-feared Independent Socialists twenty-two and the People's Party fourteen. At Weimar in February, Ebert the saddle-maker succeeded the Kaiser and the republican constitution was adopted.

But the people starved. Unhappy, hungry and betrayed, they listened to many voices. The Kaiser, announcing the war from his palace balcony, had said, "*Ich führe euch herrliche Zeiten entgegen,*" but he had led them towards no noble times. Yet the monarchists could always tell empty-bellied masses about the full-bellied "*gute alte Zeiten*" and find followers, as Doctor Hugenberg and Hitler were to demonstrate much later on. The first inevitable monarchist reaction in March, 1920, found the Republic unprepared. The leaders had not been reading up on the French Revolution.

At 6.30 in the morning of the thirteenth, gray and misty, watchers saw the gray mist begin to move and turn blacker and take form in men and steel helmets. Suddenly there was martial music, the beating of military drums, as through the Tiergarten, coming toward the Brandenburg Gate, Doctor Kapp in an automobile led a monarchist army.

The government had found evidences of this plot only the night before and had given orders to arrest three men, Wolfgang Kapp, General von Lüttwitz and Captain Pabst (whom the year before it had defended, despite his brutality in putting down the Spartacists). Admiral Trotha, sent as an emissary to the monarchist camp at Döberitz, told Kapp his movement was politically insane. No one listened. Captain Ehrhardt of the naval brigade sent an ultimatum asking for the resignation of Ebert and his Cabinet.

Thus American newspaper representatives on the roof of the Hotel Adlon could see the government fleeing in automobiles from the Wilhelmstrasse on the right, and the Baltic adventurers marching under the Brandenburg Gate on the left. As the monarchists marched by the Adlon before turning into the Wilhelmstrasse to seize the government buildings, several persons in the crowd which had gathered began to jeer. Kapp ordered the troops to fire into the crowd, which was done. It was an almost bloodless revolution at first. Taxis and street cars continued to run about. A mounted soldier rode to the Adlon at ten o'clock and distributed a proclamation signed Kapp, Imperial Chancellor and Premier of Prussia. Ignatz Trebitsch Lincoln, former member of the British Parliament, self-styled international spy in America, destined later to be advisor to one of the main armies in the Chinese War and later still a Tibetan lama, was made press censor.

The Ebert Government, before departing for Stuttgart, struck off a proclamation to the Socialist Party and the labor unions of Berlin, calling a general strike:

Everything is at stake.
No business must be run so long as Ludendorff's military dictatorship prevails.
Therefore cease work. Strike!
Cut off the resources of this reactionary clique.
Fight with all means for the maintenance of the Republic.
Let there be a general strike all along the line.
Proletarians unite!
Down with the counter-revolution!

Kapp counter-proclaimed: "Strikes and sabotage will be ruthlessly suppressed. To strike is treason against the nation and fatherland. . . . The German nation's colors are black, white and red. These are the old Imperial colors."

The call for a general strike was answered by the cutting off of the Berlin gas supply. Then water stopped running. Kapp saw failure. Then a strange thing happened. When Noske had suppressed the Spartacists, he began organizing the "Technical Emergency Organization" to replace radicals, should another communist attempt be made. This organization of potential strike breakers went over to Kapp and restored the gas, electricity, water and transportation systems.

The American people were told that Kapp was a German born in Brooklyn and that General von Lüttwitz, whom Hoover called "one of the Kaiser's old gang" when reminded he had been military governor of Brussels, was the husband of an American, Mary Curtis Cary of Cleveland. Von Lüttwitz found American enthusiasm when he waved the same red shirt which Mussolini was to use years later. "We considered it urgent to take this action for the protection of Europe against the danger from the East," he said. "Nothing is being done by the Allies to stay the advance of Bolshevism. Prussia willed it."

Kapp issued Kaiserish proclamations and Trebitsch Lincoln censored despatches; the strike breakers were restoring Berlin to normal. But General Foch called a meeting of his generals and Major General Allen, the American commander in Coblenz, to consider moving farther into Germany. This proved unnecessary. In every part of that unhappy country union labor and socialists made their choice against return of Kaiserism and its "*herrliche Zeiten*." Fighting took place in all the large cities. In Leipzig, Hamburg, Dresden, in the Ruhr, many men killed many men — but the general strike was stronger than bloodshed. It finally drove the Brooklyn Kaiser out of the Wilhelmstrasse. Lüttwitz, the pride of Cleveland aristocracy, gave his command over to General von Seeckt. The Second Empire had lasted four full days.

As Kapp moved out, proletarian anger moved against the monarchist hostelry. The Adlon was attacked. All the American and many Allied newspapermen living there found bloodshed on their own hearth. The lobby was covered with dead and dying Old Lorenz Adlon, who had loved his Kaiser, had a chance to save him that day. The mob came in, determined to break up the old images. "Who is that? It looks like the Kaiser."

"No, no. Don't you know Wagner? That is Lohengrin."

The high-whiskered Kaiser in red marble, with the funny eagle standing on his head, is still in the lobby. But in the big banqueting hall behind it a socialist waiter with a knife cut the Kaiser's head out of a $2000 painting.

The Reichswehr occupied Essen. The Associated Press of America filled the papers with stories of looting and violence. "Russian Bolsheviki prominent in the looting," was reported out of Berlin. Undoubtedly from official sources. Voigt of the *Guardian*, Mrs. Harding of the *World*, others who were actually in Essen, found no Russian Bolsheviki or German Bolsheviki. They did find Prussian officers at their worst. Paul De

Mott, an American Quaker, was arrested for fraternizing with the workers' army, murdered in prison. American diplomacy in Berlin did nothing. Letters of introduction to soviet authorities in Moscow were found on the dead journalist. That made him a "Red." The American press corps in Berlin accepted the situation.

Thus in good time was the Ruhr situation "liquidated"; thousands of men laid down their arms and again returned to their factories and mines with a feeling of hopelessness.

### PEACE AFTER 700 YEARS

There was no armistice in the seven-hundred-year war waged by the people of Ireland. The Easter Revolution of 1916 was followed by the rebellion of 1920. British leaders said anarchy was spreading. Some called it socialism, others Bolshevism. Cavalry was hurried across in May; the army of occupation numbered eighty-six thousand in June. The British forces, known as Black and Tan, unofficially waged their own war. Like many of the original Fascisti they were returned officers and soldiers out of jobs. There were many jobs in Ireland. Killing men was a steady occupation there. Savagery worse than in Flanders fields took many lives. Men were shot in the back while praying in church. Human rights and human lives meant nothing in this civil war. "It is worse than the occupation by a foreign army."

The story of how the negotiations began which brought peace to Ireland and Britain has never been told. Behind the marching and countermarching of Lloyd George, De Valera, Sir James Craig, Arthur Griffith, Michael Collins and General Smuts there walked quietly an American journalist who unassumingly had a large hand in the treaty. He is John Steele, London correspondent of the Chicago *Tribune*. Although a Dubliner by birth, he is one of the few Irishmen dead or alive who has ever been able to see both sides of the Irish question.

In 1920 there was a particularly outrageous battle at Galway which Steele reported. Galway was burned and looted by the Black and Tans. One of the chief sufferers was Pat Moylett, a grocer. But what a grocer! Beans and rifles. Food for the stomach and patriotic endeavor. Steele and Moylett watched the grocery burn and explode and Moylett told his sad, sad story.

The next day in Dublin, Steele called on Griffith, who took him to lunch at the Shelburne and introduced him to a very important Irish patriot: it was Pat Moylett, the Galway grocer. "But I know all about the fire," said Steele and Moylett said no more. One day later Steele returned to his office in Cook's Building, Pall Mall, and there was Pat Moylett sitting on the doorstep.

Now when Pat Moylett for the third time began speaking about the atrocities in Ireland and the sack of Galway, Steele was annoyed, yet he couldn't help wondering why Griffith was so deeply involved with one of many patriotic grocers who were equipping Red Mike Collins' republican army. "Whom do you represent?" asked Steele, cutting short the repetition.

"I represent nobody. I'm just Pat Moylett."

"Did Griffith send you to me?"

"Well, no, but we're good friends."

"See here," said Steele, "do you want me to take you to Downing Street?"

"I'd be killed if I went there," replied Moylett.

"Do you want to see any one in Parliament?"

"I can't go to that den of thieves."

"What DO you want me to do?"

"Could we have some talks right here in your office?"

So John Steele called up his friend Philip Kerr, who was then secretary to Lloyd George, and the conversation began in the *Tribune* office in Pall Mall which lasted six months and ended in the Irish Peace.

Lloyd George at first was suspicious. He asked Moylett for credentials. Griffith said he couldn't send them. That caused the first break. Finally Griffith found a way: he wrote a letter addressed to the American journalist which served as credentials for Moylett to Lloyd George. But the big break came later, when Griffith insisted that the Dail Eireann, the unrecognized rebel parliament of Ireland, participate in the final peace negotiations. Lloyd George, of course, refused to recognize the Dail. Steele then proposed the magic formula. The Dail was composed of some seventy-five men and the Countess Markiewicz elected to the British Parliament. Steele proposed that the seventy-five sit as the Sinn Fein party in the British Parliament so far as Lloyd George was concerned, although Ireland could consider them as sitting as the Dail Eireann. This was accepted.

Pat Moylett used to sneak in the back way to Number 10 Downing Street, but on June 24, 1921, Lloyd George invited De Valera and Sir James Craig to come in the front door for a conference. On July 8, truce was signed between the Irish republican army and the British forces, to date the tenth, at noon — the first truce since the days of Strongbow. On August 11, De Valera refused dominion home rule and on the twenty-fourth told Lloyd George that his terms were rejected by the Dail. A new conference was accepted in September; it was then that the British Premier refused to consider the Sinn Feiners as representatives of an independent State, and after the Steele-Griffith formula was found, De Valera still maintained "we can only recognize ourselves for what we are." On the eighteenth the final compromise was reached and in the early hours of the sixth of December Griffith said to Lloyd George at Number 10 Downing Street, "We will sign. It is peace." The treaty was signed. With the new year Griffith was elected President of Ireland and Michael Collins was appointed finance minister. He was in reality head of the army and guardian of the new State. "Ireland," he declared, "is now free to rebuild and reshape its national life and institutions in accord with Irish will and Irish ideals. For that blessed liberty we know how much we owe to America."

For many months Griffith did not admit he had sent Moylett

to Steele for the purpose of initiating peace negotiations. But when he did so later, Steele asked him why he had been chosen.

"I knew it had to be started by a neutral," Griffith replied, "preferably a journalist closely in touch with Lloyd George and preferably an American. I knew that a peace treaty had to be made some time. I had many friends among American journalists. They came frequently to interview me. I asked all of them if they thought we could obtain complete independence if we continued our war. Every one but you told me we could. You were the only pessimist. You were the only one honest enough to tell me the truth, that we could not obtain independence, that the best we could do would be to get dominion status. I knew you were right. I chose you."

### A BANDIT NAMED KEMAL

If there was one great satisfaction the good Christian people of the world found in the Versailles Treaty, it was the destruction of the infidel Turkish Empire. Everything was nicely divided, partitioned, mandated, occupied, destroyed. That quarter of international trouble at least would never disturb the Powers again. The Turkish people were of course not considered human beings.

Reports that "a bandit leader named Kemal is organizing bandits in Central Turkey" failed to arouse Europe. The Greeks were in Smyrna with their army. Admiral Bristol, the cold, hard, fighting man, High Commissioner to Turkey, and probably the first diplomat who ever said a kind word for the Turks, later told Ferdinand Touhy, the journalist, that he and three others had been assigned by the Peace Conference to report on Smyrna and the Anatolian coast. They had advised against Greece. "But it was given to Greece," the Admiral told the journalist, "because the enlightened way of the world to-day is first to consider what raw materials a place produces and, secondly, what human beings. That explains why nobody wants

Armenia. In Smyrna you trip over figs and tobacco; in Armenia over the outraged bodies of women and children."

The Greeks began an offensive against the Kemalist bandits in January, 1920, advancing in four columns with guns and uniforms furnished by Sir Basil Zaharoff of the firm of Vickers, Ltd., munitions makers for the British Government, and in March the British navy occupied Constantinople.

In July the Greeks made the usual charge of Turkish massacres. In November, finding their army mutinous, nearing demobilization, torn between Venizelists and monarchists, the new Greek Government decided to attack Kemal Pasha. (He was no longer called a bandit.) March and April of 1921 were marked by great Greek successes cutting the Baghdad Railroad, capturing Eski-Shehr, causing, as London had it, the abandonment of Angora by Kemal. In the counter-attack the Associated Press reported victory by two generals, Kemal and Pasha! The Manchester *Guardian* said that at Yalova, Anatolia, the Greeks had massacred Mohammedans but no one paid any attention to atrocities unless they were committed by Turks. In July the Greeks defeated the Kemalists. In August the Kemalists drove the Greeks back to Eski-Shehr with great slaughter.

Again there was ample proof that Versailles was not a peace but only a long armistice. French policy had changed. By the sale of ammunitions to the Kemalists under the Franco-Angora treaty, France found herself vicariously at war with Britain, which had backed the Greeks. Zaharoff was sending war supplies to Smyrna; French guns were now firing at British guns, French army shoes were marching against British army shoes, and frequently American bullets made for the last great war were being fired by both sides. Diplomatic stupidity and munitions makers' cupidity were again continuing the international murder.

Summer was marked by tales from American missionaries of massacre upon massacre; two thousand Christians had been killed after one battle, girls from the American schools had been abducted for Kemalist harems, there were atrocities to please every sort of connoisseur, and again no attention was given to similar acts charged against the Greeks and Armenians. On September 4, Mustapha Kemal Pasha, the Ghazi, the Victorious, sweeping into Smyrna, issued the order to kill every soldier who dared hurt a Christian civilian. Could this be last year's old Anatolian bandit? Stamboul was feverish with victory. From Saint Sophia the muezzin called:

"Hasten, O people, hasten to the mosque. The All-Powerful has smiled on his chosen people and given us victory. The infidel is overwhelmed. Hasten, O people, hasten to the mosque. Give thanks to Allah, Allah, Allah, Akbar."

French, British, and Italian warships landed marines in Smyrna and Admiral Bristol sent his destroyers to help save the civilian population. Thousands of refugees crowded the wharves; there were unparalleled scenes of horror. Men went mad. Women gave birth to children. Many jumped into the ocean and committed suicide. There was murder. As the last boat pulled out of the harbor a girl who swam several hundred yards and was clutching a ladder, was asked her nationality. She replied. It was not the nationality of the boat. Allied commanders had given orders to take aboard only their own nationals. The girl was shoved back into the sea. Thousands watched her drown.

Kemal had entered Smyrna on the ninth; on the thirteenth the fire started which destroyed most of the city. The missionaries sent their reports blaming the Turks. Kemal replied that Armenian civilians, hiding in churches and houses, had sniped his soldiers, killing many, and that he had to attack the Armenian section. The Armenians, he said, set the city on fire. No one believed him.

In America, in fact, the Hall-Mills case crowded September with sensations richer than wars and political intrigue.

The French gave "bond" Kemal would not occupy Constantinople, so the British agreed to a peace conference; Russia asked for a place but was refused. Martial law was declared in Athens as the king abdicated. Maximilian Harden blamed the intrigues of the remaining European royal families for the Greco-Turkish war. Constantine I, twice ex-king, he said, had spent ten million dollars to get his throne back, the money being supplied by Prince Christopher's bride, the former Mrs. William B. Leeds. The plebiscite which favored the return of Constantine was "made" by the dollars which W. C. Steward of Cleveland, Ohio, got out of tin plate, and willed his daughter. Add Leeds royal ambitions to Zaharoff munitions to national patriotism and you have war in Asia.

The armistice was signed at Mudania; the Turks occupied Constantinople, ordered the Allies out, deposed the Sultan, separated Church and State, and Turkey took her place as a European nation.

### FROM RED TO WHITE IN HUNGARY

To the original stupidity of dealing with the March Revolution in Russia, the greater stupidity in the November Revolution, to the cruelty and stupidity in blockading Germany, Russia, Austria and other countries for the purpose of intensifying starvation and suffering, which led inevitably to a Bolshevik reaction, the Allies sent a note to Count Karolyi, telling him that in addition to the many pieces of Hungary already occupied by enemies, the Rumanians had been awarded more purely Hungarian territory.

Karolyi, despite his title of count, despite his name, which is the most noble, despite his riches (which the present dictatorship stole from him) was a true democrat, the real representative of the people of Hungary. But neither he nor they could accept the new criminal decision. He declared it a violation of the Armistice and resigned. Like the Wilson of the first days he determined to go over the heads of rulers and appeal to the masses for justice and support. He soon found himself without a friend.

Bolshevism immediately seized Hungary. That great enemy of the Peace Conference, which every statesman feared, was let out of Asia and into Europe.

The revolution was bloodless. With shouts of "Kun Bela — Kun Bela", the masses in Budapest marched and entrenched themselves. Journalists, still uncensored, reported that the first important change was the refusal of waiters and barbers to accept tips. Bela Kun wisely judged the situation: "The continued refusal to send food and raw materials by the Entente after the Armistice was signed did more to cause the ruin and bankruptcy of the capitalistic system of Hungary than the war itself."

All reports from Budapest had Bela Kun running the country remarkably well. Editorially the American press wondered if this could be part of the same Bolshevik system that was ruling Russia in 1919, threatening Germany and Italy. Surely not. The first outrage committed was the opening of homes having private bathtubs to the use of the children of the poor.

Suddenly the Allied and Associated Powers in a note addressed "to the people of Hungary" made public by Clemenceau, threatened them with death by starvation unless they overthrew their tyrant Bela Kun. Immediately the French and later the world press was filled with stories of the Red Terror.

There was, of course, an attempt by the Bolsheviki to maintain themselves in power through military violence, which of course involved bloodshed. Bela Kun later regretted he had acted so mildly and tried to make up for it by hanging captured Wrangel officers, only to find that again he had acted stupidly, and incurred the enmity of Lenin. The terror in Budapest, despite numerous reports, was mild, and the victims few. It is interesting to note that they shared space in the American press with news of the race war in Chicago where "looting, arson and murder" were reported the first day with fourteen dead, as many killed the second day, with a total of thirty-three dead and one thousand wounded for the three-day terror.

Credit for the fall of the communist régime in Hungary was claimed by Captain Gregory, Mr. Hoover's representative in Budapest. No government could withstand a food blockade those starving days. On the first of August, 1919, Bela Kun accepted the Allied ultimatum and the Rumanian army was forty miles away. General Henry H. Bandholtz, who represented the American army, telegraphed that "the reign of terror which began in March is ended." Three days later the Rumanian army marched in and looted the capital. Stupid diplomacy achieved another victory.

That curious soldier Bandholtz then turned on the Rumanians and spoiled their little plan of annexing the whole country. When Archduke Joseph learned that the noble Balkan ally had the support of "an Allied Power" — in those days it would have been treason to name France — for its plan of uniting the two countries under King Ferdinand and the beauteous Marie, he rushed over to Bandholtz's headquarters and asked what to do.

"You tell the Rumanians to go to hell," Bandholtz replied.

The archduke thought that was not sufficient. Bandholtz called on the Rumanian general and told him the same in more careful words. With a riding whip in his hand, Bandholtz himself fought a battalion of Rumanian troops and drove them out of a palace they had come to loot. He burned up the wires to Paris. The Rumanians were eventually asked to depart.

They took with them everything they could steal. They did not confiscate; they stole! They took twenty thousand carloads of food out of a starving country. They took the seed grain for the next year's harvest. They stole the horses from famous stud farms and used them for artillery carriages, or let them drown fording a river. They stole oil paintings and silver forks.

Then Admiral Horthy marched into Budapest and restored order. He also restored the landlords and feudalism, and a peasant system very close to serfdom. And Europe cheered. The starving, unhappy Hungarians who had tried democracy and been destroyed by the Allies, who had tried communism, and been destroyed by the Allies, were now back to the good old pre-war days. Admiral Horthy instituted a "white terror" to keep them good.

## TWENTY-THREE SMALL WARS

Civil war broke out in China on the first of May, 1922, but America was not interested.

The arrest of several American missionaries, however, showed that Japan was slaughtering the Korean revolutionaries. The Peace Conference, sitting in Paris, did not find time to look into that matter. Perhaps the League of Nations, at a later date . . .

Amanullah, who rose to kingship through the assassination of his brother, raided the northern frontier, frightening the British, who had been paying all Afghan emirs blood money for decades. They believed that the Russians had offered a higher price.

The Moors fought for freedom in Morocco; Spain admitted a disastrous defeat and a retreat from Melilla in July, 1921, but the war of the victorious Allies, against the natives seeking independence, was to continue for many years.

In France there was a suspicion of a military dictatorship. In October, 1919, Clemenceau summoned General Mangin — the hero of the battle of Villers-Cotterets, the man who led the First and Second American divisions and turned the war into victory. Mangin came from Mainz. Clemenceau dismissed him from command of the Rhine.

"Are you dissatisfied with my services?" asked Mangin.

"Not at all."

"Do you disapprove of my policy on the Rhine?"

"Not in the least."

"Then do you think I am going to allow myself to be smashed between two doors without any reason?"

M. Clemenceau did not answer.

"Mangin," he said to others, "is too smart to be a general and the French army is too devoted to him. This I consider a danger to the republic."

In this way Clemenceau is said to have circumvented a military dictatorship of France.

Bonar Law, recounting the state of world progress towards peace, told the House of Commons there were twenty-three small wars now being waged: the Armistice of 1918 was lengthening into the years.

## Interlude 1922

Influenza claimed Pope Benedict, who had said, "I would willingly offer my life for the peace of the world." Cardinal Maffi, scholar, liberal, anti-Fascist, was predicted his successor. Would the conclave wait for the arrival of the American cardinals? Deadlock in Rome! Crowds waited to see the smoke rise when ballots were burned. Cardinal Ratti of Milan became Pius XI. Under thousands of umbrellas Roman crowds cried, "We have a Pope." He sent Americans this message: "I have for many years admired their youthful energy and aims. I hope they will soon learn to love me." Cardinal O'Connell arrived an hour late.

Cannibalism was reported in Russia.

Survey of two years of prohibition shows money values of $2,870,000,000 lost. Keynes placed German possibilities at five and one-half billion dollars.

Siki, Negro, was "framed" but fifty thousand white men shouting for Carpentier made him knock Georges out. "Black honor," he cried.

Two hundred thousand wireless installations in New York area. Use of radio telephone for personal communications national problem; Hoover called a conference. "Is radio becoming national vogue? Will it stay like the automobile?" Static was the great word of 1922.

Mah Jong was the fad of youth; Steinach and Voronoff of age.

Mr. Mencken wrote "The American Language." Ring Lardner, Dorothy Parker, Heywood Broun, F.P.A., contributed samples of modern slang.

Walter Rathenau's mother wrote to the mother of the monarchist lad who had assassinated the German foreign minister, "I stretch out my hand to you, the poorest of all women. Tell your son I forgive him in the name and spirit of my assassinated son, as God Almighty will forgive him if he confesses and repents. . . ."

Mr. Clemenceau came to America on a mission of hate and was welcomed enthusiastically. General Semenoff, another American idol, accused of banditry, brigandage, murdering two doughboys, was released. Ex-Premier Gounaris and four Cabinet members shot to death as traitors in Athens.

Kaiser Wilhelm married Princess Hermine of Reuss. "I know I love him," said the childhood sweetheart. "He is not so rich it can be said I am marrying for money."

The Reverend Edward Wheeler Hall and Mrs. James Mills, leader of the choir, wife of the sexton, were found dead on an abandoned farm, two miles from New Brunswick, New Jersey, on the 16th of September, and the case was discussed for the rest of the year.

M. Deibler came into his cell. M. Landru dressed. M. Deibler cut the shirt top off and shaved the neck to make the fall of the knife certain.

"Will you have a glass of rum?" — "Merci, I never drink" — "A cigarette?" — "I rarely smoke." The murderer had no bad habits. "Have you any declaration to make?" asked Judge Beguin. "To a man who scarcely belongs to this world I consider such a question an insult." Landru looked interestedly at the famous guillotine. All had been quiet. Suddenly two men seized Landru, threw him down. In two seconds the execution was over. Fifty newspapermen watched. Thus the guillotine revenged ten women who had loved France's greatest criminal.

The great mark swindle went on in Germany, costing America between nine hundred and sixty million and two billion dollars. Caillaux said, "On the rich industrialists of the Rhine lies the heaviest responsibility for the world's frightful tragedy." The tragedy went on another year. Hugo Stinnes banked his first billion dollars.

Britain fortified the Dardanelles; the Labor Party opposed a new war. "You can bet your life if we have another war we will use gas . . . and we don't care how, when or why," said Admiral Sims.

All the men who inhabit heaven are aged thirty and all the women twenty-five; the sullen and vicious ghosts are left alone; that is their punishment, reported Conan Doyle. Spiritism vied with Mah Jong.

Rory O'Connor captured the Four Courts and his best friend Michael Collins attacked him with artillery.

The first armored car for money delivery appeared in New York.

Professor Joseph Tykociner Tykocinowski of the University of Illinois demonstrated a motion-picture camera which also synchronized with the human voice, "not an experiment, a demonstrated fact."

Insulin was discovered.

The Passion Play was given in Oberammergau.

On the last day of the year in Moscow, fourteen nations dominated by Lenin and Trotsky met in the Kremlin, abolished the R. S. F. S. R. and announced the birth of the Union of Socialist Soviet Republics.

"We'll eat pie
In the sky
Bye and bye,"

sang Big Bill Haywood; "but, hell, there ain't no apple pie in Russia; we'll have to change that song."

# PART TWO: TOWARDS A NEW WORLD

## CHAPTER SIX

### THE WORLD VERSUS BOLSHEVISM

WE know now that the Treaty of Versailles was signed in fear of the Red shadow of the Kremlin. It had spread toward Asia and India and the centers of European civilization, almost engulfed Germany and Finland, gripped Hungary and threatened Italy, while the statesmen were talking colonies and frontiers in Paris. They became frightened. A treaty had to be signed, good or bad, and a lot of national houses put in order.

Bolshevism advanced with bayonets in Germany while Wilson was at sea. In the first days of the Peace Conference, while the world sank back into the old morass of fear, suspicion, rivalry, greed and intolerance, as Gibbs noted even then, not only Germans but people in Allied countries began groping for something with which to fight the Old World system the conference had failed to destroy. They tried organized labor, but organized labor was shown the door by the great statesmen; they tried socialism, but socialism was met with policemen; so eventually, at times and in certain places, the other red flag, the one with the crossed sickle and hammer, was raised.

To fight this new menace, the world diplomats in Paris, by their power of censorship and suppression, were able to continue their game. They did not fight Bolshevism for exactly what it was, — dictatorship, denial of parliamentary-democratic system, abolition of the personal and public liberties gained in centuries of struggle; they invented a bogey for Europe and America. They permitted no independent observation, no uncensored reports, no communications, and they decreed simply that any one who questioned their actions was a Bolshevik himself.

Bolshevism became a synonym of "bloodthirsty anarchy and mob rule", "nothing but massacre of all who are respectable, thrifty, educated or decent", "the greatest threat to civilization in history", to quote the press, and when Mr. Hoover proposed feeding Germany he explained that "the danger of Bolshevism was worse than the danger of war." The American army, which at first could not understand its daily drilling and marching and polishing of cannon, was informed by the generals that "You are the frontier of civilization against Bolshevism", and was kept ready to repel the invader.

No one but Wilson believed that Russia could be treated as a civilized nation — say as civilized as Poland — and he too was soon tricked out of his Prinkipo conference plan. The French frankly wanted war with Russia. In Britain, Churchill wanted war; Lloyd George, astute as usual, favored aid for one or another general fighting the Reds, then would turn to compromises and pacts. Some politicians thought promises of food, money, Constantinople, or recognition would win the Soviets for the Allied side. There had been great indecision throughout the last year of the war and this indecision continued until long after the four civil wars and the Polish war had been won by the Soviets, and the famine undergone, and Russia had emerged with a powerful army and a new economic thesis.

The Allies fought Russia in two ways: by subventioning all the military movements which sought to restore the monarchy, and by the Polish war of aggression (the most important attempt of all to upset the Soviets, the history of which will be given later in this chapter), and by a greater barrage of propaganda than Germany had suffered in its four fighting years.

The morning before the Armistice every newspaper in the Allied world published the Bolshevik proclamation of a massacre of the bourgeoisie and upper classes. In the London *Times* and *Petit Parisien,* for example, it read:

> The murder of Volodarski and Uritzky, the attempt on the life of Lenin . . . show that notwithstanding the frequent pro-

nouncements urging mass terror against the Social Revolutionaries, the White Guards and the bourgeoisie, no real terror exists.

Such a situation should decidedly be terminated and an end put to weakness and softness. All Right Social Revolutionists known to the local Soviets should be arrested immediately, numerous hostages taken from the bourgeois officer classes and at the slightest attempt to resist or the slightest movement among the White Guards, the shooting of masses of the hostages should be begun without fail. . . .

Shoot without fail anybody connected with the White Guards. . . .

Not the slightest hesitation will be tolerated in the using of mass terror.

(Signed) PETROFSKY.

In America this was not enough. To stir up moral indignation, the following paragraph was added:

The decree issued by the Bolsheviki of the government of Vladimir, declaring all unmarried girls of eighteen to be the property of the State, and requiring them to choose provisional husbands, was copied from decrees in force in the Luza and Koplin districts.

Some important papers also contained news of "the nationalization of women of the city of Hvolinsk."

The London *Daily Telegraph* reported that there was a reign of terror in Odessa accompanied by a "free love week."

The Poles sent out a statement that the Bolsheviki had captured Vilna, where "a massacre of civilians was started at once."

These stories with thousands of variations were repeated everywhere and no doubt are still believed by good citizens to-day. Proofs of falsity were not wanted by the French Foreign Office, the nations planning or paying for wars on Russia, or the munitions makers' association. It took Lincoln Eyre two years, for example, to trace the origin of the myth of the nationalization of women. He found that it had been invented in the office of the newspaper once recognized as the greatest in the world, the London *Times*. It will be remembered that the *Times* had a weak moment. During the war it passed into the hands of Lord Northcliffe, owner of the *Daily Mail*, and became the yellowest of the jingo press, remaining so until insanity and death ended the career of his lordship and restored the *Times* to sane hands again. It was Lord Northcliffe who propagated the myth of the *Kadaververwertunganstalt*, publishing corroborative testimony and photographs, all false, which accused the Germans of using the bodies of soldiers for making grease. In war, this reckless journalist believed that all weapons were justifiable — and he was now at war with Russia.

In the first weeks of Wilson's visit to Paris he could also read in the local press and in the great New York papers as they arrived, the following pleasing events: (January 8) Trotsky arrests Lenin and makes himself sole dictator; (February 1) General Korniloff's head torn off and used as football by Bolsheviki; (January 15) Trotsky flees Petrograd; (January 16) Trotsky captured with Krylenko, the bloodthirsty head of the Red Terror; (January 23) (Helsingfors) Russian Red Cross reports Bolsheviki killed three thousand in Kiev, butchered men, women and children like cattle in cellars. Orgies took place, interrupted by murder and bloodshed. Mass arrests. Doctors and lawyers murdered *en masse*. And on any day in some great newspaper the faithful prediction, "Fall of Bolsheviki believed certain", as this or that general advanced on Moscow.

What no one was allowed to publish at the time was any report of the outbreaks called mutinies among the British troops selected for reinforcements at Archangel, January 1, 1919. Lloyd George decided at once to withdraw his men and replace them with volunteers. He proposed to France that all Russian factions be invited to a truce and on the eleventh of January France refused. President Wilson was astonished. He had never heard of the British proposal. The scandal on both Continents was unbounded. Later, Assistant Secretary of State Polk took the blame, saying he had not communicated the British plan because he believed that a copy had surely been handed to Wilson in Paris.

The battle between France and the Allies thus continued, by diplomacy, perversion of the press, forged documents, censorship of the Paris newspapers, false news, and the daily tricking of Mr. Wilson, whose Prinkipo peace conference plan failed in February; and finally, in April, Maréchal Foch came to the conference with the proposal to end the Russian anomaly once and for all by making it a military question: he was prepared to organize armies and navies to capture Moscow, if necessary and — collect the Tsarist debts.

At this moment Mr. Wilson threatened to go home.

The British troops mutinied. The French troops mutinied. Even the Russian detachment, the White Russians who were supposed to take over the whole Archangel front when the Allies had established it, mutinied, but the British censorship suppressed these facts. Finally the American troops mutinied and the British gladly permitted even exaggerations to pass.

Bolshevik propaganda was blamed as usual. The outstanding fact, as all veterans testified later, was the inability of the command to answer the simple question: "What are we fighting for?" It is true that the question was first proposed by the Bolsheviki. They came over to the Allied line and said, "Comrades, why are you fighting us? We do not want to fight. We want to be let alone. You go home and we'll go home. Why are you fighting us?"

The men of the American 339th Infantry, back in Detroit, say they did not mutiny. They simply refused to load trucks with war supplies going up to the Front. Colonel Stewart arrived and made a speech.

"Why don't the Russians fight?" the men shouted.

"Why don't the French go in?"

"What are we here for, anyway?"

"We are fighting," replied the colonel, "because we will be annihilated if we don't. That is reason enough for me."

But the colonel did not answer the questions. Jay Hayden, historian of the episode, states that "the colonel asked Washington and they couldn't tell him." Hayden addressed the question to President Wilson, Colonel House and General Bliss, all busy making peace in Paris, and got no answer.

The French soldiers absolutely disobeyed their officers; they would not do outpost duty in the daytime, saying there was no sense to that at all. The White Russians "ate the bread of idleness." The Allied commanders were afraid to use them for fear they would join the Bolsheviki. The British troops mutinied at Kodish. Several detachments mutinied not once but three times.

Finally the Americans retreated from Shenkursk, a soldier reporting that "the fact of being beaten, of retreating, was lost in the ray of hope they were moving a step nearer home." They hoped they would be driven clean on to the vessels docked at Archangel, ready to carry them to the United States.

On January 18, 1920, the Allies advised Poland to abandon occupied Russian territory.

This fact is worth emphasizing. The Polish Army, outfitted with American uniforms, American supplies and French guns, had in 1918 left its own frontier behind and claimed a great victory at the opening of the New Year. It was only after the Russians had defeated them, months later, that the usual "defensive war" propaganda was loosed from Paris, with the claim that Russia had invaded Poland.

Lloyd George further advised the Polish foreign minister, Patek, to make peace. There was starvation everywhere, also typhus; Poland was crying for world charity, the nation was bankrupt and the British liberal press was asking what sinister motive backed the invasion of Russia. A wireless signed Lenin, Trotsky and Chicherin invited Patek to a friendly council, saying Russia was ready, warning Poland that "the agents of Churchill and Clemenceau are inciting Poland to a senseless criminal war."

The Polish Government rejected an armistice in April. Bolshevik resistance was broken everywhere. The Kosciusko Squadron received the plaudits of America. Colonel Charles Sweeney, known as Sweeney of the Tanks, one of our greatest soldiers of fortune, had recruited more than a hundred American aviators who, like those of the Lafayette Escadrille, were to repay a foreign soldier's service in the Revolutionary War. Major Cedric Fauntleroy of Chicago rose to the command of the Polish Second Army aviation. Captain Merian Cooper of Jacksonville commanded the Kosciusko. In the big offensive they made thirty raids, killing and wounding hundreds of Russians.

Pilsudski, making a deal with Petlura, marched to Kiev. The liberal press said it was madness to start an offensive just because the Poles couldn't agree on a suitable town for a peace conference, but the majority sang pæans of praise for Pilsudski. May 3d he announced the capture of Kiev and the church bells of Warsaw rang brazen victory. The Poles announced there was revolution in Moscow and that Lenin had shot Trotsky or vice versa. Paris announced Pilsudski would soon march on Odessa! Modestly the hero announced officially he would refrain from taking Moscow at the moment.

In Kiev, Pilsudski granted Rothay Reynolds an interview in which he said, "The Bolshevik army is badly organized. The Red soldiers fight badly. I have taken thirty thousand prisoners and my losses are less than one hundred killed. We are across the Dneiper and I can go as far as I like."

The very next day, May 22, Brusiloff attacked in a big pincher movement, Cossack cavalry on the scissors points, galloping down on Kiev, galloping through the end of May, through all June, and into July.

Defeated everywhere, Poland returned to the conference of Allied premiers sitting in Spa to divide the German billions. Its delegation applied first to Millerand, who had backed the Kiev adventure. Millerand passed them on to Lloyd George. The British Labor Party helped spike the conference by its publication of secret documents concerning the nonsinkable Winston Churchill's promises to support all White Russian armies, Kolchak, Denikin, etc., with military advisers and one hundred and twenty million dollars. Lloyd George frowned. Who was it, he asked, who first advised Pan Patek not to march into the Ukraine; who was it promised he would never send men, money or munitions? The Poles replied they were desperate; what should they do?

"You can always sue for peace," replied Lloyd George coldly.

The next day, "faced with the necessity of shortening their line", as the journalists had it, the Poles began fleeing on a seven hundred and twenty mile front.

Pilsudski's dream of empire dissolved in the Ukraine. He had tried the Napoleon and the Kaiser Wilhelm rôle; now the same gentlemen who a few weeks before had called him "the savior of civilization from the Red Peril" suggested that "he cannot career around on horseback over country occupied by peoples of other races as was done in the Middle Ages." Other of yesterday's supporters spoke of "egotism", "swell-headedness", "delusions of grandeur", "Nietzschean madness."

French diplomacy finally overcame Lloyd George's coldness; a joint note was dispatched; Russia was told trade agreements would be delayed in London unless an armistice was concluded and Poland was told it would be defended *once its troops had retreated within its own frontier*. Which happened soon enough. Russia informed Lloyd George it would accept armistice proposals directly from Warsaw. The British premier declared Russia was insincere, as usual. Russian cavalry, end of July, began circling Warsaw and threatening the German frontier. Poland asked for an armistice. Moscow ordered its generals to cease their advance and arrange the armistice. On August 27 the Allies rejected the Russian terms. The Associated Press of America was tricked by French diplomatic officials into sending a dispatch on the very day the new armistice terms were under way, stating "it is asserted in French quarters that a secret-code wireless message from Moscow gave instructions to the soviet commanders to keep pushing their offensive violently."

General Max Weygand, assistant to Foch, and a large French general staff, offered to save Poland. On the sixth of August the Russians halted their encircling movement of Warsaw and on the eighth the Soviets agreed to an armistice, provided the French agreed not to advance or support any advance against Russia, and to withdraw their support from General Wrangel in the Crimea. The Russians asked for an armistice on *all* fronts. The press in many nations proclaimed "Reds refuse armistice terms." Lloyd George and Millerand met in Hythe. The Polish general staff rejected General Weygand but accepted his ideas of regrouping. Russia sent new armistice terms, calling for Polish demilitarization. Lloyd George appealed to America to save Poland. Wilson issued a note refusing to recognize Russia, declaring the Russian people are not in sympathy with the government, expressing his faith in the Polish empire he had created.

Hardly had Lloyd George got home from Hythe when he read in his paper that France had blown the armistice and peace in Poland to smithereens by officially recognizing General Peter Wrangel in South Russia, offering support with money, guns and officers, for war on Moscow. If Mr. Lloyd George had had a knife thrust in his ribs he could not have been more surprised. The British Labor Party, not certain whether Millerand had betrayed Lloyd George, or Lloyd George had betrayed Britain by pledging union with France's new war, announced open resistance to any military intervention and threatened a general strike if Lloyd George sided with France.

Wrangel attacked on the fourteenth, defeating the thirteenth Bolshevik army, capturing four thousand prisoners, threatening to march north and disengage the Trotsky army from Warsaw. The signal was given by the Quai d'Orsay for the world press to shout its praise of Peter Wrangel, third, but not last savior of civilization in Russia. "He is bringing order out of Bolshevik chaos." "His rule is based on justice for every man," sang the press, as Wrangel marched on, restoring the land to the barons, massacring his opponents, reëstablishing the old tyranny.

Polish success on the seventeenth of August turned to national rejoicing on the nineteenth when the French plan of the Marne with French generals, and French ammunition in tremendous quantities, triumphed within sight of those on Warsaw's steeples. General Weygand and his six hundred officers received the homage of the capital. "This magnificent victory," he said honestly, "consolidates the Polish State whose existence is indispensable to France's existence."

In Washington the State Department admitted that it had sent a note to Poland, asking for a declaration of intention to abstain from occupying Russian territory.

September opened with a Polish assault in which "the Bolshevik cavalry under General Budenny has been annihilated." The victorious Poles now informed the American Government they would not halt their advance at the "artificial boundaries" specified by President Wilson. The note, signed by Prince Lubomirski, said also that "This war, which was forced upon us by the attack made on Polish cities, is a defensive war, and is waged against Bolshevism and not against the Russian people. . . . Poland guards Europe against the Bolshevik wave."

The State Department thought the Polish reply was "satisfactory."

Pilsudski determined to impose his terms on the routed foe.

Trotsky let the Poles dictate the peace of Riga in October, 1920, as Wrangel moved against him and Reuters reported revolt throughout Russia and the fall of the Soviets imminent, and the *Daily Telegraph*, "great rebellion in Moscow", which the American State Department confirmed, adding that Wrangel had captured twenty-seven thousand men and was "sweeping the Reds to east and north." Thus, with the collapse of the Soviets at last certain, the British joined by charging plots in India, and the Poles threatened to renew their war again.

But on the first of November, in a way inexplicable to daily readers, the French guns were silenced and Wrangel came to his end. Lenin sent Bela Kun to liquidate the White Army in the south, a task which Kun accomplished by many hangings, and Lenin refused to shake his hand when he returned. Addressing the All Russian Soviet Congress, Lenin not without pride announced, "All of our foes are beaten. We can now go to the work of economic reconstruction."

The era of the White Generals was over. But two greater enemies arose within the country itself: the Kronstadt sailors who represented the disillusion which Bolshevism had brought on the people of Russia, and the famine, which was an act of God aided by the peasantry.

In March, 1921, airplanes flying over Petrograd issued a proclamation to the inhabitants:

"Ultimatum: Release all the revolutionary political prisoners.

"Free speech. Free Press. Freedom of assembly.

"Freedom of organization and existence of other revolutionary although opposition parties.

"Constituent Assembly of all factions, to rule Russia."

But Petrograd did not arise. The masses were indifferent. They had had enough of promises from other leaders and feared any new régime would be as bad as the present. In the world press the first reports cheered the Red sailors as anti-Bolshevik although the wireless from Kronstadt, addressed "to all", asked aid to "fight for the election of a *free* Soviet." No one realized it was the first and almost last attempt of the Russian Revolution to replace a party dictatorship with a democratic régime. Trotsky mobilized his men and crushed the sailors without mercy.

The revolt of the peasants was silent. Refusing to pay the ten per cent. tax "in kind", they had failed to deliver the wheat and the live stock which the soviet collectors demanded, and they had reduced their cultivated acreage. Crop failures in Russia had been cyclical; fertilizers were rarely used, and due to extraordinarily severe weather conditions, the land in 1921 produced almost nothing, while the sun in the Southern Volga burned up the fields with heat that caused fissures like those of a volcanic eruption.

Facing famine, Lenin appealed to America for recognition and the resumption of trade relations, to which Secretary of State Hughes replied with a note "as near a flat refusal as diplomatic language allows", asking Litvinoff to furnish proof that there had been a radical change in the soviet system, especially as regards human life, guarantees of private property, the sanctity of contracts, and the rights of free labor.

Lenin then announced the end of grain requisitioning in March, admitting frankly that "the peasants refuse to accept any longer proletarian dictatorship" and in May the All-Russian Trades Union Congress approved the New Economic Policy, which reëstablished peasant individuality, private ownership and trade, and the middle-class merchant, or Nepman, as he was soon to be called.

The NEP did not save Russia from famine. It was too late. Millions hungered and thousands began to die. Maxim Gorki appealed to the American Government for help. Mr. Hoover, as food administrator, replied he would help on condition the seven Americans held in Russian prisons were released. "To the whole American people the absolute *sine qua non* of any assistance must be the immediate release of the Americans held prisoners in Russia. . . ." Mr. Hoover and the State Department did not inquire whether one or more of the seven had committed a robbery or a murder, or was a spy, or had contravened the laws of the country. The attitude of all governments at that time was that the Russian Government in every action was completely wrong, therefore any one jailed must, as corollary, be absolutely right.

Then began a diplomatic wrangle which lasted many weeks. It concerned chiefly Mrs. Marguerite E. Harrison, a prominent Baltimore society woman, sister-in-law of Governor Ritchie, who had crossed from the Polish to the Russian lines in June, 1920, saying she was a correspondent for the Baltimore *Sun* and the Associated Press. The Bolsheviki claimed she was a secret agent for the State Department and arrested her. The case soon became celebrated. The State Department denied Mrs. Harrison as its agent. The Associated Press said she was not a "regular" correspondent. The representative of the New York *World*, Mrs. Stan Harding, who was invited to Moscow by Mrs. Harrison and taken from the latter's home to a Cheka dungeon the moment of arrival, made accusations. The publisher Albert Boni also suspected the charming lady of giving the Cheka information leading to his imprisonment. A labor leader returning to America from Moscow was quoted as saying the Bolsheviki had threatened to execute Mrs. Harrison as a spy and that she escaped death "by taking up the work she is now in — spying on her countrymen."

But the American State Department was not interested in anything but *habeas corpus*. The ultimatum, all Americans free or no food, was repeated. Chicherin cabled in reply, "Mrs. Harrison is in good health. . . . The Associated Press statement picturing her in dire straits is untrue. She cannot be released at present in view of her activities as a self-confessed spy."

The number of starving reached twenty million. Six million men, women and children fled from the burned zone, wandering the plains, as far as the eye could see, roaming like Tartars, feeding on grass and the bark of trees, seeking for food and finding none. They abandoned three hundred thousand children along the Volga.

Then in July Lenin ordered Mrs. Harrison released. In a statement, she reasserted she came to Russia for the *Sun* and Associated Press, and "also had agreed to observe conditions and furnish confidential reports on Russia for the information of the American Military Intelligence . . . pressure was brought on me to agree to work for the Soviet Government. For certain imperative reasons, I did not reject the offer but temporized with the soviet authorities, furnishing them worthless information, thus affording ample justification for my subsequent arrest."

Finally in September, months after Gorki had appealed to Hoover, the first food train started for Moscow with American relief workers. In the course of a year they fed ten million of the twenty million they found hungry, but still millions died. How many of these could have been saved had there been no diplomatic wrangling, no one can tell. Certainly hundreds of thousands. Early in 1922, Nansen, who headed the Geneva relief mission, telegraphed from Orenburg that the famine was so bad that people were killing each other and parents were also eating their children, and the National Civic Federation of America asked that Congress investigate the relief work because it felt certain that food was helping to keep the Bolsheviki in power. Some time later Mrs. Harding asked the British Government to press charges against Mrs. Harrison; Downing Street did demand that the Soviets acknowledge Mrs. Harding's case as one of false arrest, which was done, and two thousand pounds given in recompense. Floyd Gibbons distinguished himself by beating the world with four daily cables from the famine zone, the first eyewitness accounts. He quoted a peasant as saying, "We fought with the birds for the last seeds in the fields." Colonel Haskell established thirty-five thousand relief stations, fifteen thousand hospitals, fought the plague, fought the Soviets, when they attempted to divert the food so that party communists would benefit, and in saving millions of people, incidentally had to save the Soviets.

### HOW AMERICA FACED THE RED MENACE

The American position, therefore, is somewhat of a grim paradox. The sixty million dollars which the government and the public subscribed for the Russian people were not intended for subtle work in undermining and destroying the communist system or in spying out markets for cotton goods, cameras and canned peaches, as the Bolsheviki had charged. That the high officials of the Hoover Relief "entertained" a hope that feeding would reform the Russian communist ideas may perhaps be accepted, but altogether it was the usual typical noble action of the American people, stirred emotionally by some great disaster in any part of the world. Even when it was known that the feeding of the population would preserve the Soviets, the work went along unchecked.

But the action of exterminating Bolshevism in America was prosecuted even more fiercely. The American people were not permitted to learn anything about Russia except its terror and its horrors.

"It is not compatible with public interest," said Secretary Lansing a few days after the Armistice, to reply to questions regarding Russia. The State Department had been asked if it was true the American Government knew Lenin and Trotsky opposed the Brest-Litovsk treaty but signed it because the Allies were not coming to Russia's aid, as promised; was it true that Lenin and Trotsky, before signing, gave Colonel Robins a letter to Wilson which said the treaty would not be signed if Wilson would assure moral support, food and arms; was it true the letter reached Lansing, but not Wilson, until after the decision to intervene against the Soviets; was it true that Colonel Robins, on returning to Washington, was refused an interview by Wilson; was it true that Robins was told to shut up by his organization, the American Red Cross, and by the State Department?

It is certainly true that Colonel Raymond Robins, "our principal witness about Russia", came out of Moscow, the first to say that Lenin and Trotsky were not German agents and the first to oppose America's sending troops to help the Allied wars on Russia. It is certainly true that Colonel Robins immediately was denounced as a Red by all good patriots, and it is certainly true that the State Department, besides issuing news about Russia which did not correspond to the facts, suppressed all attempts at getting at the truth of the situation, diplomatic and military.

America, where the words radical, liberal, socialist, anarchist and Bolshevik are synonymous to millions of newspaper-educated gentlemen, therefore indulged in a mad hysteria about everything Red. Opponents of anything, persons, ideas, had but to utter the word Bolshevik and it was damned eternally. Senator La Follette asked that the American troops be withdrawn from Archangel. (Leading generals had done likewise.) La Follette's opponents branded him as "the Bolshevik spokesman in America." In Seattle the men on the Stone and Webster lines went out on strike for decent wages; Mayor Ole Hanson called them Bolsheviki, crushed them, became a national lecturer, might have been President if the Coolidge-Boston-strike hysteria had persisted in the State of Washington. In Butte, Montana, the Sailors and Soldiers Association endorsed the strike of the miners but Major A. M. Jones called them I.W.W.'s and Bolsheviki, led the Forty-fourth Infantry against them, warning the friendly soldiers he was armed to the teeth with machine guns, "and there will be no dallying."

Great press investigations led to alarming exposures of the spread of Bolshevism in America. Not content with finding that the I.W.W. had several thousand members and was urging "go slow" to men in industry, it was discovered that the intellectual group representing Moscow was publishing the *World To-morrow*, the *Nation*, the *Dial*, the *New Republic*, the *Call*, the *Liberator*. "There is no question about the sincerity of the different editors connected with these various publications, which include Norman Thomas, an ex-minister, John Haynes Holmes, Oswald Garrison Villard, Henry Raymond Mussey, Lincoln Colcord, Martin Johnson, Herbert Crowley, Walter Weyl, Walter Lippmann, Signe Toksvig, H. W. L. Dana", declared one crusader; it was deplorable that the intellectuals were Americans who could not be deported. All foreign radicals were to be sent from the United States. How many were there? About six hundred thousand, raged one noble patriot. Actually only a few hundred were found deportable and the total "undesirables" numbered less than thirty thousand.

The *Buford,* or "Soviet Ark", prepared to sail with two hundred and forty-six men, three women, on December 21, 1919, taking to Soviet Russia two of America's most notorious radicals, Emma Goldman and Alexander Berkman. Berkman was at Ellis Island for the second time in his life. Henry Clay Frick lay in state, dead in his palace in Pittsburgh, lauded in the press as a great man. He was praised because he had bought Rembrandt's best canvas, the last self-portrait, and another fine picture, "The Polish Cavalier", which the Tarnowski family had kept over a hundred years before succumbing to foreign gold.

Alexander Berkman, armed with a revolver which Emma Goldman's few dollars had bought, shot Frick and went to jail for twenty-one years for it and an extra year in the workhouse after he would finish with the penitentiary. He gave the world his "Prison Memoirs", one of the great human documents written in America, and Frick gave to America all the fine paintings he had bought in Europe with all the dollars he made by employing non-union men.

The *Buford* sailed and America sighed its relief; soon it was planned to fill the ship a hundred times, and many more such ships.

"I'll be back in two years," said Emma Goldman.

"There is work for me in Soviet Russia," said Berkman.

"I do not consider it a punishment, I consider it an honor," said Emma Goldman, "and the first thing I will do is organize the Russian Friends of American Freedom."

That was in December; we next hear her telling a reporter on the Finnish border that "this is the greatest moment of my life", which is perhaps her motto for 1920; then suddenly, in mid-1921, comes a proclamation signed by her and Berkman and other radicals, accusing Lenin of filling the prisons with thousands of radicals who are not one hundred per cent. pure

Bolshevik, and of permitting tortures and executions; then 1922 begins for these most notorious American Reds with an attack on Lenin's "blood and murder régime — revolting Asiatic form of extermination; our comrades have been arrested and shot as bandits by the Cheka . . . merely holding opposing views makes you the legitimate prey of the Cheka. . . . Make haste, for the blood of our comrades is flowing in Russia."

They smuggled out their protests, then found haven in Sweden. "I came to Russia with burning enthusiasm for the revolution," confessed Emma Goldman; "I left America with rejoicing and hope, but now I have nothing left but crushed illusions. I am depressed when I think about it and the words stick in my throat. But I must talk so that the proletariat can learn by my mistake."

Thus, from one radical quarter, Bolshevism was repudiated. Certainly those who believed the miracle of Marxian idealism had been achieved in Moscow suffered a black eye and a gloomy change of view. Politically the sensation of late 1919 was the testimony of William C. Bullitt, formerly of the State Department, who as chief of the division of current intelligence of the American peace delegation had gone to Russia accompanied by Lincoln Steffens, to obtain the armistice terms on which Lenin would return to the European concert of nations. Bullitt told the Foreign Relations Committee in Washington how Colonel House, at the President's suggestion, had arranged the trip and how Wilson refused to receive him later, and how Lloyd George had repudiated him. The Lenin peace terms, which he obtained before the signing at Versailles were:

Lifting of the food blockade.
Non-interference with Soviet sovereignty.
Reciprocal rights of entry into all nations' territory.
Release of all political and war prisoners.
Withdrawal of foreign troops from Russia.

Bullitt had gone to Russia at a time the Soviets were strong; he returned at a time Kolchak was winning — Kolchak had made a hundred-mile advance and negotiations with Lenin were dropped for that reason, Bullitt believed.

The result of the Bullitt sensation was more ammunition against Wilson. There was no regret that Russia had not been brought into social and political relationship with the world on the terms asked by Lenin. The police, the Department of Justice and the daily press, with only a few exceptions, continued to encourage Red-baiting as they had Hun-baiting for several years, and although arrests were made of thousands, few were held for trial and fewer still deported. For May Day, 1920, A. Mitchell Palmer promised America that the Bolsheviki, hundreds of thousands strong, would attempt to overthrow the United States Government and plant the red flag on the Capitol in Washington, incidentally murdering all the prominent gentlemen holding government offices or having large bank accounts. May Day came. In New York and in Washington it passed as it did in Paris and Berlin, — without a shot being fired, without a drop of red or blue blood being spilled, without even a good fist fight, and for the first time since the Red scare began, people began to laugh at the Fighting Quaker.

Mr. Palmer had personal as well as national reasons for becoming the chief of "a government by hysteria." In April, 1919, a score of bombs were mailed to the leading men of the country, including the attorney-general, and some time later he was marked for assassination, but the bomb in his home only blew out the porch and a wall. (Singularly enough, a radical publication "Plain Words" was found by the side of the dead bomb-thrower, but the government kept secret the fact that "Plain Words" was published by one of its *agents provocateurs*, Andrea Salsedo, of whom we shall hear more in the Sacco-Vanzetti affair.)

Just one year later the most revolutionary step of all was taken by the peace-loving citizenry when five duly elected socialist members of the New York State Legislature were thrown out of their seats — socialist meant Red, and Red meant Bolshevik in those days.

Bernard Shaw cabled America, "It is time for the *Mayflower* to put to sea again. My old label, A Nation of Villagers, still holds. When is the Bartholdi statue to be pulled down?" But every one thought Shaw a clown, and it was none of his business to criticize the august legislature.

The greatest outrage of all charged to the Reds was the Wall Street bomb of September 16, 1920, at a time when the national sense of humor had been almost restored. Even Palmer himself did not escape the anger of the public, nor did the President. "The desperadoes," said a typical editorial, "concluded that the United States had been made safe for them by the Wilson administration and have executed the most horrible crime in the history of the United States."

In the ten years which followed this outrage there have been twenty-eight arrests announced publicly. More than one man has been beaten and tortured in police headquarters. More than once the police and the Burns Detective Agency have announced they had all the facts about the Reds who plotted the crime and sent one man with a horse and wagon and a steel safe and much dynamite into the street opposite the offices of John Pierpont Morgan. Any theory that it was the act of an individual, maniac or terrorist, or that it was not organized radicalism, has been unheeded, but in ten years and with twenty-eight arrests, the crime is still a mystery. For Thanksgiving, 1922, one Wolfe Lindenfeld, who had confessed the Wall Street crime in Warsaw, much to the satisfaction of the Burns operators, came to the United States but was ordered deported immediately as a fraud. Still, he too was a three-day Red sensation, and so far as the public press and its readers are concerned, Moscow's long fingers were in Wall Street the day of the explosion, evidence or no evidence.

By 1922 the propaganda against Russia grew thin; Germany had consolidated its republic; Hungary was fortunately reactionary; Poland more so; Mussolini had smashed all liberal thought in Italy; all of Europe had withstood Bolshevism at its doorstep, and just as the anti-German hysteria in America had collapsed, so the anti-Russian followed. America was now anti-European rather than anti-German or anti-Russian. Nor did intolerance, bigotry and hate disappear; they took new forms, — internal, national and international. The world was not at peace. The Armistice was merely lengthening. Said Woodrow Wilson to his visitors, November 11, 1922:

"Armistice is mere negation; it is refraining from force. But peace is a very positive and constructive thing as the world stands nowadays, because it must be brought about by the systematic maintenance of common understanding and by coöperation — not by amiable phrases but the active coöperation for justice." To which Henry Morganthau, spokesman for the visitors, replied, "In so far as the principles laid down by you have not been adhered to, the world has not achieved peace."

The disillusion of the times is well noted by that same Walter Lippmann who had been called a Red in 1919 and who was now writing for the bourgeois *World*. "The first of these illusions," he says, "was that the war would produce Utopia, with Utopia defined to suit the tastes and the hopes of every ambitious party in every ambitious nation. . . . The power to deal practically with the world as it is has been frustrated over and over again, now by a feeling that such a great war which cost such terrible sacrifices ought in all decency to be paid for by a peace of the heart's desire. . . .

"Two great schools of demagogy divided the public opinion of the world, appealing to hope, to greed, or to weariness — but not to truth — catching votes, playing for applause, catering to passion, menacing reason, climbing upon any band wagon that led to public office.

"Normalcy . . . consisted of the following beliefs:

"That the fate of America is in no important way connected with the fate of Europe.

"That Europe should stew in its own juice.

"That Europe is plotting to take away our independence.

"That safety for America consists in excluding European goods, European ships if possible, European labor and European ideas.

"That we can sell to Europe, without buying from Europe.

". . . And that if Europe doesn't like it she can lump it, but she had better not.

" . . . Out of the fears and in the midst of this disorder a kind of hysteria has been generated. It has evoked armies, crazy tariffs, wildcat diplomacy, every variety of morbid nationalism, Fascisti and Ku-Kluxers. . . . Protestant plots by the Masons, Catholic plots by the Pope, Jewish plots, Japanese plots, alien plots, Bolshevik plots. . . ."

## Red Interludes

1918. Professor Edward Alsworth Ross warned us: "America will not prove immune to anti-capitalist agitation." *Vide* the post-crash years. Socially prominent women resolved: "We believe that by playing bridge men and women of wealth and leisure give to the advocates of class hatred a weapon against the unity of the United States."

1919. Boris Sidis, Harvard prodigy, was sent to jail for favoring the Bolsheviki. Vinson McLean, the hundred-million-dollar baby, was killed by an automobile at the age of ten, the first day of his life he ever crossed the streets of Washington alone. Guards, tutors, paid playmates, high walls, armored cars, huskies to foil kidnapers, five nurses, failed. He had no street psychology, no self-reliance. His death, opined the press, gives "stimulus to the spread of Bolshevism." Three Polacks in Chattanooga, Tennessee, were caught red-handed reprinting the Karl Marx Manifesto of 1846 and were headlined, "Alien Reds plot overthrow of American Government." Good news was getting scarce. Small outbreaks ("mutinies?") were reported in the British Army. "We won't go to Russia," the men cried. Bolo propaganda, shouted Northcliffe. Victor Berger and four other socialists were found guilty of sedition under the wartime Espionage Act. The Espionage Act was interpreted to prevent New York harbor steamers from blowing whistles for returning soldiers.

1920. Depression year. Red scare year. "Red rule in Russia will collapse within six months," declared ex-Ambassador Francis. Japan alone was winner in the anti-Bolshevik war of the Allies in Asia. Max Eastman and Rose Pastor Stokes are "at large on bail." The legislative committee (Senator Clayton Lusk's) raided the Rand School of Social Science and confiscated the archives and books for sale, also the contents of a safe. A Congressional committee reported that the melting pot was "a delusion and a snare."

Anatole France told America, "Europe is very ill, dying. Out of the disintegration, I think, but one nation may recover, — Russia." Joseph Gollomb quoted France, saying "Socialism (but not this Red Russian business.) is the hope of the world."

"The greatest scandal in history": the "throwing" of the 1919 World's Series: Comiskey of the White Sox had known about it but had kept quiet. The indictments came, then the published confession of Eddie Cicotte, star pitcher: "Eight of us got together before the game . . . talked about throwing the series . . . decided we could get away with it. I was thinking of my wife and kids and how I needed the money. I told them to have the cash in advance. I didn't want any checks. . . . That night I found the money under my pillow . . . ten thousand dollars. It was my price. I had sold out Commy; I had sold out the other boys; sold them for ten thousand dollars to pay off a mortgage on a farm. . . . All the runs scored against me were due to my own deliberate errors. I did not try to win." The scandal was too horrible for honorable baseball fans to contemplate. What could have been back of it? Only one sensible cause: the Bolshevik virus. Accordingly for weeks Bolshevism and baseball were the national topic and emotion.

Alfred Noyes, temporary professor in Princeton, found that Bolshevism had eaten into the brains of the intellectuals of the country, who more than all others are responsible "for the peril of civilization." Even in poetry, found Poet Noyes, "we see signs of an ignorant Bolshevism, often . . . crudely ungrammatical, taking upon itself to dismiss not only all former English metrical poetry, but the metrical poetry of all ages, from Homer and Sophocles down to the present day. . . ."

Mr. Calvin Coolidge wrote for the *Delineator* on "Enemies of the Republic", shocked and grieved to find radicalism in women's colleges. He disclosed that a certain Miss Smith of Vassar had attended the trial in Washington of the Soviet representative Martens, and this same Miss Smith had declared that the Soviet "ambassador" had more intelligence than many of the committee trying him. (Surely this was treason.) He also found that the girls of Radcliffe had a Socialist Club, and some one there had actually delivered a lecture entitled "The United States of the World."

And the National Civic Federation reported that "Red doctrines are being spread from the pulpit", naming the Labor Temple, supported by honest Presbyterians, and the Forum of the Protestant Episcopal Church of the Ascension, and the Community Church. Oxford went Bolo also. Gibbon had found the university steeped in port and prejudice; Matthew Arnold thought it was the home of lost causes; now the appointment of R. H. Tawney as lecturer makes Oxford an annex to the Fabian Society; the British press believes it "not merely an academic but a national outrage."

1921. Bolshevism is really an American phenomenon. Lenin says so. In 1892, the Red Czar tells an interviewer, Daniel de Leon broke from the Socialist Party in America, founded the Socialist Labor Party in Chicago, and in 1905 joined the I.W.W. It is the De Leon interpretation which Lenin has adopted. Bill Haywood in Moscow says apples, potatoes, rich and full crops, are rotting in America, "a capitalist conspiracy to starve the workingmen"; investigation confirms the first statement, repudiates the allegation. In April, America is informed that Lenin has had all the American deportees executed; in October, Lenin sends a note to all the powers offering to pay the Russian debts up to 1914 in return for recognition; he announces his "retreat from Communism" or NEP, a reorganization to advance against capitalism, and for Christmas the Department of Commerce gives the American people a gift, — the announcement that socialism has been abandoned in Russia; and a new economic policy is being evolved, the Department learns, after reading the October speeches from Moscow which have now arrived.

1922. Lloyd George saved his government and himself by a remarkable speech to the House, saying armed intervention has been tried in Russia and failed, blockade has been tried, isolation has been tried — why not try to make peace? Acting Foreign Minister Karakhan, replying to American journalists who report America proposes sending a commission to investigate Russia, says, "It's fine with me, boys, if America will let a Bolshevik commission come to investigate America." We consider this outrageous.

The American Defense Society saw another plot to overthrow the government in the arrival of the Moscow Art Theater, despite the fact that Thomas Lamont, Otto Kahn, Paul Cravath and Doctor Nicholas Murray Butler were the sponsors. Ah! hissed the American Defense Society in reply, there is a clause in the contract by which the artists from Moscow pledge themselves not to conduct propaganda against the Soviets; what can that mean except that they must conduct propaganda *for* the Soviets? It asked the American Legion to arise and do something.

Lenin said to a peasant: "Well, *dedushka,* little grandfather, you should be satisfied now; you have the land, the cattle, the fowls; you have everything."

The peasant said to Lenin: "Yes, God be praised, little father; the land is mine, but you get the bread; the cow is mine, but yours the milk; the chickens are mine, but yours the eggs. The Lord be praised, little father."

# CHAPTER SEVEN

## The March of the Dictators

As centripetal and centrifugal forces are balanced, so extreme reaction or extreme radicalism, when the failure of the peace-making was clear, were followed by dictatorships of every form and color, Red in Russia, Black in Italy, Green in Bulgaria, an attempted Brown in Germany, White in Spain, Finland, Hungary, Poland, and many other lands. In every instance, monarchist or communist, neither the will of the people nor the law of the land was considered. "Where law ends, there tyranny begins." It was an age of tyranny.

Although in many respects the greatest of the dictators, most successful in achievements, most daring in action and most liberal in his relation to individuals and the mass, was Kemal Pasha, the dramatic figures of the Great Years were Lenin and Mussolini. The one was the most hated of men the world had known for centuries, the other the bright economic star of American bankers and American tourists. Millions, hundreds of millions of words of abuse of the former and praise of the latter filled the press of the world but only a score or two of writers honestly analyzed their programs and their philosophies, questioning whether the dictators were suppressing peoples or planning the ultimate freedom from the slavery of mind and body which has been the common fate of mankind from the days of the apple episode in Eden.

Lenin, only a few days before he died, was still referred to as "one of the greatest wreckers in history", or "the Judas of the real Russian revolution", or "another scourge of God", and Mussolini, before his complicity in the assassination of Matteotti in 1924, was glorified as the *deus ex machina* who had made the Italian trains run on time. Certainly Mussolini, confronted in the Chigi Palace majestic map room at his grand desk crowded with telephones, over which J. Caesar smiled benignly, made the best impression. He was certainly a *deus ex* something — if only theater, while Lenin, as the American journalists knew him in 1922 and 1923, was the most disarming of strong men. If he conquered, it was through the mind, because he was pure logic, just as Mussolini seemed pure theater.

Lenin was small and simple, with a fine zest for life and he never posed. He had no need to pose. He had lived his life consistently as a rebel, and never switched parties, betrayed a friend, dropped an ideal. When he said "I am not a great man" to Cesare, the artist, he gave his own true estimate. He hated power. But the logic of its use in Russia was evident, and he used power, sometimes ruthlessly, so that soon one could regard with Homeric humor the American deported communists and anarchists accusing him of bloodthirstiness. He hated bloodshed but used it. Every dictatorship sooner or later has to shoot and kill. But one cannot imagine Lenin conspiring with a St. Louis gunman to take a personal enemy for a ride in a government automobile and stab him to death; one can not only imagine, but one can actually find the evidence of Mussolini doing just that — for there are many sorts of dictators and their ways are varied, as we shall see.

## LIFE AND DEATH OF TAVARISH LENIN

He was a good bourgeois child who read his Bible every day and worshiped the way his parents had gone for generations. In school he was deficient in logic; he set himself to developing his mind and triumphed. He won a gold medal, he was head of his class, he shone. His elder brother, Alexander, was a good shot. Vladimir was a poor one. But he became a huntsman and a swimmer, although he never equaled his brother, whom he worshiped somewhat for his physical superiority.

One day Alexander was implicated in revolutionary activities. Tsar Alexander II. had been assassinated and thousands were arrested. Lenin's brother was accused unjustly and executed; Lenin became a radical. He was therefore barred from attending Moscow University, went to Kazan, mingled with his brother Alexander's friends and was expelled. As a student, he loved to sing. He was not a good singer. His group, in their Dostoievskyian manner, sang the sad songs of Russia's sad fate—Lenin once leaped up and cried, "To hell with Fate." He was a great lover of cats but never liked to play with children.

In his Swiss exile he became a great debater. His first biographer, Lepichinsky, states, "It is dangerous to interfere with the orderly thought processes of his mind. His dialectic is destructive. He picks upon unfortunate words and phrases, all potential errors, and plays his sharp sarcasm upon them. He laughs, emitting occasional sparks of demolishing irony." He was one of the very few rebels in the history of the world who had a sense of humor.

In 1917, in Switzerland, the Tsar overthrown, he wrote, "You can imagine what a torture it is for us all to sit here at such a time." He proposed the exchange in Switzerland of Russians for German prisoners, and thus came through Berlin in a sealed car. Kerensky later ordered his arrest because Lenin headed the Bolshevik wing of the revolution against the Menshevik wing in power, demanding the maximum experiment in social revolution. Lenin fled into the country, hid in a haystack, worked as a farm laborer. Beside the haystack Lenin and Zinovieff built a rude stove of stones, baked potatoes and brewed tea, on which they lived. "I am being bitten to death by mosquitoes," Lenin complained. A worker named Yemelianoff saved him from the reward of $100,000, dead or alive.

Bolshevik leaders came every night over circuitous routes, through swamps and water, to sit up with Lenin all night discussing party strategy.

Autumn came with cold winds and cold rain. The haystack

dripped and rotted. Again and again Lenin put fresh hay in it and again and again it clotted with mud. In desperation he determined to flee the country. Mrs. Yemelianoff shaved his beard, cut his hair, a photograph was taken and a passport forged. At the Finnish border he was recognized. He thought betrayal and death imminent. But the inspector winked at him and said, "I am no friend of Kerensky." Lenin reached his haven.

When the Germans began marching on Petrograd, he gave the signal for the Bolshevik uprising. "It would be naïve to wait for a majority. No revolution waits for it."

When he returned to Petrograd the rumor was spread that the Germans had financed him. "It is absolutely untrue that I was in any relation with Parvus [the German Socialist]. I always held Parvus a renegade, a social chauvinist. As a revolutionary internationalist, I could have nothing to do with German social traitors."

In June, 1922, Professor Kemperer of Berlin was asked to attend Lenin when he had his first paralytic stroke which made him speechless. A blood clot had paralyzed the brain system; he was already in a state of living death. Kemperer examined all seven of the rulers of Russia, found them all suffering from overwork, but Lenin alone fatally so. "Lenin was suffering from clotting of the brain due to overwork, which has been the cause of death of Pasteur and many other famous men," Kemperer explained, to hints of diseases caused by youthful excesses.

In November, the fifth anniversary of the revolution, Lenin, seemingly completely alive, addressed the conventions — "We have brought Utopia down within the reach of our own generation." But in March, the following year, he suffered a second stroke. On January 21, 1924, the Russian dictator, Lenin, a man, died, and a god was born.

Kalenin, president of the Union, shuddering with emotion, announced the death the following day at the All Soviet Congress session. There was silence. Thousands began to weep. The orchestra then played the Red Funeral March. The soviet wireless flashed to all parts of the world, "Lenin is dead; his work lives." Banners with this inscription appeared by the thousand for the funeral.

Lenin's body in its old, worn, threadbare khaki uniform rested on a crimson catafalque. Stalin, with folded arms, and Dzerdzinsky, chief of the dread Cheka, in a long monkish robe, stood beside it.

The Hall of the Unions gradually filled with men. It was thirty below zero outside and there was a continuous stamping of half-frozen feet. Outside, the sentries' breath froze in icicles. Krupskaya, Lenin's widow, came and looked at her dead husband's face in silence and without emotion. A requiem was played, then the Internationale. "I had a feeling that I was present at the founding of a new religion," Arthur Ransome wrote that day, and he was right.

When the coffin was taken outside few could bare their heads for fear of freezing. — A thousand persons were taken to hospitals. — The place chosen for the mausoleum was outside the crenelated Kremlin walls, not far from the black boulder which marks the grave of John Reed, the first American delegate to the Third Internationale. In New York the Reverend Doctor John Haynes Holmes said to the consternation of every one in America that Lenin was "the greatest man produced by the war . . . as years go by his name will dominate this terrific era."

Petrograd was renamed Leningrad and Trotsky wired from Tiflis for all the factions to unite, but the battle for the dictator's toga, which had begun in his lifetime, soon became acute. Stalin did not hesitate to suppress the letters or so-called will, which Lenin left for the guidance of communism. The following excerpts, smuggled out of Moscow, published abroad, are Lenin's cold appraisals of his comrades:

Kamineff is hesitating and unstable; he is an uncertain man who should be observed and spied upon constantly.

Zinovieff is a talentless individual, but he is an ambitious man who constitutes a great danger for our party and should be closely watched in all his movements.

Stalin is a silly sort of person. This man aims at being Dictator of Russia, a thing which would be a catastrophe if it were to happen. My successor should never allow, in any case, that this man be appointed secretary of the Communist Party.

Bucharin is just as much of a booby as Stalin; he does not possess the slightest notions of dialectics, but he delights in writing, although he does it so badly.

Trotsky possesses considerable talent, but he is addicted to posing; he is the only one who is destined to become leader of the Communist Party, because he knows how to make himself respected and to maintain discipline.

It was not until 1925, when Stalin had beaten Trotsky, that the full text of the Lenin "will" was published by Max Eastman, Trotsky's friend and translator.

### THUS MUSSOLINI CAPTURED ROME!

Fascism had been organized in 1919 to bring "the assurance of Liberty to the People", but in 1922 its motto, shouted by scores of thousands of Blackshirts, was the one the Arditi had used in Fiume: "*Me ne frego* — I don't give a damn." Not a damn for anything! All it wanted now was power. "Our program," said Mussolini in reply to daily questions, "is quite simple: we want to govern Italy. It is not programs which are lacking, it is Men of Will."

In the summer of 1922 cabinets arose and fell, there was the usual flood and avalanche of parliamentary talk and Mussolini was a member of the Chamber of Deputies. He threatened that august body. "Soon the Fascisti will have to decide whether to continue their struggle in a legal or an insurrectionary form. . . . I prefer a legal struggle for national, humane reasons, but I feel in conscience bound to warn you against the other eventuality."

There was no Bolshevism in Italy. But there was idle, gossipy parliamentarism, and there was the Catholic party, or Popolari, which challenged the Fascisti as the dominant element in public life. Even the socialists had grown weak. The great test came in August when the socialists and the united labor unions called another general strike because the Fascisti had assaulted their members, plundered their coöperatives, burned their newspapers; but this strike was a two-day fiasco.

On October 24, the Fascist national congress opened in Naples with no intention of marching on Rome. Deputy Mussolini made a speech saying it would be satisfied with an offer to participate in a coalition government. But the hot-bloods began yelling "To Rome! To Rome!" and the leader could do nothing but follow the hysteria. "I take a solemn oath," he replied, "that either the government of the country must be given peacefully to the Fascisti or we will take it by force." In all the speeches there was almost no mention of Bolshevism or socialism or the labor unions: the liberal, coalition, democratic, parliamentary form of government was attacked. On the twenty-sixth an ultimatum was sent to Premier Facta, who replied by offering the King his resignation. Mussolini went back to his office in Milan and on the twenty-seventh the Fascist *squadristi* or gangs, began occupying government headquarters in Florence, Pisa and Cremona. Milan and Rome were quiet.

Under the command of many generals, the "troops" began to move on Rome in three columns. From Umbria, Romagna and Tuscany the Blackshirts came to Foligno, where General Fara took command and led them to Monterotondo, north of Rome. The men from D'Annunzio's Abruzzi assembled at Tivoli, under Bottai. Genoa, Milan, Bologna, and western seaboard cities and towns, north and south, sent delegations to meet at Santa Marinella, and as their open trucks went slowly along the dusty roads, the Fascist civilians praised the adventure, as friendly opponents said simply it was child's play.

But where was our Hero all this time? "I put on the black shirt. I barricaded the *Popolo d'Italia*." He stayed in Milan judiciously until the telegrams and telephone calls from Rome doubly assured him he could have a chance at the premiership in place of old Facta. "On the night of October 31, 1922, I left the direction of the *Popolo d'Italia*. . . . I was off to Rome. . . ."

Mussolini got off the Pullman sleeper, motored to the Quirinal, put on the black shirt, was introduced "without formalities" to the King. "I beg your Majesty to forgive me for appearing in your presence in uniform. I have just come from a bloodless battle which had to be fought." The King smiled. The next day the twenty, or more, thousand Fascisti who had arrived by train, truck and horse-carriage and the thousands who had arrived after the "capture", were reviewed by Premier Mussolini and King Victor Emmanuel. "I was then triumphant in Rome," the dictator writes triumphantly. These are the facts, vouched for mainly by himself, on which the legend of a "march" on Rome, a revolution, bloodshed, and victory, have gone around the world. But it must be noted that the day the Fascisti seized the government buildings in Northern Italy, and the day Mussolini became dictator, the Hall-Mills case, so far as America was concerned, was all there was in the press.

Mussolini began the promulgation of the long series of royal decrees by which the dictatorship outlawed its enemies and suppressed the liberal newspapers.

"Both in Russia and in Italy," Mussolini wrote, summing up the situation, "it has been demonstrated that it is possible to govern outside, above and against all liberal ideas. Neither Communism nor Fascism has anything in common with liberty.

"Fascism is not afraid to declare itself illiberal or anti-liberal. It has already passed, and if necessary will again pass without the slightest hesitation, over the body, more or less decomposed, of the Goddess of Liberty."

Said Judge Gary, head of the United States Steel Corporation, in Rome: "I feel like turning to my American friends and asking them whether they do not think that we too need a man like Mussolini." A thousand other American bankers, tourists,

*Underwood and Underwood*

MUSSOLINI'S ENTRY INTO ROME AS THE HEAD OF THE FASCISTI

politicians and power-worshipers made similar statements in the next ten years.

### BEER, BRATWURST, AND THE BEGINNING OF HITLER

Trotsky at the Winter Palace in St. Petersburg, the Mussolini lads at Monterotondo, could have been defeated by a belt or two of machine-gun bullets. Not all revolutions are successful. When they fail they are frequently ludicrous. Witness the *putsch* of the Little Mussolini of Munich, who first comes to our astonished notice as "Otto Hitler, who is marching on the Bavarian capital with his Fascisti", January 28, 1923.

The French had occupied the Ruhr; Cuno had ordered passive resistance; the American troops had quit the Rhine, to the dismay of the German burgomaster, who said, "We are sorry to see you leave, we do not know how we can do without you nor what will happen to us soon"; the French had seized the banks; British labor had protested; German labor had declared a general strike; Doctor Dorten was trying to establish a Rhineland Republic; Germany was struggling between life and death.

Three thousand men carrying banners, red with a black swastika in a circular field of white, followed Adolf Hitler into Munich and his friend, Count Hugo Lerchenfeld, the former premier, was chosen to explain him to America because Countess Lerchenfeld was an American woman, née Ethel Louise Wyman. Wrote the Count:

> In Bavaria a new prophet has arisen and preached a faith which has filled thousands with enthusiasm and new hope. Who is this man Adolf Hitler? . . . A slight boyish figure with intense gray eyes, an impassioned orator. . . . Upon the outbreak of war he joined as a volunteer and received all the medals and decorations for extraordinary bravery. Lack of higher schooling prevented his rising above the rank of non-commissioned officer.
>
> At the close of the war Hitler settled in Munich and founded the National Socialist Labor Party. . . . The first and most important dogma in Hitler's creed from the very beginning has been anti-Semitism. Jewish influence is the root of all social

and moral evil; eliminate international Jewry from capitalism and capitalism will cease to be a menace to humanity!

. . . Like Mussolini, he has unfolded the banner of nationalism. The spirit of the trenches, the spirit of unswerving fidelity to the Fatherland, must be revived in order to strengthen and unite the German people.

Hitler looks upon Socialism and Internationalism as purely Jewish inventions. "Let us begin fighting the Jews and their supremacy at home and we will strike at the root of all evil!"

The N.S.L.P. has increased from 5000 registered members last July to 50,000 at the present time and is spreading like a forest fire to other parts of the empire.

The mark fell with another of its terrible thuds to fifty thousand to the dollar; the French isolated Germany; no coal was shipped; Mussolini alone stood by Poincaré and sent his men into the Ruhr; the Belgian Labor Party issued a manifesto against the occupation and the United States Government made it known to France in nice diplomatic words that it considered the new war unwarranted. What is your program of German renaissance? Mr. Hitler was asked. He willingly replied:

As the national resurrection movement has reached its greatest momentum in Southern Germany, dictatorship and martial law may first be looked for here. Its first duty will be to court-martial all Jews, traitors, hoarders, war and reparation profiteers. The Teuton atmosphere filled with alien currents must first be purified before we go on with our war of liberation against France. . . .

We Teutons will not be slaves forever. We demand above all that the treaties of Versailles and St. Germain be annulled. Here is our program:

1. Only men with Teuton blood in their veins shall be permitted to call themselves German citizens. No Jew will be permitted to call himself a German citizen because there flows no Teuton blood in his veins.

2. Non-Teutons shall only be permitted in Germany with the special consent of the Government.

In September Hitler marched into Nuremburg. By his side was the Baroness von Wrede, the former Ray Beveridge, daughter of a governor of Illinois, veteran of a stock-company production of "The College Widow", the original of the statue "The American Venus", ex-war correspondent in Germany, ex-Red Cross nurse, passionate monarchist, passionate Hitlerite. (One American involved makes news; this was news.)

The evening of November eighth was like any other Bavarian evening: Bavaria was gathered in the beer saloons, drinking stein after stein, making slighting remarks about Prussia and digesting bratwurst heavily. Enter Adolf Hitler with three hundred followers. With revolver in each hand, Handsome Adolf rushed into the Burgerbrau, pushed his way through the beery crowds and atmosphere, followed by two lieutenants whose hands also were full of revolvers, rushed to the back of the saloon, leaped on a table, fired three shots, and announced the Fascist revolution.

"Five years ago the revolution was started. To-night it is ended. A new government is taking power."

Everybody began to laugh. Handsome Adolf fired his revolver again. There was a commotion and he was put out.

With three hundred followers and every kind of pick-up rifle and gun, Hitler marched towards the war ministry. Fifty city policemen appeared marching towards them.

"I order you to surrender to the Nationalist Army," cried Hitler.

The policemen began firing instead. At the first sound of guns, the Hitlerites began running.

As quiet followed the first and only salvo, those who were not running stood with upraised arms. Among them was General von Ludendorff, "one of the greatest soldiers in the history of the world."

Two policemen came up and led him away.

At another café Hitlerites spied King Ferdinand of Bulgaria. "Kill the old Jew," they cried. Ferdinand of Hohenzollern replied, "It is evident I have a very prominent nasal organ, but I am the Czar of Bulgaria, temporarily, alas, without my throne." They let him live.

The Berlin Government was frightened. It was perhaps the

long-feared separation of Bavaria from the Reich. President Ebert and Chancellor Stresemann issued a proclamation to the people: "In these critical times, deceived forces are disrupting the Reich. In Munich armed hordes overthrew the government, arrested Premier von Knilling and built a government around Ludendorff and Hitler. . . . Those who support the movement are traitors. . . . All measures for the reëstablishment of order and the quelling of the *putsch* are taken. . . ." General von Seeckt (later a Hitlerite) was given extraordinary dictatorial powers. The Hitlerites who had held out in government buildings found themselves surrounded in the morning.

Before his arrest Hitler told the press that he acted because Bolshevism was brewing in Germany. "Let not France rejoice in Germany's downfall; when Bolshevism destroys Germany it will envelop France as well. This will be the curse of Poincaré's victory in the Ruhr." For the benefit of the American journalists, Hitler declared the American he admired most was Theodore Roosevelt. He had read all of Mussolini's speeches.

The next evening Munich, minus Ludendorff and Hitler, was back at its beer and its bratwurst. The first Fascist revolution was over.

The mark went to eight quintillion to the dollar one morning, and back to four quintillion that afternoon, and the next day was stabilized at four rentenmark to the dollar, while thousands of foreigners who had been buying and living and speculating, were angry when under the new monetary system an omelet cost five marks, while the natives said, "Well, it's cheap; it cost hundreds of millions the day before yesterday, now it's only five."

The new year opened with the trial of Hitler and Ludendorff for treason. Hitler, testifying in his defense, said, "I joined the National Socialist Labor Party and organized the movement because of my desire to exterminate Marxism and drive the Jews out of Germany. For the spiritual, my party has spiritual weapons; for those without spirit, only the mailed fist. Germany is lost forever if the German people are unable to realize politics is not tailwagging but the ability to use the sword."

Hitler was found guilty of treason and sentenced to five years' imprisonment, provided that within six months he was again found guilty of committing treason. Munich justice was at work. Ludendorff was acquitted. Cavalry with blackjacks controlled the crowds of patriots, frenzied monarchists bedecked in the old colors, who cheered the decision as a victory for the Kaiser. Crowds went back to the breweries again. Ludendorff told an American journalist, "You entered the war for the worst motives; you fought for gold." He thought the German-Americans the worst of the lot. The British Empire is doomed and will be the next to disappear. The German people will have a monarchy again because "they have monarchy in their bones." He attacked all the leading religions. "We must abandon not only Jehovah but Christ and Christianity, which have reduced our once strong and powerful people to whimpering and humility. We must go back to worshiping Wotan." Thus and more. Honorably beaten in the greatest war in history, he had been ludicrously defeated in the largest beer hall in Bavaria as Hitler's lieutenant, with the new title, "Commander of the German Nationalist Army."

### DE RIVERA, A SPANISH MUSSOLINI

In September, 1923, Dempsey knocked out Firpo, and that was about all the Spanish news America could stand. Among the items eclipsed was the military coup in Spain under Primo de Rivera, captain general of Barcelona. Two or three days later the world, European democracies especially, asked, Is it Fascism? It was at the beginning a military uprising of officers who were being made scapegoats for the Morocco disasters.

Barely had he warmed his dictatorial hands at King Alfonso's fire before Primo slipped into Rome to take lessons. In November, Mussolini told him that the ideals of humanity were organization, discipline, obedience, hierarchy, all power to the State and death to individualism. It would go fine in Spain. Both dictators agreed to curb the United States' influence in South America, where Spanish is spoken, Italians emigrate, and export markets have been in the hands of the Yankees ever since the war. It was decided to send sample shiploads of Spanish and Italian wares, spaghetti and oranges, artificial silks and olive oil and whatnots — they took their dictatorships like a couple of traveling salesmen in those days — and they concluded secretly a military pact against France which Santiago Alba, former diplomat, exposed when in exile.

Ibañez, Unamuno, rector of Salamanca University, and other intellectuals were also exiled. They accused the king and dictator of debauchery and corruption. Contrast them with the night-life ambassador, Moore, who is responsible for the myth that Alfonso was the best royal sport in the world.

Arriving in Madrid, the first day of his embassy the American ex-newspaper editor turned plenipotentiary called up the palace by telephone: "Is that you, King? This is Alec." Startled chamberlains bowed before his Bourbon majesty, breathlessly announcing the American diplomat on the wire.

"Hello, Alec, this is King," Alfonso replied, capturing the American humor. ("You see what a sport the King was," Moore commented, relating the story at Ciro's, Paris, later.) "Well, Alf, I like your country, but I don't like the house I'm in — you haven't got a little palace for rent, have you?" And the King did have a little palace, one of his old aunt's they couldn't get rid of for years. "So the King rented the palace to me." One of Alec's best stories. But better yet:

"Say, Alec, I've been thinking: You might have been right about Cuba; old Weyler, the one you call the Butcher, was a bit rough out there; you did take the Philippines, but you paid us $25,000,000 for them. Okay with me. But what about Porto Rico — you stole Porto Rico!"

This was in the midst of the disastrous Riffian war. Alec

began to think. Yes, it was true, the United States had seized Porto Rico willy-nilly.

"I'll tell you what, Alf," said the diplomat, "I've got friends in Congress — I'll see that you get Porto Rico back."

"Like hell you will," replied King Alf; "I'll make you a present of Morocco."

"You see what a humorist the King is," commented Alec to the newspaper boys who loved him because he was such a good sport.

The myth flourished. Ambassador Moore, friend of the press, an old newspaper man himself, spread the propaganda for old Alf and old Primo. Meanwhile the dictatorship abolished public and personal liberties and robbed the country, covering its fiscal excesses by borrowing abroad. (The same system practiced under Fascism, Greek dictatorship, most South American dictatorships, all nicely veiled by false reports of "balanced" budgets.) Eventually economics, ruthless and inevitable, overtook king and dictator, as we shall see in the history of the Thirties, and crushed Bourbonism in Spain.

### PANGALOS

Greece was bankrupted by the Smyrna adventure. British aid and the Zaharoff millions could not prevent it. But somehow in 1923 here was Greece with a brand-new army, well outfitted, under General Pangalos. In two years he built up a military conspiracy and one morning fired a fusillade of blank shots, occupied the telegraph office in Athens, went to the military barracks, received a pledge of loyalty, and asked the government to go away. He became dictator for a while. (His fall, and the return of constitutional government are matters for a later chapter.)

### KAROLYI, BELA KUN, HORTHY AND CHARLES

We have seen the Karolyi democracy ruined by Allied stupidity and the Kun dictatorship annulled by American food. When

Admiral Horthy became dictator of Hungary he told the American press: "So long as I am alive, Bolshevism will never raise its head again in my country. At its first sign of life, I will suffocate it in blood. I will not tolerate another Red terror and my armies are ready to fight. The time will come when the Entente leaders will go down on their knees and plead with me to save Europe from Bolshevism."

But, after instituting his White terror, Horthy did not have to face Red Bolshevism — his first problem was the runaway emperor, Karl. This poor, weak, shy, deluded Habsburg thought he could accomplish a "slow" *coup d'état*. He took the promises of French royalists to mean more than the notification of the Council of Ambassadors that it would "neither recognize nor tolerate" the return to the throne of the Habsburgs. Karl, in exile in Switzerland, stayed in his room three weeks and grew a beard. He left for Basle on the twenty-third of March, 1921, met Prince Louis Windischgrätz, coming from Paris; they traveled to Vienna, gave a dinner to fourteen notable monarchists, went by car to Hartberg in Styria, came to the bishop's palace in Steinamanger, West Hungary, bowing to the acclaim of a few peasants *en route*.

Count Teleky was sent on a mission to Horthy: would he give up the dictatorship to the ex-Emperor, or not? Karl would go to the telephone every hour or two, telephoning to Horthy to give Teleky a favorable answer. At dinner with the bishop, he ate the highly seasoned Hungarian paprika dishes, smacking his lips and declaring he was starving to death in exile because he was unable to get a good Hungarian cook. Horthy answered the 'phone calls himself but promised nothing.

Eventually Karl set out for the capital. He reached the Horthy palace in Buda and sent Count Sigray in to announce him. Horthy was very polite. They talked two hours and a half, when the Emperor was persuaded to return to Steinamanger. He came back Easter Monday, after many breakdowns on the road, without having slept for three nights. The Swiss Government presented the Allies with proof that Prince Sixtus of Bourbon was the chief conspirator, having obtained from the Spanish Ambassador in Berne the false passport for the bearded pretender. That was the March *coup d'état.*

In October, Karl the Indefatigable tried it again. Profiting by experiences in automobile breakdowns, this time he flew. He landed at Raab, where a provisional legitimist cabinet was formed which tried to bribe Horthy by offering him the title of prince. With five thousand royalist troops and armed peasants, Karl moved against the Budapest garrison of seven hundred. One report had it that Horthy had promised not to fight, another that Horthy, finding the Karlists few, mobilized the capital's garrison at the last minute and rushed up troops from other centers. Three miles from Budapest there was an encounter. The Horthy army fired a few rounds. Karl actually saw men killed before his eyes. He trembled. The weakling, the second-rate king, had made two attempts for a throne, just to please Zita. "I would not spill a drop of blood for a thousand thrones," he had said at a tea interview in Esterhazy castle.

Horthy captured Karl and Zita and imprisoned them in Tata Tovaros castle, after an encounter at Komorn where the Karlists left two hundred dead. The Little Entente meanwhile had threatened to invade the country unless the Habsburgs were expelled within twenty-four hours. Poor Count Andrassy, who had backed the second coup, was found "worn, frail, almost transparent" from worry. In April, 1922, Karl I., Emperor of Austria, died in exile, in Funchal, Madeira, and the Hungarian crown went up in all the stock exchanges of Europe and America.

"Where laws end, there tyranny begins."

Of the progress and failures of these and other dictators we shall hear more at the end of the decade of the Twenties.

## INTERLUDE 1923

Charles A. Lindbergh is "a red-hot radical", "a Bolshevik", "a socialist", "a dangerous Red", "a traitor to the Republican Party." He ran for governor of Minnesota on the Farmer-Labor ticket. In 1916 he introduced a resolution in Congress to investigate "this inhuman and senseless war now raging." Charles A. Lindbergh also wanted to investigate the "Money Trust." "I am an enemy of Wall Street."

October 3. International Air Races, St. Louis. Among those present: Charles A. Lindbergh, Jr., "shy, rustic, awkward, and badly outfitted." "Slim" has been flying since he quit the University of Wisconsin in 1921. In 1922 he went barnstorming as a parachute jumper. "He neither smokes nor drinks, and has no use for women."

The bobbed-hair question is being answered around the world.

The reigning fashion: Tut-ank-hamen.

Paris decrees slim figures. First death from dieting in America.

Joe Cook refuses to imitate *four* Hawaiians.

Justice Ford finds D. H. Lawrence's "Women in Love" too awful for words.

"Love, Mr. Gallagher? Money, Mr. Shean."

The Prince of Wales, in the midst of world chaos, makes an address: "I would say that the popularity of fox hunting, far from being reduced, has been increased. I have hunted with ten packs this season (loud cheers) and have come across very little barbed wire (cheers). We are very grateful to the farmers for the help they have given to keep going a sport without which I do not think this country would be what it is to-day." (Prolonged cheers.)

In Palm Beach only three men or one per cent. wore soft collars.

In 1921 the belt line dropped until it was in danger of disappearing; in 1923 there is simplicity of line and the waist is higher.

Silent boycott of American goods in Mexico worries Mr. Hughes more than French occupation of the Ruhr.

After years of useless digging Howard Carter in 1922 came upon a tomb. January 11, 1923, they removed a wall. Carter lit a candle and stuck his head in. Minutes went by. Lord Carnarvon in suspense said, "For heaven's sake, Carter, say something; can you see anything?" "Yes," replied Carter, "it's wonderful." Carnarvon then stuck his head in. At first he could see nothing but streaks of lightning. They were lines of gold.

After five years in jail for participation in the Bavarian revolution, Ernst Toller, playwright, released, says, "I have nothing in my head."

A Greek named G. S. Gurdjieff establishes a new religion at Fontainebleau.

Harlem is discovered by the white residents of New York! Negro jazz-banders making billions in Berlin, Negroes enjoying liberty in Europe after the war; Roland Hayes sings with the Boston Symphony.

The police were informed that "there is a murder in it, the most immoral of crimes"; they had not previously heard complaints about this show, so they sent a spy. He came back and said Barrymore was "good." The play was "Hamlet."

Chinese boycott of Japan, begun in March, cuts Nippon trade one third.

Fourteen per cent. of Paris marriages end in divorce; twice as many divorces in smoky Lyons as in sunny Marseilles. Where misconduct is charged in France sixty-two per cent. of offenders are women.

Twenty-eight amendments to the Kalamazoo dancing ordinance; one makes it criminal for dancers to look into each other's eyes.

Charles Garland refuses a million-dollar inheritance, says inherited wealth is a curse.

A seventeen-year-old girl from California drove Mrs. Molla Bjurstedt Mallory from the old 1915 tennis throne. Her name is Helen Wills.

"Yes, we have no bananas." It is a ridiculous song without any sense, reported London. "But we have pineapples," replied Paris.

Gerald Murphy had his guests take solemn oath no one would betray Antibes as a summer resort. There were no other Americans there. It was the only unruined spot on the Riviera.

Etiquette books are best sellers.

"If only we could send to Germany the food you waste in America," said "Christus" Lang in New York. Clemenceau sailed back with several grapefruit, "the only thing I had not known when I lived there after the Civil War." The famine in Russia being over, Colonel Haskell will quit Moscow.

Cleveland Marathon dance lasts fifty-two hours, sixteen minutes. New York girl beats Marathon record; sixty-nine hours; loses seven pounds.

Radio only link with Japan during earthquake.

It costs forty marks to print each new one-mark note. Berlin issues two thousand billion marks a week. Mark goes to billion for one dollar. Astronomical chaos in German money. Get baby buggy full of marks for a dollar. Old marks worth more as waste paper than money.

The world's greatest mathematician went into the Berlin subway and handed in a ten-mark note. The fare was five and one-half marks. "Have you got a half mark," asked fräulein. "But I gave you a ten, not a five-mark note," replied Einstein. "Have you got a half-mark piece," shouted fräulein. Desperately the professor produced it, and got five marks back. Puzzled, he went to his train, counting on his fingers.

Frank Vanderlip cured of diabetes by discovery of Canadian named Banting. Sir William Bells lists most needed inventions, — glass that will bend, a pipe that can be cleaned, and pictures that will talk.

Tin-can tourists overrun Florida.

Short skirts overrun Paris; Patou capitulates at last.

Owing to wage reductions totaling three billion dollars and lowering of the standard of living below the 1914 level, the British Labor Party membership has increased to almost seven million.

Farmer-Labor Party of Minnesota elects Magnus Johnson Senator. American Defense Society believes it is a safe venture; the returns for the first time in the history of a State were watched with more interest in Moscow than America.

# CHAPTER EIGHT

## The "Wars" of Religion and Morals

> Over and above the spectacle of a world amazed at the prevalence of dissent from acknowledged dogma in art and science and religion, we have the widespread attack upon social notions not a decade ago conceived as fundamental. . . .
>
> — HAROLD J. LASKI in 1920

DICTATORS pretend to be very busy people. Although they concern themselves foremostly with materialism, balanced budgets, military prowess, and train schedules, they find a spare moment to regulate the morals of nations and poke a finger into the question of art, utter a dictum on esthetics.

Thus we find at this epoch Mussolini saying magnificently, "Let there be Art — but Fascist art," and ruling that some Blackshirt symbol or ideology glow from each canvas at the Venice show, and the Bolsheviki censoring Tsarist sculpture by blowing up statues of old rulers and demolishing religious shrines.

In the United States, where every man is free and equal, dictatorship had hard going, but had its own sweet successes. The movies and baseball not only submitted, they appealed for dictators and gloried in having them; the theater considered a Tsar, triumvirate or dictatorial committees, and literature barely escaped them. Intoxication was prohibited by law in America and the fight to make the whole world dry moved on to London.

Beginning with a handful of patriots, the new Ku-Klux Klan enveloped five million men, a larger force than the Blackshirts and the Red Army combined, in an attempt to dictate white Protestant supremacy. With fire and sword and the law and manifesto and with terroristic methods, the dictatorial idea marched into the moral and religious and artistic world, seeking power, as it had elsewhere in throne rooms and palaces.

In Moscow anti-religion raged in the law courts and spat upon the images millions held sacred, while in Rome Methodist chose to settle a hill higher than the Vatican. Fundamentalism was *en route* to Mecca and Dayton. The movements had one thing in common, the salvation of religious peoples from the decay and degeneration of the post-bellum world.

### MECCA AND DAYTON

In 1924, Sultan Ibn Sa'ud, who came with his tribesmen out of the Nejd, victoriously gained control of a large part of Arabia, captured the holiest of the four holy cities, raised the banner of Mohammed in Mecca and proclaimed himself dictator of Arabia. His first acts were moral and religious reforms.

Alarmed by reports that the Wahabite leader had destroyed the tomb of Mohammed, hundreds of millions of followers in all the countries from Morocco to China sent a mission of inquiry to Mecca. This mission was headed by Ain-el-Mulk Habib Allah Khan, "the eye of God", Persian consul general in Damascus, who promised to bring back a report on the Puritan renaissance in the forbidden city from which only twelve Christians have returned alive.

Sultan Ibn Sa'ud being a prohibitionist and a hater of nicotine was able as dictator to abolish smoking and drinking immediately. His fanatical soldiers burned up one hundred thousand hookahs, narghiles, hubble-bubbles, as the water pipes are variously called, banned alcohol in accordance with the dictates of the Koran, also forbade the use of silk or rustling garments by women, as froufrous took the minds of soldiers off their work, and decreed bloodshed, if necessary, to enforce these reforms.

But even a wild dictator found he could not defy the will and desire of the masses by edicts. Bootlegging set in. Sa'ud decreed that all persons caught drunk should receive several lashes of the whip. Several gentlemen soon found themselves being whipped every morning — and having a good time at night. The no-smoking law had to be changed too. Smoking is now permitted in private homes and a heavy duty on tobacco swells the dictatorial coffers. Phonographs, so dear to Arab ears, were next prohibited, with the chanting of prayers in the public streets. The few radios found were seized. Finally music and musical instruments were declared immoral, the law being enforced so logically that the military bugle ceased blowing reveille for the soldiers. Mecca is now a paradise for Mr. Irving Berlin, who wanted to murder a bugler.

The marriage customs of Mohammedanism were a great problem to the Sultan, who likes his woman young, fresh and frequent. The rule of Mohammed limiting polygamy to four is strictly enforced. Ibn Sa'ud never has more than four wives at a time. However, he divorces one and marries one almost every month, so that in the course of the last twenty years he has made more than a hundred and fifty ladies temporary sultanas and temporarily happy. Each divorced wife who has had a child must never marry again, and all receive pensions. Thus is morality preserved in Arabia.

The Mecca electric-light system and the telephone network have been destroyed. One telephone and its few connections remain. Any reader desiring to speak to the Sultan-Reformer may now call MECCA-1, and he will answer. He got six airplanes and several tanks from British munitions makers but decided to sell them. "I can win without modern mechanisms," he adds, "but ever since Colonel Lawrence introduced me to the telephone and radio I have found them useful — for myself."

It might also be recalled that the British Government paid

Ibn Sa'ud, through Colonel Lawrence, the sum of three hundred thousand dollars for fighting the Turks, and that the Persian official found Sir Gilbert Clayton in the town of Bahred, drawing up a new contract. Like many other reformers the Sultan needs a lot of cash.

In Zion City, Voliva announced that the earth is flat and flanked by icebergs to keep foolish sailors from falling into space; the sky is a solid dome from which hang sun and moon and stars, like so many chandeliers. The State legislature in Kentucky had a bill making it a criminal offense to teach in any State-supported institution "any theory of evolution that derives man from the brute or any other form of life or that eliminates God as the Creator of man by a direct creative act."

In 1923 the University of Tennessee dismissals for teaching evolution totaled ten. "In Sverdloff University, Moscow, only Communists may teach; in Tennessee, only Fundamentalists." When Professor Jesse William Sprowls was refused reëngagement because he had used a textbook on evolution the students protested.

"We, the undersigned" —forty distinguished American citizens, including Herbert Hoover — declared there was no antagonism between science and religion. Other signers were Professor Millikan, Rear Admiral Sims, Professor Pupin, Bishops Manning and Lawrence, Frank Vanderlip.

Controversies raged. Bryan led the fundamentalists, assisted by Doctor Stetson, Doctor Stires, Doctor John Roach Straton. "Evolution," said the Reverend Dr. Straton "is a lie out of Hell." The modernists were led by Doctor Parks, Bishop Lawrence, Doctor Woelfkin, in 1923.

In his New Year's sermon Doctor Percy Stickney Grant thought "Heresy in one age often proves truth in another. Science does not support virgin birth or bodily resurrection"; Doctor Guthrie believed "Christians will die of boredom if there is not some mixture of paganism in their religion", and

Doctor Joseph G. H. Barry declared "The Bishop must discipline the modernist clergyman. Cain was the first modernist."

Governor Cameron Morrison and the board of education (sic) of North Carolina prohibited the teaching of evolution in public schools. For entertaining "individualistic beliefs in the theory of evolution", Doctor Henry Fox was asked to resign from Mercer University in Georgia.

But the best stunt of all belongs to the Reverend Z. Colin O'Farrell of Butte, Montana, who brought a monkey into his church and himself into the front page of every newspaper in America. Illustrating his attack on evolution, the reverend gentleman declaimed:

> "Backward, turn backward, O Time in thy flight,
> "Make me a monkey again, just for to-night."

The church was pitch-dark. A spotlight played on the preacher. The monkey chattered. The preacher had to shout at it and to beat it at times. It was a grand show. But grander yet was the Dayton monkey show which we shall find in 1925.

Monsignor Abbotti refused holy communion in St. Praxed's Church to two women who wore low-necked gowns.

Bishop Manning of the Protestant Episcopal Diocese of New York asked Reverend William Norman Guthrie to explain the Greek dancing which had been permitted in St. Mark's-in-the-Bouwerie in November, 1923, reports having "greatly shocked and scandalized" the Bishop. The defenders said the dancing was "classical and symbolical" — "beauty with which to fight the filth and prurience of New York to-day", in the words of Doctor Guthrie — but these were "half-naked girls", according to some newspapers.

The Reverend Thomas Kirkwood of Syracuse thought it "a sad commentary on our democracy to see our youth spoiling their good hats by turning down the brim in front because the Prince of Wales turns down the brim" and another eminent reformer, A. K. Fillmore, "president of the Society for the Uplift of Moral Virtue and the Suppression of Unwarranted Pleasure" warned the world against coffee drinking.

In 1919, Senator Sherman expressed the fear many good Protestants entertained, — that the Vatican would dominate the League of Nations. Some time later the Evangelical Protestant Society was organized to "wage war on the Pope" and the Methodists of America bought a plot of ground on Monte Mario in Rome and planned to build a Protestant Church which would dominate the Catholic St. Peter's.

In 1920 the Holy Office issued a decree asking Catholic bishops to watch "an organization which . . . instils indifferentism and apostacy to the Catholic religion." The Young Men's Christian Association is named; and in February, 1921, Cardinal Merry Del Val's attack on the same institution was published. Soon after the Fascisti came into power and atheistic leaders learned the Machiavellian truth that it is best to rule *with* the Church, the Fascisti forced the American Methodists to refrain from the o'ertopping Monte Mario adventure, and one by one the American Young Men's Christian Associations closed their doors.

Thirty members of the French Academy of Science threatened to bolt if Professor Einstein was permitted to speak on relativity. In the University of Berlin, Einstein was denounced by Hitlerite monarchist students as a "Sau Jude." Harvard denied it was banning Jews, reaffirming it planned restrictions in the manner of Rumanian universities.

S. Stanwood Menken, head of the National Security League, and Governor Al Smith debated the maintenance of the Lusk Bill, the governor favoring repeal. Doctor Alexander Meiklejohn was ousted as president of Amherst, being too liberal in his ideas on education. Judge Gary, insisting that labor keep at it twelve hours a day, collapsed during a speech in 1923.

### RED INTOLERANCE

As you face the spot once occupied by the most holy shrine in Moscow, that of the Iberian Virgin, you can see in a niche replacing a religious statue, in a wall on your left, the words in Greek characters: RELIGIA OPIUM DLYA NORODAH, "Religion is opium for the people," a quotation from Karl Marx, which incidentally was frequently used by Mussolini in his Swiss exile.

Long before Leninism as a religion was born, the Bolsheviki attempted to destroy the faiths of all people by teaching atheism in all its public schools, its universities, even in the army camps, where illiterate peasant soldiers first learn their alphabet. Christmas, 1922, and Easter, 1923, anti-religion held ribald festivals comparable only to Carmagnole in the French Revolution.

Between these dates occurred an event that shocked the world. Numerous Catholic priests, mostly Polish citizens, were arrested for treason. They were accused of being Polish politicians, of having sympathized with the enemy during Pilsudski's advance into Kiev, of having intrigued and given aid to the enemy. Archbishop Zepliak and the vicar general, Monsignor Butchkavitch, were first on trial.

Indignation enveloped Europe and America. Few questioned the facts, few were interested in the justice or injustice of the case. Led by the Archbishop of Canterbury and the Polish General Sikorski, public opinion was marshaled against the bloodthirsty Bolsheviki. The accused denied giving comfort and aid to Poland but admitted violating the covenant made by Cardinal Roop which placed Church property in the hands of the congregations, not the priests. Krylenko, the dread prosecutor, then produced his evidence of treason.

Christmas, 1922, the students of Sverdloff University made mock of all religions in the Red Square. Five thousand boys and girls carried a hundred effigies of Jesus and Moses, Buddha and Confucius, Mohammed, Osiris, Saint Gabriel, Saint George,

Abraham and the Virgin Mary, and an enormous figure labeled "Almighty God", all of which they burned at night in a great bonfire opposite the Shrine of the Iberian Virgin. Here, in the snow, the remnants of nobility, some clad in their last sables and ermine, others in rags, gathered defensively. They knelt in the snow in prayer; their breath was white, it was zero weather and the sun was moribund. The godless marched by, jeering and mocking and imitating the prayers with a ribald litany while one labeled Mohammed turned somersaults and one dressed as the Patriarch of the Russian Church drank vodka out of a huge bottle and pretended he was drunk.

In March, 1923, Zepliak and Butchkavitch were found guilty of treason and sentenced to death. Krylenko, the public prosecutor, was called in the world press "the worst of all bloodthirsty beasts", who had asked the death penalty "like a wild animal stinted in its allowance of blood." Gentle Cardinal Mercier said, "In four years the World War mowed down, I believe, ten million human lives. In a little more than that time the Bolshevist Socialism has sacrificed from twenty to thirty million."

Polish Minister to Moscow, M. Knoll, Mr. Hodgson, the British trade commissioner, and Father Edmund Walsh, the American priest in charge of the Papal famine relief work, visited Chicherin, who assured them the priests would be pardoned. The sentence of death had been a gesture. On April first and second the Minister of Justice, Kursky, informed the press — and Chicherin confirmed the report — that the death sentence had not been carried out. On April third, *Pravda* carried a note saying Monsignor Butchkavitch had been executed. The Cheka had acted without notifying the ministers of foreign affairs and justice. This is how the Red terror works. An official blamed the war threats of General Sikorski and the war-on-Russia movement in other lands for the pique of the Cheka leaders which had resulted in this death. A little while later the Riga representative of the Associated Press reported that Patriarch Tikhon had been poisoned in prison and the Moscow representative of the same news association reported that Tikhon had been pardoned. The second report was true. Archbishop Zepliak was permitted to return to Warsaw. In Washington, the State Department retaliated by issuing the following note: "The Department of State has canceled the authorization for a visa for Mme. Kalenin, wife of the president of the so-called Soviet Republic of Russia. The presence of Mme. Kalenin in this country is rendered wholly undesirable by the deep feeling which has been aroused by the execution of Vicar General Butchkavitch." Mme. Kalenin had intended visiting the Red Cross.

Easter came early in April, 1923; the prosecutions of the Church waned; from Moscow's forty times forty blue and white and golden churches the bells sang the resurrection; crowds pulled at the bells with a spirit defying soviet authority; bearded Bishop Antonin in the marble Cathedral of the Holy Savior lifted his hands to the golden ikon, the colorful painting of a haloed Christ, and in a voice of pain exclaimed, "Father, forgive them, for they know not what they do", while outside the students chanted, "Down with the priests; down with God", keeping time with the bells. On the steps of the cathedral, communist soap-box speakers preached atheism.

But beyond and above these visible demonstrations, two powerful elements were attempting to gain, reform and control the Russian Church. It had never gone through a reformation and the time was propitious. None saw this more clearly than Bishop Edgar Blake, who represented the Methodist Episcopal church of America, and Father Walsh, who represented the Vatican. Here were more than one hundred and fifty million religious people who could easily be led into another formula. Rarely in history was such a vast field of soul-saving open in an established religion. (The Soviets approved and smiled; what they wanted was the breaking up of the Russian Orthodox Church into many smaller churches, as in America.)

In June, Bishop Blake gave his blessing to the Living Church.

But Bishop Blake had reckoned without his colleagues. Suddenly he was recalled by cable, when indignation in America followed all that talk about "Russia is in the midst of a stupendous social experiment", and the government trying to establish "a human brotherhood", and Methodism lost its chance for one hundred and fifty million souls. In October, 1923, there were reports from Rome that "union of the Roman and the Russian church is believed near at hand" but that too failed. Year after year, however, the students marched and chanted "Down with God" and sang ribald litanies, and there was indignation throughout the world — and the Soviets continued to smile and to divide and weaken the established Tsarist Church.

## INTOLERANCE RAISES ITS KU-KLUX KLAN BANNER

A negro employee of the Cecil Hotel, Atlanta, had been murdered and the Council of Christian Churches had protested it was the work of a revived Ku-Klux Klan. Thus in September, 1920, the Ku-Klux Klan was nothing but a good, human-interest feature story up North. An ex-Methodist minister named Simmons was found who claimed "several thousand members", and stated: "its purpose is to inculcate the sacred principle of noble ideals of chivalry, the development of character, the protection of the home and the chastity of womanhood, the exemplification of a pure patriotism towards our glorious country, the preservation of American ideals, and the maintenance of white supremacy, and to provide a vital, perpetual memorial to the men who served so valiantly in the ranks of the original Ku-Klux Klan." (In the original credo was written "We avow the distinction between the races of mankind as same has been decreed by the Creator. . . .")

What about the murder of George King? Colonel and Ex-Rev. William K. Simmons knew nothing about it.

What about membership? "Membership cannot be bought; it is awarded for faithful services." In the "A.B.C. of the Invisible Empire", one of the Klan's first publications, however, were the words "If you really believe in the order . . . and contribute the sum of $10 . . . membership is awarded you."

Between Armistice Day and late 1920, one hundred and seventy-eight thousand Negroes had quit Georgia. Suffrage had enfranchised the negro woman and war-time training had placed rifles and revolvers in the hands of Negroes. Many thought there was greater danger than during the Reconstruction.

In just one year the Klan passed from a feature story to a "national menace" to the salvation of "white supremacy"; the ambiguous "several thousand" of 1920 became six hundred and fifty thousand in 1921. The great campaign was rolling over the prairies and down metropolitan streets. Kleagles sold memberships by wholesale, pocketing four dollars of the ten dollar "donation", sending a dollar to the King Kleagle and letting five dollars disappear mysteriously into the imperial treasury. The Klan operated a great printing press and a nightgown factory, making its six dollar and fifty cent wares for one dollar and twenty-five cents, as its enemies claimed. With Simmons were associated in triumvirate Edward Young Clarke, Imperial Kleagle, professional publicity man and drive promoter, and his partner in the Southern Publicity Association, Mrs. Elizabeth Tyler. The Kloran was the Klan bible.

Years of prosecution and exposure began. The first came largely through the confessions of Henry P. Fry of Chattanooga, an old Southerner, captain in the Tennessee National Guard, who had got his commission as a Kleagle on April 7, 1921. Congress was called upon to act, every man running for office had to declare himself, the Republican and Democratic National conventions had to go on record, ministers preached for and against it, politicians sounded their constituencies. And the writers did their stuff.

"A great deal of moral indignation," wrote Mencken, "will be wasted over the effort of a horde of tin-roofers and shoe clerks to make themselves mysterious and important. Congress will begin an unintelligent and dishonest inquiry into their grotesque cavortings, Draconian laws will be passed to put them down and in the end the promoters of the show will escape with comfortable fortunes, their dupes will go back to the poolrooms and the movies, and the way will be open for starting all over again."

Congress did investigate and almost immediately there were reports from everywhere that the Klan had split internally, was disintegrating and was dead, but it gained a victory in Texas in July, 1922, when Mayfield, whom the Klan favored, won over Culbertson for the United States Senate.

Although at least eighty per cent. of the American press declared against the new Ku-Klux Klan, it continued to grow; "nightgown tyranny" came north, even to New York, where, at the opening of its drive in November, 1922, Heywood Broun declared:

"The formation of the Ku-Klux Klan seems to us a happy development in American life. Before the birth of this organization the business of hating was difficult. There was no single group which included all the illiberal elements in America. But now they are all together. We do not understand just what common bond fuses these divergent actions — bigots, patrioteers, braggarts, busybodies, censors — but there they are."

On the other hand, Senator John Sharp Williams declared himself, *vide* the *Congressional Record*, "I go as far in the pathways of peace as any man who was ever born. I am willing to arbitrate nearly everything in the world, except one thing, and that is the attempt to outrage a white woman by any man, whether white, black or red. I surrender him at once as being beyond the pale of law, to the first crowd that can get to him. . . . Not only is blood thicker than water, but race is greater than law, now and then."

May 23, 1923, Governor Smith of New York signed a bill practically outlawing the Klan from his State. "You have signed your own political death warrant so far as your aspirations for the Presidency are concerned," the Klan told him. He did not believe it.

On the eve of the 1924 political conventions, after another year of daily reports that the Klan had disappeared or died, an audit showed a gain of four hundred and fifty thousand in the past twelve months. The Klan reached its apex with millions of members (it claimed six) and vast political powers. From this 1924 apex there was only one road and that led downward. Laws were passed against it but one may doubt their effectiveness. The Menckens and the Brouns laughed, and this laughter was symptomatic of the new spirit of American tolerance. In the great year 1925 the Klan lost battle after battle, and took off its masquerade, and returned to its poolrooms and its movies.

### ORIGIN AND SUCCESS OF PROHIBITION

The prohibition movement began with dynamite, ended with legislation. In 1880 a man named Corbin brought the blessings and delights of booze to the few hundred inhabitants of Westerville, Ohio, but found no welcome. Tradesmen refused to deal with him, the best citizens crossed to the other side of the street, but Corbin declined invitations to leave town. So one dark night the good citizens dynamited the Corbin saloon, and Corbin, unharmed, took his wife and children away.

The Reverend Howard H. Russell organized the Anti-Saloon League of America in Westerville in 1894. The spiritual backers came from the Oberlin Temperance Alliance. In 1919, the Reverend Purley A. Baker, D.D., was general superintendent and Bishop Luther B. Wilson, D.D., LL.D., of New York was president. Ernest H. Cherrington of Westerville, general manager of the publishing interests, explaining the success of the movement, said that a record had been kept of every Congressman. "The lobbyists in the employ of the League are instructed to whip the stray legislators into the way they should go. If that method fails, the League sets to work to make that Congressman's chance of reëlection nil. If he is a Republican, we aim to have him defeated by a 'dry' Republican, or we turn to a 'dry' Democrat in the same district.

"Look at the fight the League put up to defeat 'Uncle Joe' Cannon. It took three skirmishes. But we did it.

"Our speakers go into churches. We explain the necessity of funds. Most of our income is derived from the churches which are solidly lined up back of the League.

"The League is sufficiently opportune to seek results.

"We have a complete list of church voters of every town, city, county and State.

"In addition, in the last few years, the League has received support in a large way from men of large means."

Investigation showed the Anti-Saloon League maintained the finest lobby in Washington. "It is the best working organization in the country," said Senator Sheppard. Congress obeyed it.

In the flush of national victory, the League announced its old motto, "America bone dry by 1920" would be replaced with "A Saloonless and Drunkenless World." Two million dollars a year had been spent in state and national work; now it needed five million dollars a year to dry up the world.

Rather belatedly in January, 1919, the liquor interests began fighting the inevitable. A billion-dollar fund was reported but never quite seen. An alarming series of advertisements began. To make them effective, the clever publicity men advised linking up booze with personal freedom; prohibition with Bolshevism! "Will Bolshevism come with National Prohibition?" America was asked.

January 15, 1919, needed only one more State to make the nation dry; at 10.32 A.M. Thursday morning, January 16, Nebraska ratified, with Missouri an hour later and Wyoming only twenty minutes behind. America had gone dry. Frank L. Polk, Acting Secretary of State, declared the amendment valid.

The ceremony was simple. Bryan was present. Said the great Commoner: "In the future we shall deal with individuals who are merely lawbreakers because it will be impossible to organize a national bootleggers' association any more than a national pick-pockets' association." The Reverend Billy Sunday wept. "The rain of tears is over; the slums will soon be a memory; we will turn our prisons into factories, our jails into storehouses and corncribs; men will walk upright now, women will smile, children will laugh, hell will be for rent."

Then came Mr. Volstead, a mild man who couldn't hurt a fly, a gray-eyed little man born of immigrant Norwegian parents, who had risen to fame by being for fourteen years prosecutor in Yellow Medicine County, Minnesota, and finally got himself elected into the House of Representatives. He had been asked to write a law in which he did not believe whole-heartedly. He wrote the act which defined intoxicating liquor as one-half per cent. alcohol and provided enforcement, putting teeth into the Eighteenth Amendment. Andrew J. Volstead became the most hated man in America.

In Wall Street, Scotch went to thirty cents, doubled; rye likewise; cocktails to thirty-five cents, an increase of twenty; mint juleps, the drink of modern Dionysians, forty-five cents instead of thirty; but there was one bright spot: beer, steady at ten cents.

The press asked, What will become of such words as "tight" and "lit" and "three sheets in the wind", next year? In May the brewers turned to "near beer"; the man who invented that term, said a comedian, was a bad judge of distances.

The night of June 30, 1919, saw the greatest collective spree in the annals of intoxication, the greatest wake in the history of the world, in which both Armistice-night celebrations and all New Years' Eves were tea parties by comparison; on the stroke of midnight millions of persons raised a glass to poor old John Barleycorn. For the first and last time probably, bartenders and waiters were as drunk as their clients. "Parades broke out like measles." Dignified persons noted there was an "unpleasant note of wantonness" in the great debauch. Thus was the war-time prohibition law celebrated.

"Pussyfoot" Johnson went to London to begin the work of making the universe dry. In a friendly encounter with students he unfortunately had one of his eyes put out. "Pussyfoot's eye will make England Dry", the posters then announced. But the five million dollar international prohibition movement which began in Westerville, Ohio, seems to have ended in Washington, D. C.

### THE BATTLE OF THE BOOKS

The literary lynching of James Joyce was an international event. He was burned on the docks of London and arrested on the piers of New York. The *Little Review,* where "Ulysses" was appearing in chapters, was barred from the mails in 1921. At the same time Germany confiscated Georg Grosz' "Ecce Homo", and Daudet, in the face of French criticism (but not censorship) withdrew "The Procuress." D. H. Lawrence's "The Rainbow" was prohibited in England, later in America.

In 1922 the battle over censorship was on. Some publishers favored a committee on ethics at the head of which would be a Tsar or dictator, like Mr. Hays of the movies and Judge Landis of baseball.

Sinclair Lewis suggested that Sumner appoint a committee of sub-dictators composed of Bryan on biology, Billy Sunday on morality, Pussyfoot Johnson on law, Fatty Arbuckle on the theater and Ponzi on business. Mencken suggested a committee of the heads of the Elks, Rotary, Ku-Klux Klan, a Methodist bishop chosen by rolling dice, the Honorable Calvin Coolidge, Schwab, Otto Kahn, Rabbi Wise and young Rockefeller. Hamlin Garland, on the other hand, admitted he thought the new books cheap, tawdry and pornographic. When Chief Justice Ford of New York found his daughter reading a certain book which was a best seller, he was so shocked he then and there determined that only by suppressive laws could he clean out "the Augean stables of modern literature."

In the midst of this moral holocaust, it was found that the

year's best sellers were "Black Oxen" by Gertrude Atherton, "The Mine with the Iron Door" by Harold Bell Wright, "The White Flag" by Gene Stratton Porter, "The Alaskan" by James Oliver Curwood, "His Children's Children" by Arthur Train, "The Covered Wagon" by Emerson Hough, "The Enchanted April" by Elizabeth, "Faint Perfume" by Zona Gale, "The Cathedral" by Hugh Walpole and "One of Ours" by Willa Cather. The non-fiction list, according to the *Bookman*, was led by Papini's "Life of Christ." What was all that shootin' for?

The *Dial*, *Broom* and a few minor modern magazines were booming. The *American Mercury* was founded. Books on the war began to appear free from the sentimental garbage of the 1919 reaction. The country began to quiet down.

In defeated Germany the era of disillusion was marked decidedly with war books. Generals and admirals wrote confessions, explanations, apologies; the Kaiser did likewise, and they all fell flat in America. In Germany fiction, personal narratives, pacifist literature flourished. In England Sassoon, unable to awaken the country with poems, published his prose opinions on the war, asking what had become of the idealism which was supposed to be the redeeming feature of war; what had become of patriotism, the devotion and the brotherhood of man in war time; had the brutalization been only temporary; were the nations really "exalted, spiritualized, by the baptism of blood?"

So fed up was America on any story dealing realistically with the recent bloodshed that the publishers of John Dos Passos' "Three Soldiers" advertised it in 1921 as "NOT a war book."

In April Lytton Strachey published "Queen Victoria", opening a new era for enlightened biography. E. E. Cummings published "The Enormous Room"; O'Neill produced "The Hairy Ape." Philip Gibbs' "Now It Can Be Told", exposing the stupidity, filth, horror and uselessness of the Great War, opened the road for many truthful revelations.

Sinclair Lewis's 1919 effort was "Free Air", which had been reviewed under the rubric "mere mention" as "a chatty story"; he wrote "Main Street" in 1920. The Nobel Committee, considering Anatole France, D'Annunzio and Hardy, chose France, despite protests from everywhere calling him a dirty Bolshevik. In America the fact was mourned that we had no candidate for Nobel honors, probably would not have one for generations. "America never produced as many books as now, but not often have her letters been at a lower level," said the old New York *Tribune*. The younger generation hailed "Main Street" and "The Beautiful and Damned", where it found itself portrayed alarmingly by F(rancis) Scott (Key) Fitzgerald.

Who were America's leading literary stars? The *Literary Digest* published its poll July, 1922. The winners were: Hergesheimer twenty-two votes, O'Neill fourteen; Anderson thirteen; Cather twelve; Frost and Cabell tied for fifth place with eight each. The losers were: Masters seven; Sinclair Lewis and Edna Millay six each; Sandburg, Van Loon and Robinson five each. The booby prizes went to T. S. Eliot, Santayana and Ring Lardner, one each. Hemingway was not known; Dreiser had come under the statute of limitations, as belonging to the past generation.

The super-realists, or Surrealists as they called themselves, were triumphant in Paris, fighting the conventional writers and the Dadaists, but it was a member of the Chicago group who furnished the greatest delight to friends and foes by the publication of his "Triget of Griva", which Ford Madox Ford, editor of the *Transatlantic Review*, in Paris, printing it in 1924, called better Dadaism than the work of Aragon, Desnos, Soupault, André Breton *et al.* Here it is:

I GASPIRI

(The Upholsterers)

A DRAMA IN THREE ACTS

BY RING LARDNER

*Adapted from the Bukovinan of Casper Redmond*

## CHARACTERS

IAN OBRI — *A Blotter Salesman*
JOHAN WASPER — *His wife*
GRETA — *Their daughter*
HERBERT SWOPE
FFENA — *Their daughter, later their wife*
EGSO — *A Pencil Guster*
TONO — *A Typical Wastebasket*

### ACT I

A public street in a bathroom. A man named Tupper has evidently just taken a bath. A man named Brindle is now taking a bath. A man named Newburn comes out of the faucet which has been left running. He exits through the exhaust. Two strangers to each other meet on the bath mat.

*First Stranger:* Where was you born?
*Second Stranger:* Out of wedlock.
*First Stranger:* That's mighty pretty country around there.
*Second Stranger:* Are you married?
*First Stranger:* I don't know. There's a woman living with me, but I can't place her.

*(Three outsiders named Klein go across the stage three times. They think they are in a public library. A woman's cough is heard off-stage left.)*

*A New Character:* Who is that cough?
*Two Moors:* That is my mother. She died a little while ago in a haphazard way.
*A Greek:* And what a woman she was!

*(The curtain is lowered for seven days to denote the lapse of a week.)*

### ACT III

(The Lincoln Highway. Two bearded glue lifters are seated at one side of the road.)

TRANSLATOR'S NOTE: — The principal industry in Phlace is hoarding hay. Peasants sit alongside of a road on which hay wagons are likely to pass. When a hay wagon does pass, the hay hoarders leap from their points of vintage and help themselves to a wisp of hay. On an average a hay hoarder accumulates a ton of hay every four years. (This is called Mah Jong.)

*First Glue Lifter:* Well, my man, how goes it?
*Second Glue Lifter:* (Sings "My Man" to show how it goes.)
*(Eight realtors cross the stage in a friendly way. They are out of place.)*

CURTAIN

## THE CRITIQUE OF PURE ART

The otherwise sterile German revolution gave birth to Dadaism in 1919, and the greatest movement in painting since Cézanne, Expressionism, which Hermann Bahr described in a slender volume "Expressionismus", in 1920. "The emphasis," Sheldon Cheney explains the movement, "is on any sort of expressiveness as against imitativeness." Kandinsky, Klee, Franz Marc and the giant Oskar Kokoschka, Chagall and Campendonk were noted expressionists.

Not since the mass excitement of 1913, when Marcel Duchamp's "Nude Descending the Stairs" drove thousands to the New York Sixty-ninth Infantry Regiment's armory and the Chicago police had been asked to close Jerome Blum's post-impressionism show, was there such excitement as 1921 produced when modern exhibitions were held in many cities. The uproar in Philadelphia became so great a "commission in lunacy" visited the Pennsylvania Academy exhibition.

But most alarming of all was the movement "to kill modernist pictures." One was always killing something in those days, liquor, immoral books, Reds, jazz or Negroes. The strange, diverse, unchanneled forces liberated by the war, in 1921 suddenly turned on new enemies, "satanists, degenerates, madmen who were destroying our civilization with paint and canvas." Who were these underminers? They were named and their works too: Paul Cézanne ("Sorrow", "The Bathers", and a still life of fruit); Degas ("Before the Race", "The Bather", "Two Women Seated" — showing either mental or moral eclipse); Derain ("Woman Half-length"); Gauguin ("Hina-Tefatou"); Matisse ("Spanish Girl"); Picasso ("Woman Dressing Her Hair",

"Woman at a Window"); all described as pathological in conception, drawing, perspective and color. Renoir's "Girl Arranging Her Chemise", owned by Joseph Stransky, was especially disapproved as vulgar in subject, ugly in face and form, weird in color.

In England, in 1923, Jacob Epstein, the American sculptor whose every new style caused a scandal, was told his was "art for the devil's sake"; he was "an artist Lenin, bolshevizing art", and no less an authority than Chesterton asked despairingly, "Are the Artists Going Mad?" The town of New Rochelle put pieces of canvas on MacMonnies' "Venus and Adonis."

Was there no sanity left among critics? Did no one rise to the defense of modern art? Hear then the decision of Willard Huntington Wright (who fortunately for readers of detective stories but unhappily for the seekers of artistic appreciation, later turned into S. S. Van Dine): "During the past decade," wrote Wright in that same fatal 1923 of art hysteria, "the younger painters of this century, in the face of constant hostility, ignorance, indifference and ridicule, have produced a body of creative work which outweighs in originality and significance the output of any European nation, with the one exception of France; and even that nation need not be excepted if we bar four or five preëminent names such as Cézanne, Renoir, Matisse and Picasso."

## CHAPTER NINE

### NEW MEN FOR OLD

WHEN Lloyd George laid down the premiership on October 19, 1922, the last of the Big Four of the Versailles days was driven from power. President Wilson had been the first to be repudiated; his two colleagues, Messrs. Orlando and Clemenceau, were overthrown because Italy and even France thought they had not got enough land and spoils out of the peacemaking, and Lloyd George finally had to surrender to a nation disillusioned, tired of promises, and ready soon to make the socialistic-labor experiment.

New men and new ideas were replacing the great names of Armistice time. In America there was a rapid procession of Presidents: Theodore Roosevelt's death being followed by Harding's, and then by Wilson's, leaving a strange new occupant of the White House who had won the Vice Presidency largely through a myth. In this unstable epoch arose Gandhi of India, whose new gospel of peace now resulted in his being acknowledged one of the four great men of the century, while the recently despised German scientist Einstein was admitted to be another of the caryatids upholding the modern world.

Two sinister figures came into tremendous wealth, power and fame, both as secretly as possible, because their achievements were wrung out of the blood and sweat of millions of people: Hugo Stinnes in Germany and Sir Basil Zaharoff in England, France, Greece and Asia Minor. In France two men driven into prison as traitors early in the war came back into public life: MM. Caillaux and Malvy. Grandeur and misery mingled in the lives of the new men who were replacing the old men.

## FOUR AMERICAN PRESIDENTS

Roosevelt hardly comes within this chronicle. Having done his best to destroy Woodrow Wilson, he died peacefully in his sleep January 6, 1919, leaving for America the memory of a tradition breaker, the incarnation of the new spirit in aggressive success, a new idol for timid youth, a new conception of Yankee statesmanship.

Try as he would, Mr. Wilson could not be "human", he could never have the Roosevelt appeal, he remained a solitary, he never touched the heart of the people he had led into war but could not lead to peace. He tried his best. He used slang, he went to vaudeville shows and applauded with the masses, he read detective thrillers, but it all seemed such an effort. It was as if consciously he was trying to show the world he was not a cold personification of the conventional professorial type. His secretary, Tumulty, lets the real man out of Fate's bag with the account of the visit of a noted journalist come to instruct Wilson in "public relations", suggesting stunts for winning public sympathy.

"Tumulty, you must realize that I am not built for these things," said the President; "I do not want to be displayed before the public. If I tried to do it, I would do it badly. I want people to love me, but they never will. . . ."

They never did.

He tried to be friendly to the press but he feared the reporters. He thought he could perhaps get close to them by talking their language, which for him meant talking down to their level, and they resented it and laughed at him afterwards. He once astonished every one with his outburst, "I'll get their scalps yet", but he was armed not with a tomahawk but with fine phrases. One day, after his breakdown, he appeared at a window of his house to greet admirers, and leaning heavily on a Negro servant, recited:

For beauty I am not a star,
There are others more handsome by far,
But my face, I don't mind it,
For I am behind it,
It's the people in front that I jar.

If in Paris he realized he was being beaten, if he suffered, if he went through the agony in the garden, he gave no sign of it outwardly.

September 3, 1919, he collapsed in the middle of a tour of the country in which he sought favor for his treaty and his League.

On March 19, 1920, the Senate rejected the treaty forty-nine to thirty-five, twenty-one Democrats having deserted Wilson. Armistice Day, 1921, he stood in his doorway and burst into tears when twenty thousand persons called him "the greatest soldier in the World War."

February 3, 1924, Admiral Grayson, watching at the bedside, felt the exact moment when life departed. He looked across the room to the wife and daughter, who understood with bowed heads. No word was spoken.

The world knew that the great war President was dying. On the sidewalk a hundred persons knelt and prayed.

Grayson had told him the truth. "I am ready," Wilson replied; "I am a piece of broken machinery."

Newspapers which had fought him now called him "the greatest figure in world history risen from American soil."

He was the most beloved and the most hated man of the century.

His successor was a man whom no one hated. Warren Gamaliel Harding, Senator from Ohio, publisher of a provincial newspaper, was chosen, June 12, 1920, according to Colonel Harvey, who told the inside story later, "because there was nothing against him and because the delegates wanted to go home." On July 5, Harding struck the ungrammatical keynote of the campaign and his own personality. Normal men, he said, not supermen, must rule; he was against one-man government, meaning of course Wilson. "Normal men," he said, "and back to normalcy will steady a civilization which has been fevered by the supreme upheaval of all the world."

Wilson rode with Harding on March 4, and the Ohio Gang moved in force into Washington. The first hint of scandal came in the request of Senator Kendrick of Wyoming, April 15, 1922, that an oil lease be investigated. From a private corporation's office came the statement, "Mr. H. F. Sinclair . . . welcomes the fullest investigation" of the leasing "by the proper departments of the government of the naval reserve Number 3 in Wyoming, known as the Teapot Dome."

In June, 1923, Harding went on a speaking tour. July 28, Harding was reported suffering from ptomaine poisoning. It was said he ate something two days earlier which did not agree with him, something out of a can, "thereby making an alibi for the Alaskan crabs that had been unjustly accused." Some had it the crabs had been Japanese. It was not thought serious.

The press August 3 was bordered with the conventional black and there was great national sadness. "President Harding Dies; Apoplexy brings the end while wife reads to him." After all the reports of recovery!

Looking back on these days with a historic, suspicious eye, one must find much that is inexplicable in the death of the President.

At that time, it must be remembered, Harding was the Galahad of Presidents. Harding the Immaculate. Harding the Spotless One. The one dark rumor, the one ugly whisper, the one dirty ghost of his life, had been laid just before the election. Harding was not an octoroon; had not, in fact, any Negro blood in his Puritan Ohio veins. The story of his elopement with Florence Kling was nobody's business and the few who knew of the Nan Britton "romance" were not exploiting it.

To-day, it is said, Harding died just in the nick of time. Another month or two, with renomination imminent, everything would have been in a typhoon of scandal, — Teapot Dome,

Fall, Daugherty, Sinclair, Nan Britton, the Ohio Gang, the Hamon murder, Gaston Means, all whirled into the most disillusioning muddy spectacle since the days of presidential impeachment.

As for the death of the man, the mere rereading of the official medical bulletins and eyewitness accounts is disquieting enough. On the night of July 31, Harding had passed the pneumonia crisis. General Sawyer was going for a walk, his first departure from the bedside. The President's temperature was 99 3/5, pulse 118, the lowest since he was taken ill, respiration 36, a decrease of 8 from the last previous report; the cough had been dissipated. The President was cheerful, was reading the papers, even the reports of his illness. On the night of August 1, the President's temperature was normal.

"The fire is out. We can't say it will stay out. Nobody can say that," said Doctor Sawyer.

"What do you think about our starting home Sunday?" the President had asked his physician. His physician thought it was pushing things too fast.

At 7.30 o'clock on the evening of August 2, the President stretched out his hand to his wife, who was sitting by him, shuddered, and passed away almost instantly, in a stroke of apoplexy.

The last bulletin had stated: "The President has had the most satisfactory day since his illness began."

Doctor Sawyer told correspondents it was safe now to say that the President was convalescing. The temperature had been normal, the pulse near the President's normal of 80, and the respiration had decreased to 34. None of the "downs" the physician had feared had interrupted the "ups" during the day. Tension, strain and anxiety in the household had vanished.

Harding died the nation's hero.

The rise of Calvin Coolidge was a phenomenon. The Boston police strike of September, 1919, was followed by the election on

November 4 when he carried Massachusetts by one hundred and thirty thousand; from then on it was only a matter of time before he would be in Washington, as he had become a national hero.

To this day it is generally accepted as fact that Coolidge broke the police strike. His fame rested on that until he became President and brought prosperity. The facts in the Boston strike as reported by the Citizens' Committee headed by Banker J. J. Storrow, are:

> On September 9, the day the strike began, Mayor Peters asked the governor to send 3000 troops, Coolidge declining in a letter saying: "There is no authority in the office of the governor for interference in the making of orders by the police commissioner or in the action of the mayor and the city council. I am unable to discover any action that I can take."
>
> That Tuesday a small boy threw a brick through a downtown window and rioting began. The damage was $300,000. There were crap games on the Common and only 400 police were on duty.
>
> On Wednesday, according to the report, Mayor Peters called out troops and asked Coolidge for three additional regiments of infantry because "it was clear that the situation was a military one." By Thursday morning order had been generally restored in the city. On Thursday afternoon, September 11, the governor assumed control of the situation as indicated by his proclamation of that date.

The report concludes: "In justice to the governor it should be stated that at all times he assured the members of your committee that whenever called upon for a military force he would procure sufficient men — if they could be secured — to maintain law and order."

The strike was broken the morning of Thursday, September 11, by Mayor Peters, the governor not acting until that afternoon.

## THE FATHER OF VICTORY

Within a year Georges Clemenceau, *Père-la-Victoire,* became known as *Perd-la-Victoire*. Foch, Tardieu, Poincaré, the

*Underwood and Underwood*

EUROPE'S "MYSTERY MAN", SIR BASIL ZAHAROFF

militarists, the haters, the jingo press, accused him of having given in to President Wilson because the two had permitted Germany to come out alive after defeat. M. Clemenceau was repudiated. He had not a friend left.

M. Clemenceau received a great welcome in America in 1922 when he came to damn pro-German sentiment.

The old Tiger lived on quietly in retirement in Vendée until November 21, 1929, when he died, his last words being, "I am suffering atrociously in my intestines." He had ordered that all women leave the house. "I want no tears; let me die before men." In his will he directed: "Let me be carried in the silence of daybreak to my Vendéean forest, and there, beside the coffin of my father, let mine be placed upright like his. Even in death I wish to remain standing." There was no national funeral. There was no religious ceremony. He was buried, standing up, facing his enemy, Germany.

### THE MAN WHO WINS EVERY WAR

In Constantinople in the old days, before the Allies brought in their red, motorized fire engines, fire-fighting usually followed this formula:

The victim would shout, the shouting would be heard up and down the streets, and a squad of riffraff Greek and Armenians would arrive with a little wooden machine into which buckets of water were poured. By working handles on both sides, this water could be made to squirt up a storey or two. Before this was done, however, bargaining was in order. "How much?" the fire-fighters asked. "Two pounds," the victim would say, watching his home burning down. "Ten pounds," the firemen would ask. "Give you five." And so on. If the deal went through, well and good; otherwise the firemen would stand around until the moment the house was given up. Then every one, firemen included, would dash in and loot.

One of these Greco-Armenian firemen who ran around Constantinople clad in a breechcloth in those days was Sir Basil

Zaharoff, now "one of the few legendary figures left in a skeptical age", the greatest munitions maker in the world, multimillionaire, maker of governments and wars, the one man who wins every war. That Zaharoff owns half or more of the firm of Vickers-Armstrong and sells guns and battleships and tanks is fact; that he was a fireman; is the secret owner of the gambling casinos of Monte Carlo; that he was part owner of Krupps before the war and enjoyed the profits from both sides are speculations he has never confirmed or denied. He has chosen mystery as his rôle.

In the 1870's, however, there is a record of a young Greek named Basilieos Zacharoff appearing in the Old Bailey prison court, London, to plead not guilty to a charge of theft. Thanks to a wealthy uncle who came from Turkey, and a clever lawyer, the lad was saved from punishment. Fifty years later King George knighted him for services in winning the war.

After the London episode, Zaharoff returned to Greece, where he got a small job with Nordenfelt and Company. As luck would have it, the Balkans, Russia and Turkey went to war and every nation bought munitions. The twenty-five dollar a week agent soon had several hundred thousand in the bank and nothing could stop his progress.

Vickers, which had absorbed Nordenfelt, promised Zaharoff a partnership if he got a five million dollar order from Spain, which he did promptly. He became a millionaire and the most important munitions salesman in the world. He then did what the Krupps, the Schneiders, the American munitions makers and the British have done and do: he sold the means of bloodshed to both sides. In addition, Zaharoff visited the prime ministers of all the Balkan countries, the kings of Continental Europe, sowing the seeds of suspicion and hatred, and selling large orders of guns "for the purpose of national defense." He is also charged with fomenting the disputes which led to various wars. He sold the machine guns which killed British soldiers to the Boers and he made most of the British munitions for use against the Boers. Spain used up his goods in the dispute with the United States and had to buy more. The Balkan Wars were fought with Zaharoff guns against Zaharoff guns. Being a Greek patriot, he spent his own money on two wars, the Greeks against the Turks in 1911 and the disastrous march against Kemal Pasha. In the World War he served the Allies well by intimidating Greece into being friendly; then he subsidized the Venezilist movement and drove King Constantine from the throne.

He also gave large sums to war charities and established hospitals for the wounded and dying.

### STINNES, THE GERMAN COLOSSUS

The other great mystery of the epoch was Hugo Stinnes, a man who spoke in sixty-three newspapers anonymously but maintained an almost unbroken silence otherwise.

He came into international importance as the first German to defy the Allies after the war. He refused to give up his coal. When he banged his fist on the table at the Spa conference, he jolted all Europe.

Because he had amassed a billion-dollar fortune, because the Stinnes "Empire" extended by rail and ship lines and newspapers and coal and iron mines from Berlin to Buenos Aires, from Moscow to Constantinople, he was soon written up in the popular million-circulation American weeklies as a "success story." Here was a man to study and emulate. (Ten years later Ivar Kreuger was a similar subject.)

Stinnes' great exploit, not included in laudatory biographies, was participation in the looting of Germany through the inflation. The McKenna report to the House of Commons, 1924, showed that between $1,808,000,000 and $2,070,000,000 in German marks had been sold to foreigners, American buyers alone losing about one billion dollars, and that one million persons having money on deposit in German banks were wiped clean. Those two billion dollars lost were gained by some one.

One of the big gainers was Hugo Stinnes. He paid in worthless paper marks "borrowed" from the government, and repaid the government months later with a handful of dollars, thereby profiteering millions per month.

Between Armistice Day and May 1, 1924, when he died, Stinnes dominated German politics equally with the changing chancellors. He influenced Wirth, Cuno, Marx and Stresemann and their cabinets.

### MAHATMA GANDHI AND THE COW CRISIS

The name of Mohandas Karamchand Gandhi now became known around the world as the teacher of non-violent means for gaining national liberties. He was being called Mahatma, great sage. He disowned the title. "There is not a moment I can recall when it may be said to have tickled me."

Gandhi is not a Brahman, but a member of the third caste, Vaisyas. Physically weak as a child, cowardly and shy, he gave up eating meat in seeking to cure himself. He lied to his mother about a lost appetite and stole money to buy cigarettes. Once in despair he contemplated suicide. Betrothed at eight, he married at thirteen, taking advantage of a relative's wedding to make it a double ceremony and save money.

At the age of nineteen he went to London to study law and was excommunicated from his caste. For three months he attempted to become an English gentleman, taking lessons in dancing, elocution, French and the violin. "It only cultivated disappointment," he wrote later; "I have no ear for Western music, and the result was a ludicrous failure." He tried to read the Bible, Genesis and Exodus, and did not like it. Later on, the Sermon on the Mount meant almost as much to him as the Bhagavad-gita.

He returned to India, practiced law a while, and was sent to South Africa to try a case. He stayed twenty-one years and fought the color line and indentured labor, establishing his own newspaper for those ideals. Some Britons supported him, others did not; he was stoned in Durban, Natal, and saved by an Englishwoman with an umbrella.

After the passage of the Asiatic Law Amendment Act, all his work having proved futile, he began passive resistance and was in jail three times. In 1914 he thought the Indian Relief Bill settled all problems and returned to England to find the World War beginning. Bad health kept him from organizing his Indian ambulance corps, so he returned to India in January, 1915, accompanied by his faithful wife, and was received as a leader. The British Government decorated him for services to the Crown. He denounced radicalism in Bengal. Throughout the war he was loyal to Britain, urging Indians to respond to the call to the colors.

In India he now published "The Story of My Experiments with Truth", a philosophical biography. He professed himself a believer in the Hindu doctrine of *maya* (illusion of all material things). He does not think his political experiments important. He is still seeking self-realization, "to see God face to face", to attain *moksha* (salvation), to realize Absolute Truth. He devotes two chapters to *brahmacharya* or celibacy within the marriage state, for the purpose of realizing God. Control of the palate being the first essential to such a vow, he discusses dietetics at length.

In 1922 Gandhi passed his greatest crisis as leader of the *swaraj* or self-rule movement, when he ordered a sick cow to be killed. "To the orthodox Hindu," Sarat Mukerji explained, "a cow is a cow, sick or well; and as the cow gives milk to the babe and takes the place of the mother, she is considered sacred by the Hindu. They love her as a mother; they worship her as a goddess. As no one would think of killing a sick mother, so the Hindu argues no one should think of killing a sick cow. It is a sin. No matter who commits the sin, whether a Mahatma or even a saint, he is a great sinner. A sinner has no right to be the leader."

Millions of Hindus were shocked, thousands protested, minor

leaders attacked Gandhi. The cow incident was explained, debated, defended by few. It was now a long time since Amritsar had made Gandhi the leader of the non-violence, non-resistance nationalist independence movement, and little had been gained politically. Disillusion took up the case of the sick cow. Gandhi defended himself:

"I knew that public opinion, especially in Ahmedabad, would not approve of my action and that it would read nothing but *himsa* (violence) in it. But I know too that performance of one's duty should be independent of public opinion."

"Would the Mahatma apply this theory of his to human beings as well?"

He replied "Yes" decisively, adding, "Suppose, for instance, that I find my daughter — whose wish at the moment I have no means of ascertaining — is threatened with violation and there is no way by which I can save her. Then it would be the purest form of *himsa* on my part to put an end to her life and surrender myself to the fury of the incensed ruffian."

In time, it was found, the cow-eating Mussulmans and cow-worshiping Hindus came in greater numbers to Saint Gandhi's shrine, and he had made a beginning in bringing them together out of this strange incident.

## Interlude 1924

Chinese Christians send America warning against Mah Jong and "the terrible curse which comes through gambling."

February 1: Britain recognizes the Soviets; President Wilson near death's door; Alexei Rykoff named Lenin's successor; Howard Carter certain Tut's mummy is intact.

The undertakers, Carter proved, had cheated by substituting granite for expensive white sandstone in the coffin lid.

> Who shall doubt the secret hid,
> Under Cheops' pyramid
> Was that the contractor did
> Cheops out of several millions?

On the twelfth the lid was lifted, revealing a solid gold coffin. On the inside Carter deciphered:

> LET ALL WHO LOVE LIFE
> AND HATE DEATH
> WISH THOUSANDS OF GEESE
> AND BREAD AND BEER
> TO MY SOUL

The Charleston, via Harlem, begins the conquest of the world.

Dion — or Dean — O'Banion loved flowers and originated dinner-dress gangsterism, and when he was killed tens of thousands of persons attended his funeral. He had a ten thousand dollar coffin, his age's rival to Tut's, and twenty-five beer-running trucks carried the flowers. He had killed eight men, it was said, but helped cripples and newsboys.

In May, Marguerite Upton, Mrs. Peggy Archer-Hopkins-Hopkins-Joyce became Countess Morner. (June 16, 1921, Alfred

Austrian, attorney for James Stanley Joyce, pleading with the Cook County court to bring Mrs. Joyce to Chicago, told the judge: "My client had one shortcoming. His great error was that he fell in love with Peggy. He believed in the sanctity of womanhood and he believed that she would make him a good wife. He has found out his mistake.")

July 29, 1924: Count Morner sought annulment of the marriage.

"The title was a liability," said Peggy. "The hairdressers did not know me. I rarely used the title Countess Morner. As far as I am concerned, you can spell it m-o-u-r-n-e-r hereafter."

The finding of a pair of glasses, "probably a woman's, because small", solved the "perfect" murder. Richard Loeb, seventeen, and Nathan Leopold, eighteen, wealthy college students, were arrested for kidnaping and killing their neighbor, Robert Franks, aged fourteen.

The case was tried in the press and the accused condemned to death before the hearing.

Clarence Darrow, defending, said Leopold had "the most brilliant intellect that I ever met in a boy. . . . Both were incipient paranoiacs. The whole case discloses no motive that could induce a sane mind and normal person to commit such a crime."

"No rich man ever hanged for murder," screamed those papers which had already tried the case.

September 10, Loeb and Leopold were sentenced to life imprisonment with no parole ever.

"Gun Moll", latest word in underworld.

Crossword puzzles replacing Mah Jong.

Spiritualists produced epigrams just received from Oscar Wilde; for example, "Being dead is the most boring experience in life."

Houdini had "Margery" (Mrs. Le Roi G. Crandon) try her stuff in a laboratory. It was a blank. She "produced" nothing but her voice.

President Doumergue gave a reception to American advertising men and forty-seven gold spoons disappeared. Souvenirs, it was said.

Major Imbrie, taking pictures for souvenirs in Teheran, was killed by a mob. America sent a Mussolinic ultimatum to Persia.

March 24, Patrick Joseph Hayes and George William Mundelein made cardinals.

The Methodist Episcopal General Conference, five to one, lifted the ban on amusements, except those "which cannot be used in the name of Jesus Christ." The Pope accepted a radio outfit.

Duse died in America.

Elizabeth Bergner played Shaw's "Saint Joan" in Berlin, proving to international critics she was the world's greatest actress.

Great Bernard saw his first American baseball game in London, Giants *v.* Chicago White Sox (the King almost got hit but he ducked a foul) and said, "The only way of preventing civilized men from kicking and beating their wives is to organize games in which they can kick and beat balls."

The Lord Chamberlain lifted the ban on "Mrs. Warren's Profession."

At the Olympic Games in Paris, the United States as usual won the honors in victories, first places, points scored. United States ninety-four; France sixty-four; Sweden forty-four and one-half; Britain forty-one and one-half; Finland thirty-four.

Florida amended its constitution, prohibiting inheritance and income taxes.

The Coolidge victory in November was followed by the five biggest days the Stock Exchange had ever seen.

Prosperity bells rang throughout the land.

## CHAPTER TEN

### Five Years of Wars — and Peace Conferences

Whichever direction we go, we are marching into a fog.

— Lloyd George, 1921

The perpetrators of the crime of the Treaty of Versailles, as if conscience-stricken, began in the year 1920 the series of peace conferences to which the term "greatest in the history of the world" has on more than one occasion been used in the past thirteen years. They were punctuated always with the cannon shot of the dictators marching to power, enlivened by the cries of civilian massacres, stained with the blood of civil war and small wars of aggression, while desperate peoples groaned and sweated and called for revenge.

September, 1919, the Treaty of St. Germain was signed, forcing Austria to become an independent State. A neat interpretation of Wilson's program. The Austrians, left stranded in Vienna with a long, narrow strip of country, had realized their economic salvation lay in union with Germany; but Italy, afraid of a common frontier, and France, fearful of any added military strength, denied Vienna and the peasants the right to decide their own fate. In November, the Neuilly Treaty robbed Bulgaria of its rich lands and in June, 1921, the Trianon Treaty cut two thirds of Hungary away and distributed the pieces to her enemies.

Each of the four treaties created better causes for war than could have been found in 1914. Rumania, Poland and Italy were presented with land and people which they cannot absorb but have to subjugate. Through Germany the Danzig Corridor was cut, severing East Prussia from the Reich so that Poland could have President Wilson's promised highway to the world's seas and oceans — and incidentally a naval base for future wars. Where plebiscites in German territory were held, the Allies took part or all the land voting for the Fatherland and gave it to the enemy. Eupen and Malmedy were awarded to Belgium. The Saar coal basin was occupied by France. Two hundred and fifty thousand German-speaking Austrians were awarded to Italy in the Tyrol, where they enjoyed some liberties until Fascism created an Alsace-Lorraine there by abolishing the language, schools, newspapers and freedom of the people. Transylvania, parts of which were one hundred per cent. Hungarian, came under the crude, corrupt sway of "victorious" Rumania.

The treaties divided factories from workers, producers from consumers, towns from their railroad stations, pigs from their pastures, and patriots from their homes. In many cases stupidly, unnecessarily, in others with malicious forethought.

The reaction in Europe was militarism, hatred, super-patriotism, revenge policies, preparations for new wars, unions of the victors to hold their spoils, secret military organizations, rebellions, uprisings, and new plans for wars which may in time mature.

On Germany reparations were imposed which equaled a penal sentence. Year after year the war guilt clause becomes more important in Germany's struggle. Article Number 231 of the Versailles Treaty states: "The Allied and Associated governments affirm and Germany accepts the responsibility of Germany and her Allies for causing all the loss and damage to which the Allied and Associated governments and their nations have been subjected, as a consequence of the war imposed upon them by the aggression of Germany and her Allies." Germany continues to fight this clause. If once it were stricken out, there would remain little moral ground for the punishment, monetary and material, inflicted on the losers.

France, left almost solitary by the defection of America and the whirligigs of Mr. Lloyd George, found reparations its strongest weapon for continuing the destruction of Germany — for nothing less than destruction could make France secure, according to her then political program — and money she proceeded to collect with her bayonets.

In 1919, Lloyd George's committee reported the total cost of the war to the Allies had been one hundred and twenty billion dollars. The American experts declared, according to Tardieu, that sixty-five billion dollars could be expected and was fair. J. M. Keynes reported that ten billion dollars was all Germany could pay. Keynes, however, was an economist, and in those days, as in these days, politicians and soldiers, not economists, settle financial questions.

The French, through M. Loucheur, presented a bill for the reconstruction of the war zone, for fifteen billion dollars and later M. Klotz, Finance Minister, changed this to read twenty-six billion dollars. Mr. Lloyd George, however, found that in 1917 all of France was worth just twelve billion dollars according to her own estimate, and the war zone was only four per cent. of the country, and he wanted an explanation. In 1928 an official British report showed that the entire reconstruction had been accomplished for a little more than four billion dollars. France could not openly explain that what she wanted was destruction of Germany, not reconstruction of France.

At San Remo in April, 1920, it was announced that all the difficulties between the French politicians and Mr. Lloyd George had been patched up, in the face of a new German menace. The French press was again ordered to glow with tributes to the great Welshman. It glowed. The statesmen created Armenia a free State. Its mandate had been offered and refused by the United States, much to the chagrin of the churchmen who played the sad symphony of Armenian massacres. While the Allies were arguing who would get the mandate, the Russians annexed the country. So that problem was off their hands.

In July, the Allied premiers met at Brussels and Spa to divide the spoils of war. It must be remembered that no amount of indemnity had been fixed. It was part of the French idea to keep Germany guessing, forever if possible, making her pay her utmost annually but never saying when the end would be. It was agreed that France get fifty-two per cent. of the German reparations.

In 1921, the Allies struck Germany a great blow. Despite murder, looting, rioting, fire and sword, torture and terrorism, mostly on the part of the Polish irregular troops; despite the fact that eight thousand French infantry looked after the Polish interests and the two thousand Italians had been traded to the French cause in return for French aid in the Adriatic, the Upper Silesian plebiscite resulted in 716,408 votes for Germany and 471,406 for Poland. The vote being sixty per cent. in favor of Germany, the Allies gave sixty per cent. of the country to Poland. The whole world, with the exception of one nation, thought the decision unjust. Germany has never stopped complaining; in 1931, for instance, her charge of continued Polish terrorism was answered by "a sharp rebuke" to Poland from the League of Nations.

Among the justifications offered by Poland is the charge that Prussian Junkers, owners of the mines and factories, have for a century tyrannically exploited the workmen, all of whom are Polish. This is probably true.

Berlin's rejoicing over the vote turned next morning to rage when it was announced the frontier would be so drawn that the Polish farming lands, in being joined to Poland, would include the mineral deposits, the coal, and the factories and mines. Poland did not wait for official action. Adalbert Korfanty, the commissioner sent from Warsaw, seized the zone. The French and Italians looked sideways. The British alone were left to preserve law and order. Colonel Pepys Cockrell led four British battalions against Korfanty.

The Polish Government went through the form of dismissing

Korfanty; Germany sneered, Britain and America thought it was a transparent joke. Various minor battles were fought between German irregulars, Polish irregulars, and the Allied troops. But in most instances the Allied troops were not all on the same side. The British frequently came to the aid of the Germans in driving off the Korfanty bands who were being aided by regular French troops. Once Cockrell was captured by a Polish company which prepared to shoot him. Said the Colonel, "Although invisible, the Union Jack envelops me. If you shoot me, you fire on the British flag. Now do what you damn please." The Poles set him free.

On August 25, the United States and Germany signed a peace treaty in the office of Foreign Minister Rosen in the Wilhelmstrasse. The ceremony began at 5.20 P.M. and closed at 5.22 P.M. The signers of the treaty stood up. The American commissioner, Ellis Loring Dresel, suffered an unfortunately situated carbuncle. The German diplomat therefore also stood. Dresel signed both copies, shoved them across the desk, and Rosen signed. One journalist was present; he had also seen the signing of the Versailles Treaty.

Armistice Day, 1921, the first great effort to establish peace was made by the American Government. President Harding had called the nations together for a disarmament conference. He had promised, as presidential candidate, to do something to make up for our failure to participate in the Versailles fiasco and this was it. Sober Mr. H. G. Wells thought it "may become a cardinal event in the history of mankind. It may mark a turning point in the history of human affairs." M. Briand wirelessed from his boat, "France has confidence that the conference will give to the world definite peace, and . . . the assurance to our country of that security to which she has a right." An American cynic remarked that the United States would participate with a delegation "the left wing of which will be represented by Elihu Root", but all the rest of the world was optimistic.

Marshal Diaz of Italy, Admiral Lord Beatty of England and

General Foch of France arrived amidst unparalleled enthusiasm. But Mr. Wilson refused to see General Foch, his physicians saying he was too ill, and it was recalled that just after the Versailles Treaty the President had said that "a militaristic party, under the most influential leadership, was seeking to gain ascendancy in the counsels of France. They were defeated then, but are in control now."

Nobly President Harding opened the conference and Secretary Hughes electrified every one with his proposal of a ten-year naval holiday, the scrapping of sixty-six warships, and the ratio for England, the United States and Japan of six, five, three, in capital ships. Mr. Balfour replied the next day and Briand spoke for disarmament. France was prepared to cut down its army to five hundred and twenty-five thousand men! And military service would be reduced from three to two years.

"This is not disarmament, it is economy," cried H. G. Wells in wrath.

"Germany has refused to disarm," continued M. Briand; "she still has seven million men who made the war."

In December, naval experts produced the six, six, three plan but there was pessimism. Then Japan accepted the five, five, three plan, expecting concessions in the East for so doing. The press complained of too much secrecy, too much going on behind closed doors. But the American labor unions and the British labor party endorsed Hughes' proposals and Schwab exclaimed, "I'd sink my steel plant to end war."

Mr. Wells was the only one to call attention to the future of the munitions interests. Why not have the governments take over the private interests, so that arms would really be controlled? And why was Russia, which was continuing to build up an army and navy, absent? "Why punish peoples for sins of their rulers?" asked Mr. Wells.

Northcliffe's *Daily Mail* replied by firing Mr. Wells as conference correspondent. The cable read: "Tell Mr. Wells I am not asking him to change his opinions but to express them more decorously with regard to France." *Le Petit Parisien* threw Wells out too, and its owner, M. Dupuy, raised the question of the "growing responsibility of the press in international politics." This same newspaper was one of ten which had accepted money from the Tsar for pro-Russian propaganda for years. The *World* rebuked the *Mail:* "Mr. Wells is under the same instructions as every member of the staff . . . no policy except publication of the truth." The Manchester *Guardian* was sure France had no reason to take offense, but Jacques Bainville, "foremost political writer", did, saying, "Wells is a socialist. . . . Our greatest friends in all countries are the reactionaries."

On the eighth of December, Britain gave up the Anglo-Japanese treaty and on the thirteenth the nations signed a Four Power treaty for peace in the Pacific. Success was obtained to the limitation of battleships, because Britain sacrificed her pact with Japan and the United States agreed not to fortify the Philippines.

The Washington Conference treaties were signed August 17, 1923. In 1932, startling disclosures were published by Major Herbert O. Yardley of the "American Black Chamber", a part of the military intelligence division of the United States army which, organized for war in 1917, continued until 1929. During the conference, Major Yardley wrote, the dispatches between Britain and Japan were deciphered by his bureau; he learned that both nations had arrived "with no great sincerity of purpose" but with plans for the usual diplomatic horse trading. By knowing the real sentiment and plans of these nations, Major Yardley gave the information to the American Government which armed it for a successful result.

In January, 1922, a conference at Cannes at which M. Briand made the issue militarism or peace was wrecked by M. Poincaré and his press. In April, Europe again decided a world conference was necessary and came to Genoa to establish peace on a solid basis, to restore economic confidence, rehabilitate Europe financially, and end the wars which were following the World

War. For the first time the two ex-enemies, Germany and Russia, were present. Absent was the United States, President Harding refusing, in March, to participate in an event at which Bolsheviki would have an equal voice. Thirty-three nations met at Genoa. Keynes saw them divided in two camps, the liberal or radical, for peace and freedom of trade, *versus* the old world of militarism or diplomacy, which wanted power, prestige and national glory.

There were four hundred and sixty journalists present, many more than diplomats, and all but three or four poured out the daily news of peace on earth, good will to men. The three or four cynics gathered in a little trattoria around a two-gallon flask of Chianti to listen to Lincoln Steffens' history of ostracism which comes to a man who exposes corruption and to Ernest Hemingway singing the prohibited song of the Italian Army:

> The General Cadorna
> Wrote a letter to the Queen:
> If you ever want to see Trieste,
> Buy yourself a picture postcard.

The town had been cleaned up and all the Fascisti told to stop beating up people; all the street women were driven out, the soldiers put in new uniforms and good shoes, the railroad station was draped with flags and spread with a great red carpet, and amidst festivity, Premier Facta of Italy on April tenth read the King's welcome. Mr. Lloyd George replied with an optimistic speech. M. Barthou, the French Minister of Justice, spoke for Poincaré, if not for France; the Germans caused a thrill by their appearance, and then Georges Chicherin arose and simply declared that Washington was fine for naval disarmament, and now the time had come to disarm on land. Europe should disarm, he said.

If he had thrown a Bolshevik bomb into the hall there could hardly have been a greater scandal. What? Disarmament? M. Barthou shouted, "Disarmament is not on the agenda." Mr.

Lloyd George took charge of the confusion and from then on ruled the conference. Disarmament was not on the agenda — it must not be mentioned again.

Sunday the sixteenth, however, the Russians threw a bomb again. They met the Germans at Santa Margherita near Rapallo (the Italian Government, Chicherin had said, has arranged for us to live not in Genoa but in Rapallo, thirty miles away, with the only communication a long road especially convenient for assassination) and signed a peace treaty, providing for recognition, cancellation of all debts, and trade arrangements.

Mr. Lloyd George thought this was disloyal. M. Barthou rushed to the telegraph office asking M. Poincaré what to do with this disaster. The French howled there were secret military clauses, a union between Germany and Russia to crush France — all of which was of course untrue. The treaty was the only definite peacemaking effort of the whole conference — and it just about ruined the conference.

What was left of it Sam Spewack, an American reporter, crushed in his own long-fingered hand. He cabled to America that the British had got an oil monopoly in Russia; that the Shell group, dominated by London, had beaten the American Standard Oil in the race for the greatest prize Moscow had; that the British Government and its oil syndicate had formed a partnership to beat the United States; that the contract ran for five years, with an option of similar renewal — and that oil was the secret beneath the critical days in world diplomacy.

Mr. Spewack's private bomb exploded just as the Allies had completed an ultimatum to Russia which would have wrecked the conference willy-nilly. Russia was about to be told to recognize private property, the war debts, renounce Germany, and all that. Every one turned now to oil. Every one denied everything. Mr. Lloyd George performed all sorts of prestidigitation, rope-walking, somersaulting and parlor magic in the great diplomatic circus, keeping all three rings going. In one, France, helped by Poland and the Little Entente, played their parts.

M. Barthou had received orders from Poincaré to smash things up and come home. Mr. Lloyd George snapped his whip and told him "what a fool he'd be" to follow such instructions. The Russians played in their ring, with oil as the main attraction, and the press had a ring of its own. The newspaper circus at times rose to six hundred performers.

The oil situation cleared when the principals admitted only *initialing*, not *signing*, the treaty.

May 11, the Russians replied to Barthou, asking for a loan, a commission of experts to study the question of confiscated private property; they promised to discontinue Bolshevik propaganda in countries where it conflicts with the law but to maintain it internally. The French said this was altogether "insolent." They had prepared that reply to whatever statement came out of Russia. Poincaré had demanded complete surrender. A French newspaper printed a forged military convention between Germany and Russia dated April 3. Every one knew the conference was a fiasco.

But Mr. Lloyd George said he ought to have something in his hands to take home, so he insisted on keeping the conference open until he got every one to agree on a six months' (instead of a ten-year) non-aggression pact and a committee of experts "to study problems." The big result of Genoa was a bad temper for all nations.

In London, in August, a conference on German reparations, the thirteenth meeting to discuss it, ended in failure.

In November, France decided to occupy the Ruhr if Germany defaulted on the coming January 15. At this time Clemenceau was in America, saying France was not militaristic and Germany was arming; and at this time Mussolini was establishing himself in Rome. Christmas, 1922, France got Belgium and Mussolini to vote that Germany was in illegal default. Britain refused. Poincaré, however, prepared to carry the old war into new German territory.

January 1, 1923, the French obtained Britain's neutrality. In

London it was denied this was an exchange for French support to British claims for Mosul oil. The Senate voted to withdraw the American Army of Occupation and American disapproval of the new war was transmitted to France by Ambassador Herrick, "who made it clear the American Government considered the invasion a grave blunder." France denied this. She had determined to put Germans to work in the mines and factories to earn money for France under French bayonets. On the tenth, as the American troops were ordered home, the French advanced, "occupying Essen and other Ruhr towns peacefully, the Moroccan troops, not Negroes, leading, and Mussolini sending engineers."

Taking a thought from Gandhi, Premier Cuno of Germany ordered passive resistance but no sabotage. The French seized the Reichsbank and arrested German officials. German engineers walked out of the mines as French and Italians walked in. British labor, in eight hundred meetings, protested Poincaré's actions. German labor tried a general strike and Doctor Dorten began plotting a Rhineland republic. The mark went down. The franc went down. The French accused Britain and America of selling money short. German telephone and railroad men went on strike, tying up the French movements. The last American troops left the Rhineland and women wept.

The conference meeting in Lausanne decided to drive a million persons in and out of Asia Minor, an expulsion equaled only by that of the Huguenots from France and the Moors and Jews from Spain. An exchange of populations was arranged, six hundred thousand Greeks to leave Asia Minor, four hundred and fifty thousand Turks to come there from Macedonia.

The Belgian Labor Party issued a manifesto against France. In British political and financial circles, as well as in labor and liberal organizations, Poincaré's invasion was considered wanton wreckage of government and materials, mad and unjustified. In France a few liberal voices were heard. Said General Sarrail, "The present policy of the French Government in the Ruhr will destroy forever that reputation for justice and fairness we held among nations."

The French Government granted a loan of four hundred million francs for the Polish army. American Senators said it meant war and asked why France had not used that sum to pay her debts. The Allied Council of Ambassadors awarded Vilna, ancient Lithuanian capital, to Poland.

In June, Germany offered to pay one billion, two hundred million marks yearly and to mortgage the nation. In July, the Lausanne treaty of peace with Turkey was signed. In August, Stresemann tried to form a cabinet to save the nation Cuno had wrecked. He slated Rudolf Hilferding for finance minister and planned wages and taxes on a gold basis, thus destroying the game by which Stinnes was filching millions. Stresemann faced the Reichstag on August 14, while Messrs. Stinnes, Thyssen, Haniel and Stumm dealt with Loucheur and his *Comité des Forges* — the German and French coal and iron kings were running both nations in those days. The highest British legal authorities advised the government the Ruhr occupation was an illegal action, an act of war, which was communicated to the French Government without effect.

August 29, the German Government abandoned passive resistance and sued for peace.

October 25, when the destruction of Germany seemed imminent, Secretary Hughes proposed an economic conference in which the United States would participate, which would determine what Germany could pay. The French, who had also been suffering an economic debacle through the Occupation, agreed, providing the total of one hundred and thirty-two billion gold marks due was not changed. On December 15, the Reparations Commission announced it would invite General Dawes and Owen D. Young to be unofficial representatives of the United States to the experts' committee which would investigate Germany's financial position.

The State Department approved the appointment of Messrs.

Dawes, Young and Henry M. Robinson, and the committees met in Paris, January 14, 1924, to find practical means "not imposition of penalties" and proposed guarantees which "are economic and not political." The Dawes plan provided for a unified stable currency, a new bank of issue, payments from budget, railway bonds and transport tax, industrial debentures, and recommended taxation at least equal to that in the Allied nations. A first mortgage bond for eleven billion gold marks on railroads and another for five billions on industries were also proposed and a two-year budget moratorium, a two-year transition period, payments becoming standard the fifth year. Payments contemplated ranged from one billion gold marks the first year to two and a half billions the fifth. The economic experts were certain Germany could pay. The committee reported:

"The task would be hopeless if the present situation of Germany accurately reflected her potential capacity; the proceeds from Germany's national production could not in that case enable her both to meet the national needs and to ensure the payment of her foreign debts.

"But Germany's growing and industrious population, her great technical skill, the wealth of her material resources, the development of her agriculture on progressive lines, her eminence in industrial science, all these factors enable us to be hopeful with regard to her future production."

Said General Dawes: "The plan if accepted will lead to an ultimate and lasting peace."

The Allied premiers called a conference in London. Chancellor Marx arrived August 5, asking the Ruhr evacuation in six months instead of two years. A compromise of one year was accepted. Agreement was signed the sixteenth. The Reichstag accepted the twenty-ninth. The Dawes plan was declared in operation the first of September. Mr. Young was made agent general for reparations and Parker Gilbert appointed to succeed him October 31. He was called the dictator of Germany.

In September, 1924, the League of Nations drew up the Geneva Protocol, hailed as "the Magna Carta of national security", "the first practical move for disarmament" and "civilization's boldest advance against barbarism." It was soon forgotten.

At the same time the Spaniards were completely defeated in Morocco and the Riffians came to the gates of Tangiers. Primo de Rivera turned desperately to French aid and Islam called for a holy war to free two continents from Christian domination. The events were generally overlooked in America, due to the excitement caused by the Loeb-Leopold case in Chicago.

Britain and Colonel Lawrence had made the promise "Arabia for the Arabians", but failed to keep it. India was in a revolutionary state. Kemal was victorious. Now Abd-el-Krim had won over Spain and in Syria the natives were fighting the French, who were forgetting that mandated citizens are not exploitable colonial subjects. The British policy in Arab lands, as explained by Colonel Lawrence, had been to fill a derby hat with gold pieces and let small patriot leaders grab a handful, big patriot emirs a double handful, but the Spanish and the economic French thought it cheaper to use the army and navy. The French joined the Spaniards in the Riff, continuing the war through 1925. In May of that year the Quai d'Orsay loosed its propaganda: Abd-el-Krim had attacked the French without warning or reason; the war (as usual) was defensive; soviet money was supporting the Moroccans. And America believed all this claptrap. At least, until Larry Rue and Vincent Sheean, two non-gullible war correspondents, penetrated the Riffian lines and told quite another story.

In the sixth post-armistice rebellion in Syria, August 7, 1925, the French suffered eight hundred casualties at Suwayda, capital of a pagan tribe known as Druses, one of whose emirs, found guilty of robbing his subjects, was put to work by General

Sarrail on the public road where every one could see his downfall. The helots of course followed their masters into war.

In October, the civilized world was shocked by the news of the bombardment of Damascus. The Associated Press reported (from Haifa) there were five thousand casualties; the Arab Executive (in Jerusalem) announced twenty-five thousand dead and dying in the destruction of the oldest inhabited city in the world. Later the Associated Press and other agencies cabled (from Cairo) that "a traveler . . . describes days and nights of 'unforgettable horror' . . . hundreds lying in the streets, two thousand buried in the débris."

Against these fantastic reports disseminated everywhere the facts recorded by the one journalist eyewitness in one Chicago newspaper made no impression. They are quite simple. Druses and Syrian nationalists (who may have had just cause) broke through the gates at night and fighting began. Some fifty Armenians, French mercenaries, were killed at once. When the successful revolutionaries began marching against the Christian-European section, General Sarrail, fearing massacre and having insufficient troops, ordered Fort Gouraud on the brown bare hills behind the city to fire eight shots on October 10. This warning gave the Mohammedan slum population time to evacuate. The next day one hundred and twenty shells were fired into the swarming bazaars around the Street Called Straight and the uprising ended. In his official report, Sarrail says one hundred and thirty-five persons were killed and two hundred and fifty houses destroyed, and Damascus saved from murder and looting. A similar statement was made to the League of Nations. Sarrail was recalled. But the myth of barbaric massacre remains.

The year 1924 found 24,018,328 men under arms, 18,000,000 of whom were in Europe and 752,000 in the French army. Wars were still being waged and peace conferences still being held every six months or every year. Little had been done to right the wrongs of Versailles. The world was not disarming nor was peace secure. The most important achievement was the Dawes Plan. But, although it was hardly realized by any person or any nation, much ground had been sown for the fruitful results which made 1925 the great year in world progress towards a peace of good will and international coöperation.

## Interlude 1925

Stock Market sales biggest in nine years; United States Steel soars; Sir Robert Horne says "Real prosperity"; Ford says "Century of prosperity"; Gary says, "We are on the verge of a great era of prosperity." America drunk with prosperity. Report of Herbert Hoover: "The standard of living in the United States is the highest in the country's history and therefore in all history." Imports and exports between four and five billion dollars, exports exceeding by seven hundred million, all quantity records broken. No other nation has regained pre-war trade, Hoover shows. "Gentlemen Prefer Blondes." Red Grange, wonder man of the West, conquers the East.

John D. Rockefeller wrote poetry on his eighty-sixth birthday:

> I was early taught to work as well as play.
> My life has been one long, happy holiday;
> Full of work and full of play —
> I dropped the worry on the way —
> And God was good to me every day.

The Prince of Wales also wrote poetry declining the daughter offered by Neptune, when crossing the equator on H.M.S. *Repulse.*

An American woman motor-boating in Lake Geneva lost a ring and said "Drain the lake; I'll pay for it."

Nacktkultur flourished in Germany.

Tut's coffin disclosed false whiskers but a solid gold crown.

"A Million Inhabitants by 1935!" Miami, Magic City, slogan. "This bubble will not burst."

To-day the United States is producing, reported the Washington *Post:*

55 per cent. of the world's iron ore
51 per cent. of the world's pig iron
66 per cent. of the world's steel
51 per cent. of the world's copper
62 per cent. of the world's petroleum
43 per cent. of the world's coal
55 per cent. of the world's cotton
95 per cent. of the world's automobiles

What is America like to a foreigner capable of describing? Listen then to Aldous Huxley, visiting Los Angeles:

Jazz it up, jazz it up. Keep moving. Step on the gas. Say it with dancing. The Charleston, the Baptists. Radios and Revivals. Uplift and Gilda Grey. The pipe organ, the nigger with the saxophone, the Giant Marimbaphone. Hymns and the movies and Irving Berlin. Petting Parties and the First Free United Episcopal Methodist Church. Jazz it up! . . . The celebrated Farmyard imitations. 10 — Evangelists — 10. The finest troupe of Serio-Comic Cyclists ever. Onward Christian Soldiers. Abide with me. I'm gonna bring a watermelon to my girl to-night. . . .

. . . The Charleston, the fox trot. "There is only one first-class civilization in the world to-day. It is right here, in the United States and the Dominion of Canada." Monkeyville, Bryan, the Ku-Klux Klan. "Europe is hardly second-class, and Asia's is fourth to sixth class." (Jazz it up; jazz it up!)

. . . The national motto should fit the national facts. What I would write under America's flapping eagle would be: Vitality, Prosperity, Modernity.

The day Mr. Bryan died, London barred "Desire Under the Elms", Mussolini banished the representative of the Chicago *Tribune,* Poland expelled twenty thousand Germans from German territory under Polish rule.

"A dollar down" idea engulfs America.

"Freak art has passed: there are almost no nudes in the Chicago show."

A Harvard Heretic published the Harvard Credo:

That T. R. is the greatest Harvard graduate,
That all Gordon Gin is false,
That Calvin Coolidge saved Boston,
That free speech, love, and verse, are just about the same.

# PART THREE: THE AGE OF REASON

# CHAPTER ELEVEN

## The Locarno Era

Somewhere in the Decade of the Twenties many tides turned. The greatest failure in the history of the world, Versailles, was partly retrieved by the Locarno Conference; the Ku-Klux Klan waned; the League of Nations won its first great victory in stopping the Greco-Bulgarian war; the world began to disarm itself mentally; Hindenburg saved the republic in Germany. Surrealism replaced Dada among the advanced thinkers; "It" became the synonym of sex appeal, and Sex moved out of the Pullman smokers; Freud became a parlor sport and the stock market had the greatest boom in history; the French evacuated the Ruhr; one-piece bathing suits were no longer arrested; Fundamentalism reached its Barnum and Bailey apogee in Dayton . . . a thousand climaxes and a few anti-climaxes were recorded.

By a coincidence, almost every one of these important events dividing the decade happened in its middle year, 1925, which we will now consider.

What had happened to the world between the Armistice and the end of 1924? Nothing tells the truer inner story better than the secret memorandum drafted by the British Foreign Office for the Prime Minister and the members of his Cabinet, a document of historic importance which in some mysterious way Mr. John L. Balderston, now better known as the author of "Berkeley Square", obtained in May, 1925.

Following are some of the most significant statements in the document:

Europe to-day is divided into three main elements, namely, the victors, the vanquished, and Russia. The feeling of uncertainty which is sapping the health of Western Europe is caused to no small extent by the disappearance of Russia as a power accountable in the European concert. The most menacing of our uncertainties.

All our late enemies continue full of resentment at what they have lost; all our late Allies are fearful of losing what they have won. One half of Europe is dangerously angry, the other half is dangerously afraid. Fear begets provocation, armaments, secret alliances, ill-treatment of minorities. These in turn beget a greater hatred, and stimulate a desire for revenge, whereby fear is intensified and its consequences are enhanced. The vicious circle is thus established.

Although Germany is at present quite incapable of undertaking aggressive action, it is certain that with great military chemical potentialities she will sooner or later again become a powerful military factor. There are but few Germans who seriously hope to exert this strength, when reacquired, against the British Empire. It may be doubted if the majority of Germans to-day desire a war of revenge against France; but it may be confidently asserted that as soon as Germany recovers, there will be a steady movement towards the righting of what are for a German the two most objectionable provisions of the peace settlement, namely the Polish Corridor and the partition of Silesia.

France is afraid of Germany because:

1. She is Germany's neighbor.
2. She has within living memory been twice invaded by Germany.
3. The birth rate in France is declining.
4. The birth rate in Germany is increasing.

These circumstances have inevitably and justifiably led France to place her security above all other considerations.

Marshal Foch, having defeated Germany, insisted that if there was to be any security for France or peace for Europe, the German frontier must cease at the Rhine. That, he stated, was the only effective guarantee of French security.

What then are the essential conditions of the security of the British Empire?

The policy known as isolation is not to-day a practical policy.

*Underwood and Underwood*

THE SIGNING OF THE LOCARNO TREATY, 1925

At the far end of the table on the left may be seen Stanley Baldwin, Britain's Premier, and to his immediate right is Sir Austen Chamberlain, Foreign Minister of Britain. At the right side of the table, second from the rear (with mustache and hunched shoulders) is Aristide Briand, of France. On the left side of the table, second from the front, is Dr. Stresemann, and next him (third) Dr. Luther, both of Germany.

For America, powerful and aloof, such a course is still perhaps a possibility. For the British Empire no such escape is feasible. History and economics show that isolation in present conditions spells danger, vulnerability and impotence. Geography and aëronautics show that isolation is not in our case a scientific fact.

The defense of Great Britain necessitates:

1. That no single power shall be in a position to occupy or to dominate all the Channel and North Sea ports.

2. That the hostility of France, Belgium, and, more incidentally, the Netherlands, Germany and Denmark, who now possess these ports, or of any combination of them, is to be avoided.

3. That no third power at war with France or Belgium should be allowed to invade those countries so as to threaten the *status quo* of the Channel ports or of such French or Belgian territory as would expose Great Britain to aërial invasion.

4. That it is consequently a necessity of British and, therefore, of imperial defense, to reach some understanding with France and Belgium which may entail a guarantee on our part that these territories shall not fall into other hands.

Although in the present mood of Europe it would be useless even to mention the revision of the peace treaty, yet, if the concert of Europe can thus gradually be created, saner counsels may prevail. It is conceivable, especially if Germany with French good will becomes a member of the League of Nations and obtains a permanent seat on the Council, that it may become possible eventually to revise by European agreement the dangerous conditions involved in the Silesian settlement and the Polish Corridor.

## THE LOCARNO ERA

Dismal as the British Foreign Office memorandum is, the situation was still more fearful, as could be admitted only after the conference at Locarno, when the greatest result in peacemaking was achieved. In fact, the Locarno era was not, as had been hoped, the final episode of the Versailles Peace Conference: it was peace, but peace for just five years, or, another long armistice, to be broken with the death of its great co-author, Gustav Stresemann, the German chancellor.

The conference opened October 5; its purpose was to write security pacts for Germany and France, and also for other great and smaller powers. (Germany ratified November 27, and the treaties went into effect September, 1926. More important than the ratifications was the feeling of coöperation, almost friendship, which was noted between Briand and Stresemann, France and Germany, a spirit which led to greater progress for peace in Europe than any treaty, law, act or use of force since the first armistice.)

Almost unnoticed in America was the fact that the last French troops left the town of Ruhrort on Locarno day—the Ruhr was completely evacuated. France had made a noble gesture at last.

The world felt that the war was now over, peace had come, universal disarmament could begin, universal peace might follow. So Austen Chamberlain explained the results of the conference, inviting the press to meet with him in Paris. Speaking of the beginning of the year when he thought war imminent, and now, he said, "When I came to the Foreign Office, I was aghast at the nearness of this danger. National passions were seething over irritating problems. Suspicion, jealousy, hatred, unrest were everywhere. Nations talked war and it was evident beyond doubt that if the current were not checked the world would drift into another Armageddon even more catastrophic for the universe than the last conflagration."

When Mr. Chamberlain had finished, the astute among the journalists realized something perhaps more important than the Locarno pacts, the clue to the situation: Britain was back in her historic rôle of three centuries of keeping the peace in Europe, just as the memorandum had predicted.

On September 8, 1926, at Geneva, the chairman posed the question: Shall Germany be admitted to the League of Nations and given a seat on the Council, as an equal of the Great Powers?

The roll was called. France spoke first. Briand said "Yes." The other nations followed. The decision was unanimous.

One week later there was a lunch at Thoiry which lasted four hours. Then two middle-aged gentlemen stepped out from the Hotel Leger, feeling that more had been done to heal Franco-German wounds than anything since Versailles.

Messrs. Briand and Stresemann had succeeded in harmonizing opposing views — for the first time — between chicken and fruit. But the nationalists in France and their press shouted that Briand had gone too far; the nationalists in Germany accused Stresemann of being taken in by fine French words and subtle flattery, instead of action. The two statesmen said nothing. But the results were apparent for five years.

### THE ZEITGEIST HITS COOLIDGE

In 1925 one hundred and fifty thousand miners quit Pennsylvania anthracite fields, asking ten per cent. increase in wages, and President Coolidge, seeing no "national emergency", did not threaten to call out the army, as Harding had done.

In 1925 the President declared against loans to foreign nations for war purposes.

In 1925, addressing the national convention of the American Legion in Omaha, the President of the United States talked on the folly of hysterias and the perils of intolerance. If not the conductor of the symphony, he was at least in key with the new spirit of the times. He amazed the country.

The era of shuddering, of course, was not quite over, but when the real one hundred per cent. Americans like the President could publicly appeal for mental disarmament, the tide of hysteria had surely turned back. It was marked by the defeat of the Ku-Klux Klan in Detroit, where the election was really a national test, and it was followed soon after by a complete debacle which was aptly alliterated: "K.K.K. gets Kan in Kansas."

The War Department's "Spider Chart", although largely repudiated, was still being circulated. It linked the Women's Congregational Committee, the National Council for the

Prevention of War, as branches of Soviet publicity. The Girls' Friendly Society, the Needlework Guild of America (sic), the Woman's Christian Temperance Union, the Ladies of the Grand Army of the Republic and the Young Women's Christian Association are also "linked with Soviet Russia in a dastardly plot to undermine American institutions." What had all these patriotic and sewing societies in common? They were entirely composed of women, millions of them, and these women were opposed to future wars, therefore enemies of the War Department — apparently.

In 1925, Roger Baldwin, of the American Civil Liberties Union, got six months in jail for unlawful assembly; he had tried to read the Bill of Rights in public without a license. Young La Follette overwhelmed three conservative rivals in the Wisconsin election for nomination to the Senate. A great test of sentiment came in the appointment of Colonel Haskell by Governor Al Smith as major general commanding the New York National Guard.

Colonel Haskell, as Hoover's man, had saved ten million human beings in Russia from death by starvation, and incidentally the Soviet régime. He had expressed himself favorably about Lenin and had dared to report that the Bolshevik Government was not going to fall "in six months." When the appointment was announced, the great American Defense Society protested, "it has been alleged Colonel Haskell's sympathies are for Soviet Russia."

This time, instead of the usual hysteria in the press in favor of the American Defense Society, quite the opposite editorial reaction followed. The Defenders ran for cover, apologized, praised Haskell as a fine soldier and a fine man, also a good American.

Here is part of the record of this society:

In armistice time: campaign for American boycott of "goods made by bloodstained hands", to avoid "the risks of poisons and germs in German products."

1919: warned America in June of nation-wide revolution, the

opening of our jails, the seizure of the government by "an autocratic minority of anarchists."

Objected to the restoration of German opera.

Urged recognition of the terrorist Kolchak as the real Russian.

1923, in November, without consulting the Allies, the Society decided that the amount Germany could pay was just one hundred and thirty-three billion dollars.

From 1919 to 1925, the American Defense Society was listened to as the standard bearer of the better citizenship, the real one hundred per centers; but in the days of the successful functioning of the Dawes Plan, the Locarno pacts, and an American export trade with Europe of six hundred million dollars, the attack on Haskell was hailed as "foolish words from the American Dementia Society, which has the brains of an ostrich, the courage of a rabbit, and the manners of a polecat." Had times changed?

## ENGLAND IN 1925

James Ramsay MacDonald kissed the King's hand, January 22, 1924, and announced the first Labor Government in Great Britain. The Northcliffe press yelled "Socialist" and the laborites did not deny. The first action was the recognition of the Soviet Government. Reaction replied by forming the British Fascisti: Labor called the B.Fs. "bloody fools." A workingman named Jim Brown left a fifty dollar a year shanty to live in a castle. He was "King of Scotland" and had a real duke as Lord in Waiting. Philip Snowden recounts that "a real countess frantically asked me (she had been reading the *Morning Post*) if it was true that the first thing the Labor Government was going to do was to cut the throat of every aristocrat and steal all their property . . . the capitalist class is touching lower depths than even it has ever reached before in rousing hate and passion and class prejudice. It cares nothing for the interests of the country and would gladly see it ruined if it could destroy the Labor Party."

But in a few weeks two great changes came over England: the laborites who had talked as if they were communists, who had denounced "capitalism" and accepted the present world as a war between capital and labor, were not only kissing the King's hand but his shoe also. They were completely tamed. Facing the army and navy budget, revolt in India, the Singapore naval base problem, threats of the unions to strike, they acted just as any other political party would. The other side of the picture was the ruling class. It changed too. The scared ones were laughing at their fright. They were dining with laborites and no longer calling the movement "Glasgow sansculottism." They had dumped their British bonds on the market in alarm and were now buying them back.

In the summer, Premiers MacDonald and Herriot met to restore peace in Europe. For the first time in five years there was optimism.

In October, the Labor Government decided to defend the editor of the supplement of the *Workers' Weekly,* called *The Forces,* which appealed to "Soldiers, Sailors, Airmen. . . . Don't Shoot Strikers." The charge was treason. Parliament voted "no confidence" and the first labor experiment was at an end.

When election day came, the Tories tricked Britain the last minute by publishing a forged Zinovieff letter with the usual Third Internationale plotting against the home government, India, etc. (The Berlin trial which revealed the forgers has already been mentioned.) Austen Chamberlain insisted the Zinovieff letter was genuine and one of many incriminating documents. The British Trades Union Congress cabled from Moscow the letter was a forgery. It was too late. Labor was defeated. The vote was:

| | | |
|---|---|---|
| Conservatives | 7,300,000 | (1923) 4,700,000 |
| Liberals | 2,800,000 | 3,500,000 |
| Labor | 5,500,000 | 3,800,000 |

But although labor was defeated, liberalism was crushed. Labor in 1925 began to organize for its second attempt. It was no longer an unimportant movement. It was the second great party, the Opposition. In that remained its victory.

### HINDENBURG TURNS THE TABLES

For years the French jingoists had been singing the litany, Germany is arming, Germany is preparing for war, Germany has secret armies, Hitlerites and Steel Helmets, Germany has new gas inventions, Germany is plotting revenge; but Britain and America would not listen. Now, when Ebert died in February, and Old Hindenburg, "acting on the Kaiser's advice", proclaimed himself presidential candidate and finally was elected, the jingoists seemed justified.

German militarism rejoiced. There was jubilation in Doorn. Militarists, jingoists, war munitions makers, bankers in conservative France, prepared to meet the menace. It was noted that in Hindenburg's six-mile ride through Berlin among the cheering crowds there were thousands of monarchist banners, only one republican. That banner was on Hindenburg's car.

But it proved most significant. The week he took office, all the Ludendorff crowd, all the Junkers and the Kaiser lovers came to see him and participate in the government — they talked to him as the place-holder for the Hohenzollerns. Old Hindenburg kicked them downstairs. He not only took the oath of allegiance to the republic, but he fulfilled it sincerely. In fact, it is now evident that the acceptance by Hindenburg of the Presidency was the profoundest blow the German monarchists had suffered. Hindenburg became the republican keystone and milestone. 1925, the first year of the Dawes Plan, found Germany on the upgrade, paying in full, back at work, and apparently settled as a republic.

### STALIN CONQUERS TROTSKY

Russia, having been left solitary by the Allies, turned to inner dissension. Late in 1924, Kamineff, Trotsky's brother-in-law, and Joseph Stalin, the Georgian who held no official position in the ruling circle, issued a forty-column report, branding Trotsky, as a Red heretic, always acting, the Menshevik, which was in Bolshevik eyes treason. Stalin accused Trotsky of attempting to clothe himself in Lenin's mantle — the fact Lenin had willed it to him being suppressed. Stalin urged the Communist Party to wage relentless war on the military chief, "otherwise Trotsky's ideas may become the concentration point for all non-proletarian elements who strive to disintegrate the proletarian dictatorship." In December, Moscow announced Trotsky was seriously ill and really needed a warmer climate. It denied this meant exile. (The Pope in a Christmas allocution said he believed it his duty "to exhort all, especially men in power who love peace, the sanctity of the family, and human dignity, to make every effort to fight the grave dangers and certain injuries coming from Socialism and Communism.")

In 1925, the British Trades Union mission published its report on Russia: agriculture is recovering slowly; immorality among children is being checked; the opposition press has been destroyed and censorship is absolute; birth control, even by operation, is permitted; religious marriage has no civil validity; worship of the memory of Lenin has become a cult; the arts are extremely rugged and aim at violent, almost grotesque, expression; musicians have turned to decadent forms of syncopated noise known as American jazz; there is strong propaganda against religion in general; clergymen who conspire against the government are treated as ordinary political offenders; communism is taught in the public schools, also state capitalism.

Trotsky was tried for treason (Trotskyism) and dismissed as chairman of the Revolutionary War Council.

Max Eastman rose to Trotsky's defense, publishing Lenin's deathbed declarations favoring the war chief as his successor; Stalin, by control of the censorship, published only his own views, namely, that Trotsky was a danger because he was "thirsty for power", a Red Bonaparte. Trotsky, in order to live

# THE FORCES

*(Special Service Supplement to the Workers' Weekly)*

Vol. I. No. 1. FRIDAY, AUGUST 1, 1924

## SOLDIERS, SAILORS, AIRMEN!

### Will You Kill Your Mates?

## REMEMBER—YOU ARE WORKERS!

### The Bosses are Your Enemies.

**DON'T SHOOT STRIKERS!** They are workers like you. They are fighting for a decent living for themselves and their women and kids. If the profiteering capitalists, through their agents—your officers—tell you to murder British workers—**DON'T SHOOT.**

### THEY ARE GETTING READY

### NEXT WAR ANY TIME NOW

Preparing for war? Yes, of course, they are! It is profitable.

Winston Churchill, introducing the Army Estimates for 1920-21, said:—

Submarines, then? No scrapping of "unfair murder-weapons" here.

Only about fourteen months ago H.M. Submarine X.1 was launched at Southampton. Its

### WE APPEAL TO YOU

"Join the Army and see the world." Or join the Navy to escape unemployment. Or join the Air Force and get through your apprenticeship without starving. These are the promises and compulsion used to recruit soldiers, sailors, and airmen.

They should have said: "Join the Army and see what war is like."

The next war is being prepared, and it is you that the bosses rely on to fight it for them. They will keep clear

### FORM YOUR OWN COMMITTEES

Your fellow workers have their Trade Unions, Trade Councils, and Workshop Committees.

Are you allowed to form committees?

Yes. Sailors in the Navy, you have Welfare Committees. What can they do?

BRITAIN'S FIRST LABOR GOVERNMENT COLLAPSED ON ACCOUNT OF ITS DEFENSE OF THIS PUBLICATION

The editor had been accused of treason. Macdonald fell October 8, 1924 — after nine months in office. Labor was defeated October 29, in a general election

in Moscow, was forced to repudiate Eastman's book "Since Lenin Died."

The annual Red world scare consisted of such items as "Chinese uprisings attributed to Russian Communists in Pekin embassy"; "Red spies betray French troops in the Riff"; "Soviet agitators fomenting rebellion in Afghanistan." Bishop Cannon returned from Russia with the strange news that religion still flourished, despite Bolshevik edicts and "without any sign of espionage, interference, or fear." He actually saw Roman Catholic priests alive, walking in the street, and he spoke openly to a Methodist in Moscow. The fear that Britain had gone Red was dispelled when the Labor Party voted nine to one, refusing to permit communists to affiliate.

A great moral reform was heralded from Moscow. To prevent legally recognized polygamous marriages, or illegal wives and illegitimate children, Comrade Krylenko authorized a complete change in the marriage laws. Clara Zetkin, German communist delegate, offered this criticism: "The famous theory that in society based on communism it is just as simple to satisfy one's wish for love as it is to get a drink of water is well known. Well, to this 'drink of water' theory we owe the fact our younger generation has gone mad. This theory has ruined a good many youth. Let us be spared such 'Marxism'." Trotsky added, "The destructive period in family life is still far from ended. The process of disintegration goes on at full speed. . . . In all such cases mothers and children are the victims." Everybody agreed tragedy and trouble came from the drink-of-water theory. Laws were passed.

## THE FUNDAMENTALIST CRISIS IN AMERICA

On May 25, 1925, the following indictment was issued:

That John Thomas Scopes, heretofore on the 24th day of April, 1925, did unlawfully and willfully teach in the public schools of Rhea County, Tenn., which said public schools are supported in part and in whole by the public school funds of the State, certain theory and theories that deny the story of the Divine creation of man as taught in the Bible, and did teach instead thereof that man has descended from a lower order of animals, he, the said John Thomas Scopes, being at the time and prior thereto a teacher in the public schools of Rhea County, Tenn., aforesaid, against the peace and dignity of the State.

Mr. William Jennings Bryan had been making silver-tongued orations to sell Miami lots. Florida was booming. A New Empire — a Taxless Paradise. Bryan indignantly denied he had made a million dollars — it was only half a million. Suddenly the years of bickering over Fundamentalism and Science came to a climax and conclusion in Monkeyville in 1925, and Bryan was there "to make the world safe for Genesis." Not since the Salem witches had there been such religious hysteria. Opposing Bryan were the volunteer lawyers, Clarence Darrow, Dudley Field Malone and Arthur Garfield Hays. Bryan made the best epigram of all, however. "I am not so much interested in the age of rocks as in the Rock of Ages."

The jury brought in a verdict of guilty and the judge fined Scopes one hundred dollars. (A year later the State Supreme Court reversed the decision on the technical ground that the court instead of the jury had fixed the fine.)

In the excitement a few world affairs were overlooked.

The war in the Riff, the French defeats by Abd-el-Krim, and the Franco-Spanish alliance to fight in Morocco to a finish got a little publicity through the organization of volunteer American aviators.

The civil war in China was noticed because four Americans in a launch flying the American flag were fired on at Canton.

Fascist violence was headlined through Mussolini's apology to Ambassador Fletcher, June 11, for attack on Consul Gowen, May 24. The American press smuggled the story from London.

Mexican seizure of landed estates and division among peasants caused great concern in Washington because American property was involved and Secretary Kellogg issued a warning to President

Calles to curb the Reds, otherwise the United States would rescind its recognition.

Bolshevism's progress caused a lot of eye-lifting when the Harrimans of New York signed a manganese contract in Moscow.

On July 26, Bryan died in his sleep after too big a meal. He had come to Dayton saying, "They can't make a monkey out of me." But "they", the world in fact, did make a monkey out of the whole affair. A sense of humor triumphed. Silly legislatures continued to pass anti-evolution laws but no one ever paid any attention to them. The same gales of laughter which had torn the nightgowns from the Ku-Klux Klan were sweeping over the censors and the snoopers and the prohibition enforcers and the witch-burners and the instigators of Red fear. It was a time of recovery of sanity.

A year later a traveler reported the town of Dayton was dead; a sow and her litter were wandering aimlessly about the streets, the crops had been bad and heaven had sent a drought. There were bankruptcies and the factions in town still hated each other. Fanaticism remained. They united in hating the North for having poked so much fun at them.

### MORALS AND MANNERS

From 1917 to 1919 there were police raids and denunciations of birth-control meetings, books were confiscated, women were put in jail, some went on hunger strike. In 1921 there were lawsuits growing out of the New York police use of violence at the Town Hall. But in 1925 the National Birth Control Conference was held in Hotel McAlpin, delegates, doctors, psychologists, college presidents, Protestant preachers and editors participating. The police were absent. Colonel Theodore Roosevelt, Jr., speaking in memory of his father, called the birth controllers "hog selfish and bad citizens."

Atheism was reported disappearing from the college campus.

"It" or the Clara Bow brand of Sex Appeal was universal.

After the war the word "sex" itself could not be used in the best bourgeois society; now it was not only permissible, but it could be stated without blushing that there were two sexes, male and female. Moreover, the new sex freedom was already being cheapened by the confession magazines and the tabloid press.

The second Freudian Tide swept America. The first, dated 1912, was highbrow and Greenwich Villagy and Liberal Club, and included Floyd Dell, Max Eastman, Susan Glaspell, George Cram Cook and that crowd. The second wave embraced even Moody, Texas, and Oskaloosa and the Bronx with its Œdipus complex, its sublimations, its dreams and its unfulfilled desires.

Cardinal Du Bois, Archbishop of Paris, showed the liberal trend when he declared, "Virtue in women never depended on the length of her hair; after all, a fashion is the most popular form of art, and God is the friend of true artists." In London, Epstein's "Rima", memorial to W. H. Hudson, was attacked as "bestial and misshapen, ugly and inhuman"; but Cambridge, the university of Darwin and Newton, saved its good name when a court ruled that Trinity College could not dismiss the noted scientist J. B. S. Haldane because he had been corespondent in a divorce action. The Paris gigolos felt the spirit of the times and organized a union banning "robbers and gold-diggers and blackmailers whose chief prey are elderly American women seeking thrills." Among the organizers were waiters with clean shirts and Russian princes without.

In 1925 the ultimate in bathing suits had been reached. (No one could then dream of the Antibes idea of a two-piece suit, the brassieres and the pants, with nothing between). Shoes and stockings were discarded and the American beauty posed in a one-piece garment "with a wisp of a skirt on it."

Thus 1925 comes to a distinct end with a promise of more tolerant times. The one great international event next to Locarno was of course the League of Nation's triumph in preventing the war between Greece and Bulgaria, but as there was no war there is little to write about. One important matter, however, has intentionally been left out of this review: Fascism. Here we had in 1922 a movement marching to bring Liberty to the people, as its springtime song announced. It was meant to rival the communist system in Russia and the individualist-capitalist system of the United States; it too was supposed to be a program and a philosophy, and it too meant to grow international. The materialistic success and the complete moral-philosophic failure of Fascism is the subject therefore of a later chapter.

## Interlude 1926

When Debs died he was called, of all things, "distinctly American", the frontier or colonial type, alas, now vanishing. It was said he never understood communism or cold dialectical Marxism. He was the pure Yankee nonconformist of Washington and Franklin's time, like his own hero, John Brown.

Vanishing America (Omaha *World-Herald*): The forest primeval. The old oaken bucket. The little red schoolhouse. A gentleman, a scholar and a judge of whisky. The one-horse shay. Women's crowning glory. A large cold bottle and a small hot bird. The village smithy. Milady's petticoat. The Blue and the Gray.

The "Vitaphone" or talking picture; Mr. Nathan said let them keep it up and the theaters, not the movies, would be crowded.

Full-page advertisement by united churches of Kansas City:

FLAMING YOUTH! GET THIS NEW THRILL!
BE A SPORT AND GIVE CHRIST A CHANCE.
GET THE REAL THRILL.

"I had to lie, bribe and drink to put over prohibition in America," confessed Pussyfoot Johnson in headlines. Norway — 523,423 to 415,637 — went wet. Norway had permitted, under its dry law, light wines and beer and everything up to fourteen per cent. Drunkenness increased. Bootlegging. Rum-running. Norway's Volsteadism was changed to twenty-one per cent. Bootlegging in whisky, cognac, gin, aqua vita continued, drunkenness continued, and then came the referendum.

Maharajah Sir Chundra Shum Shere Jung bought fifty-two

thousand slaves in Nepal and set them free; twenty-three thousand were liberated voluntarily; thus ended slavery in an independent Indian State at a cost of one million, four hundred thousand dollars amidst mutterings of revolution.

Contract bridge thrills sweeping auction bridge into discard.

Professors Miethe and Stammreich obtained gold by bombarding mercury surfaces with electrons in an extremely high vacuum; there was fear Germany would fool the world by an overabundance of gold, but the process was too costly.

The Illinois commander in chief of the American Legion accused "this person, Jane Addams" of working to abolish all military training and of turning Hull House into a hotbed of Bolshevism. John Burns called Jane Addams "America's only saint."

Bernard Shaw got the Nobel peace prize. He said, "We have a genuine dread of the intellect in any form, and a conviction that art, though highly enjoyable clandestinely, is essentially immoral."

July 26, Shaw's Birthday.

Al Capone nabbed as killer in Cicero; America's rôle in world affairs transformed from savior to scapegoat; Mexico mobilizes troops to close Catholic churches; Mrs. Hall, widow of pastor, held for murder; France will tax aliens; Zinovieff ousted from Politburo.

Sinclair Lewis refused the Pulitzer prize; he disliked it because Pulitzer made it for a book "best presenting the wholesome atmosphere of American life and the highest standard of manners and manhood." Lewis denied his books represented anything of the kind. To write books for the Pulitzer prize, writers would be compelled to become "safe, polite, obedient and sterile." The committee had chosen "Arrowsmith", having passed on and up "Main Street" and "Babbitt" previously. Theodore Dreiser struck gold in "An American Tragedy."

August: France makes rapid recovery; Pig Woman testifies; General Motors reaches $213; Gertrude Ederle swims English

Channel, first woman, time record; Queen Marie will visit America this winter; Moscow denies (seventh time) Stalin assassinated.

The birth of a daughter to the Duchess of York considered as providing an heir to the British Throne, as Prince of Wales is never expected to marry.

Valentino funeral. Hysteria. Morbid crowds. Pola Negri shed tears for the movies. Magnificent Paris gowns. Aimee Semple McPherson disappeared. Ederle returned to New York. More hysteria.

Prince Windischgrätz, on trial for forging millions of French francs, pleads patriotism; defense says some day Hungary will erect monuments to him; his family motto, "Mankind begins with Barons." Verdict: four years in jail.

The eight-year struggle in Morocco ended. The French, who had occupied the Ouergha Valley, the Riff granary, without pretext, won but did not rejoice. They paid Abd-el-Krim with a palace and money, somewhere else.

The French captured Suwayda, capital of the Druses. Bennett Doty, or "Gilbert Clare" of the Foreign Legion, deserted and thus brought the war in Syria to the American breakfast table.

The Floranada Club in Florida went bankrupt for eight million dollars. An omen.

With inconceivable splendor, Mr. A. was crowned Rajah of Jammu and Kashmir, and even the donkeys in the procession wore emerald trappings.

With the general strike over, the British coal miners continued for another six months, with their slogan:

Not a penny off the pay,
Not a minute on the day.

Rayon turns trees into silk stockings.

September 21. Hurricane takes toll of four hundred dead, five thousand injured, in Florida.

September 23: In a huge downpour, one hundred and thirty thousand see Gene Tunney knock the crown off Dempsey.

December 3: Mrs. Hall acquitted.

Doctor Raymond Pearl, biologist, Johns Hopkins, proves by scientific investigation that man who takes liquor in moderation lives longer than total abstainer.

Year closes with 1,738 deaths from poisoned liquor in eleven cities; 724 in New York.

## CHAPTER TWELVE

### Fascism, a New World System

In the early days of the year 1917 a little man named Bronstein sat in the Café Boulevard, Second Avenue, New York, telling amused and tolerant fellow loungers how revolutions are made and what he would do if he were a dictator. Bronstein was then working for a Russian newspaper, *Novy Mir,* earning exactly twelve dollars a week and dreaming of Marxian conquest.

Ten weeks later Mr. Bronstein was *en route* to Russia; he succeeded finally in reaching Petrograd, and the end of the year found him, the great military genius, now called Trotsky, leading the Bolshevik revolution and building up a Red army to defeat a world of troubles.

Not only Trotsky, but Lenin and a dozen other Tsarist exiles in London, Switzerland and New York, spent their time in studying the two essential needs of a successful dictatorship: seizure of power and a program of action, once a new régime is proclaimed. Their program, of course, was based on the theories of Karl Marx, his partner, Engels, the American De Leon, the Frenchman Sorel, and other radicals.

Mussolini was the student of the very same prophets and dreamers. They were the men who made him. He confesses his debt to them, but having gone over to the Allied war party in 1914 and having been ejected from the Socialist Party, he was politically shipwrecked when the war ended. He followed his teachers in organizing and plotting; and he came into power without plans or ideas.

In the course of time Fascism acquired a program, even a "philosophy." But, in the same years in which it ruled and flourished, and influenced dictatorships from Finland to Spain, from Japan to South America, it was merely a government by bayonet and castor oil, taking from its enemy, the Russian dictatorship, all the means of suppression, such as the Cheka system, and producing no new idealogy for the guidance or amazement of a muddled world.

Mussolini's first crisis came on August 24, 1923, and he solved it in a way which warned the world that a new spirit had entered European affairs, new and extremely dangerous. General Tellini and two aides were slain by bandits at Janina, on the Greco-Albanian frontier. The assassins were Albanians. Mussolini immediately asked for fifty million lire indemnity, a salute to the Italian flag, and the punishment of the bandits, giving Greece twenty-four hours to comply. Premier Gonatas said the ultimatum would be answered within time, most points being admitted; others, he thought, might be modified. The assassins were not Greeks, the answer stated, Greek sovereignty was being infringed, and, moreover, fifty million was a lot of money. Mussolini was kindly requested to reduce the fine.

August 31, Mussolini replied by bombarding and occupying Corfu. An ultimatum to quit the long dismantled forts was given at two o'clock; firing began at five, and victory perched on the Italian colors at exactly six o'clock, the Greeks not having fired a shot in reply or offered any resistance to the Italian navy. The old fort had been used as a police school and a house of refuge for women and children protected by the American Near East Relief. The Fascists killed fifteen of them. (Ex-Ambassador Child, in one of his numerous apologies for Mussolini, hints that the authorities permitted the refugees to remain in the danger zone. Colonel Bowe of the American Relief denies this and estimates the victims at a hundred, of whom sixteen were infants.)

September dawned dramatically in many parts of the world; Pennsylvania had an anthracite strike, the Fascist Hitlerites occupied Nuremberg; Tokio and Yokohama were in flames after five hours of earthquake; Mexico was recognized after a three-year break in diplomatic relations — and the Italian navy covered itself with glory again by capturing the Greek islands of Paxos and Antipaxos and shelling a passing vessel. Indignation in London. Stupefaction in Athens. Alarm in Central Europe. Washington was semi-officially aghast and looked towards the League of Nations to do something. In Rome there was jubilation.

Greece having appealed, the League declared itself competent to solve the problem. A resolution by the Spanish representative Quiñones de Leon was approved. In official indignation, Mussolini replied, "In case the council of the League declares itself competent, the question whether to remain or to resign from the League arises in Italy. I have already voted for the second solution." Throughout the world it was known that the League of Nations would fulfill itself or founder in a week.

But it did not founder. The usual diplomatic side step was taken. The League plan was shelved but the Council of Ambassadors was told to intervene with a note to Greece and the evacuation of Corfu was traded for fulfillment of the majority of ultimatum points. Zaharoff, it was understood, found the fifty million for Greece. By this time, the attention of the world had shifted again to Japan, where the disaster had become one of the greatest in history: the dead were one hundred and ten thousand and the injured more than a million.

Celebrating, in March, 1924, the fifth anniversary of Fascism, Mussolini said, "Do not underestimate what has happened by calling it a ministerial crisis. It was a real revolution. . . . I am a tyrant. . . . Whoever is not with us is against us," and he proved the latter by ordering Italy to vote the Fascist ticket on April 6, while the militia stood by with their bludgeons at every polling booth and beat up thousands of members of the other five political parties.

The events of violence and corruption of this election soon

led to the second great crisis in the history of Mussolini and Fascism. In May, the Duce defended the grant of a monopoly to the Sinclair Oil Company of America, the Opposition having introduced a bill abrogating it. A young man named Giacomo Matteotti announced he would speak on the bloodshed during the April elections and the graft which accompanied the oil grant. In the Chamber, June 6, Mussolini shook his fist at the Matteotti group, saying that in Russia the communists knew how to deal with an opposition, "and you," he added, "would have a bullet through your spine." Four days later Matteotti was assassinated. (Of this event, which was soon to bring Italy to the verge of civil war, nothing was heard abroad, each nation having its own alarms and sensations.)

When Matteotti failed to appear in Parliament, all Rome suspected he had been killed by the Fascist Cheka. Cesare Rossi, Mussolini's closest household friend, and unofficial head of this organization, rushed to the Duce with the news that four or five of their employees had, after kidnaping the Opposition chief, murdered him and buried the body. The Fascist Cheka agents accused included Dumini, an American, born in St. Louis, the son of Adolphus and Jessie Williams Dumini.

The three days which followed were touch and go for Fascism. Every black shirt disappeared from the streets. Panic invaded Rome. Mussolini's pictures were torn down or covered with tar or with the word "Assassin" and "Morte Mussolini." Cardinal Maffi telegraphed the Duce, "As a priest I weep, as an Italian I am ashamed." Premier MacDonald attended a Labor Party meeting which condemned the assassination. Pope Pius was shocked, particularly because one of the accused, the Undersecretary Finzi, was married to the niece of Cardinal Vannutelli. The Fascists of America cabled Mussolini to clean up the party and see that justice was done.

Mussolini ordered General De Bono to resign as chief of police, imprisoned Dumini, Volpi, Filippelli, Rossi and others. On June 26, he announced the abandonment of the Fascist dictatorship, the abolition of the illegal Fascist militia, and . . . "we will enter into legality, clean out the party, follow a policy of conciliation."

The five opposition parties having failed to seize the opportunity for a revolution, Mussolini pacified the country and early in 1925 made a complete reversal of policy. Instead of deploring the assassination of his chief rival and purging and legalizing Fascismo, he boasted that "the sequestration of Matteotti, with its consequences, belongs morally, politically and historically to Fascismo."

This speech was followed by the first of twoscore decrees by which Fascism created a program. Italy was made "Totalitarian" or one hundred per cent. Fascist, Corporate State, and a sort of syndicalism introduced; the press, Freemasonry, the five opposition parties and any future opposition, the jury system, academic freedom and the commonplace rights under previous democracy and monarchy, were suppressed, censored, abolished, destroyed. Considerable violence accompanied this creation of the Fascist State, Bolitho recording that in three months sixteen men in public life were killed, thirty-six seriously injured and one hundred and seventy-two assaulted by Fascisti while forty-six homes and political clubs were invaded and destroyed.

On the first anniversary of Matteotti's death, Mussolini warned Italy against any demonstration and ordered his Blackshirts to parade with their flags and their weapons and their challenges. Franklin C. Gowen, an American vice consul at Leghorn, was assaulted for failure to salute a black banner but the Fascist Government and the American State Department and the American Ambassador in Rome decided to keep this incident secret. American citizens arriving in London described the attack, forcing the State Department publicly to ask an apology of the Palazzo Chigi; Mussolini apologized and the American Ambassador declared himself satisfied with the Fascist Government paying eight dollars for Consul Gowen's injuries. At the same time, the Italian economic system became so dangerous the government begged J. P. Morgan to save it. The leading American bankers had just told the Rome journalists "confidentially" that the dictatorship was a bad risk. However, the loan was made and a few days later the Chamber passed a law for the Fascistization of the Italian State.

In November, Deputy Zaniboni was arrested for attempted assassination of Mussolini. Testimony revealed Fascist agents, including a leader of the Cheka named Quaglia, as having suggested and planned the attempt, even to supplying a rifle and renting the room in a hotel opposite Mussolini's foreign office.

In April, Giovanni Amendola, Matteotti's successor, died in Nice from wounds inflicted by the Fascisti, and the Honorable Violet Gibson, sister of Baron Ashbourne, a lady suffering from religious hysteria, shot Mussolini in the nose with a tiny revolver. Mussolini had just emerged from the congress of surgeons. They put a piece of sticking plaster over the wound. "The bullets pass, Mussolini remains," said Mussolini. "A supernatural force entrusted me with a lofty mission," said the Honorable Violet, as she was led away. Mussolini sailed for Tripoli like a conqueror. "Rome carries the beacon lamp of strength to the shores of the African Sea. No one can stop our inexorable will. Everything has been prepared to enable Fascism to hold the destinies of the Italian people in its iron fist." Crowds shouted "Hail Cæsar."

On October 31, as he left the stadium at Bologna, Mussolini was fired upon, the bullet ripping some cloth, grazing a sleeve, but otherwise doing no harm. Bolitho declared the Duce had been wearing a steel vest for a year. The high officials in the following car lynched the supposed offender, a Fascist youth of sixteen named Zamboni. The body was smashed almost to pulp, stabbed fourteen times, dragged around town, left unburied for a day. The Premier was unruffled.

In December the Reverend Sante Scarpe was beaten to death by Fascists for refusing to disband the Catholic Boy Scouts of Vittorio Veneto, and the Pope made an address denouncing

Fascist rowdyism and the theory of the Fascist State, "which attempts to monopolize everything, making of the State an end in itself and of citizens mere means to that end." The American Federation of Labor issued a proclamation to all its branches to fight Fascism at home and abroad.

Thus the record of violence ends temporarily and permits a glance at the great constructive achievements of the new world system. In announcing the Corporate State, Mussolini said, "For the first time in the history of the world, a constructive revolution like ours realizes peacefully, in the field of production and work, incorporation of all the economic and intellectual forces of the nation." The main features of the syndicalist State are:

Prohibition of strikes and lockouts, with machinery created for arbitration, and the militia to check the workers.

Enforced coöperation between capital and labor and between classes.

Industrial competition abolished.

State control of business and industry; state control of capital.

Creation of categories for all productive citizens.

Charter of Labor.

A new Parliament composed of four hundred persons chosen by the Fascist Grand Council from lists supplied by unions, syndicates, etc. No opposition ticket or party permitted, no opposition politics permitted.

One of the first new decrees ended the eight-hour day; another forbade the migrations of men seeking work from one province to another. A thousand restrictions were put into force. At the same time the government began to extend its rule into business, until, in the Nineteen Thirties it operated most of the steamship lines, almost all the banks, silk factories, shipbuilding and other industries, somewhat after the manner of Russia under the New Economic Policy. It also engaged in large public enterprises and borrowed between eight and twelve billion lire abroad, issuing statements for several years that it had balanced its budgets. It reorganized the railroads and claimed that all trains ran on time. Motor boats were introduced into the

*Keystone View Co.*

WAR MINISTER LEON TROTSKY, BEFORE HE WAS EXILED FROM RUSSIA

Grand Canal in Venice. Magnificent auto roads were constructed. Considerable lands were drained and irrigated.

In the course of years, the first slogan, "Hierarchy, Order, Discipline", became an achievement. The Fascist hierarchy assumed all power, and order and discipline were marred only by infrequent outbursts of violence and massacre. New police and spy systems were also established. In 1925 and 1926, no less than thirty-five thousand persons were arrested for uttering non-Fascist political views. After the complete suppression of the opposition parties and newspapers, arrests dwindled to five or ten thousand a year. Fascism became absolute. It boasted of all its material progress. All the bankers of America loaned it money and praised it. It was a complete success. Everything flourished, — except old-fashioned human rights.

In the Russian dictatorship, the period was also marked with important troubles. In September, 1926, there was a repetition of the Ninth of Thermidor which had resulted in the downfall of Robespierre and the end of the French Revolution. But this time Stalin was prepared for it. He struck first. Zinovieff, President of the Third Internationale, and others, were accused of secretly organizing a faction to oust the Georgian. Trotsky and Kamineff were charged with being sympathetic, and even Lenin's widow, Krupskaya, was said to favor the faction. Stalin, addressing the party, said, "We have had enough of that idiotic slogan, 'the world revolution.' Without the assistance of the outside world, whose credit, good will and products we need, Russia can not exist much longer. Trotsky and Zinovieff are responsible for the lack of sympathy we find in America."

Trotsky, Zinovieff, Kamineff, Evodokimoff, Piatakoff and Sokolnikoff, who had maintained Lenin's policies, accused Stalin of losing sight of Russia's international mission to upset capitalism throughout the world. Trotsky also insisted on taxing the peasants, keeping them from becoming *kulaki* or agrarian capitalists. Stalin favored peasant prosperity though it involved another retreat.

One year later, just as the British Trade Union Congress by 2,551,000 to 620,000 voted to sever relations with the All-Russian Council of Trades Unions, Trotsky was expelled from the Comintern, together with Kamineff, Zinovieff, Radek and other leaders, while hundreds were arrested and sent into Tsarist Siberian exile. "They are guilty," stated the official organ *Pravda*, "of trying to split the party, of carrying on secret propaganda among workmen, of printing anti-Stalinist literature in hidden printing plants, of organizing secret meetings, and of coöperating with counter-revolutionists."

Trotsky then delivered his last challenge to Stalin:

"You want to expel us? That is but natural. The Stalin-Bukharin group which throws into the prisons of the secret police some of our best comrades, like Nechayeff, Fisheleff, and others, which has seized the control of the party machinery, which rules over the party by violence, can not tolerate us. We understand that. You have tried to prevent us from making our program known to the bulk of the party. This means that you fear the party. We have told you that, in spite of all your prohibitions, we would make our ideas known to all, and we will do it. Comrades Mrachkovsky, Fisheleff, and others, who were printing our literature in secret plants, were and are acting in keeping with our orders, and we are responsible for their work.

"By removing, expelling, arresting our comrades, you are fighting against the party itself. The situation is such that average Communists are terrorized; they dare not voice freely their disagreements with Stalin's policy. The dictatorship of Stalin and of his party machinery degrades the party. Before his death, Lenin said: 'Remove Stalin from the post of Secretary-General, for he will bring the party to rupture and ruin.' Unfortunately, these words were then concealed from the party."

But Trotsky realized his rule was over. "I shall not be astonished," he told a journalist, "if our struggle against the Stalinists ends the way the struggle between the Girondins and the Jacobins of the French Revolution ended. We of the Opposition may die as the victims of the Russian Ninth of Thermidor."

With the majority of the living leaders who made the Russian revolution, Trotsky, Zinovieff, Kamineff, Rakofsky and Radek in fear of their lives, Russia celebrated the tenth anniversary of Bolshevism. Stalin had conquered. The Georgian was now absolute dictator.

In Paris, General Simon Petlura, once dictator of the Ukraine, walked down the Boulevard St. Michel. A man named Samuel Schwartzbart, once a Petlura soldier, met him. Schwartzbart held a photograph in one hand, a revolver in the other. Making sure of the man, the ex-soldier fired, crying dramatically at the same time, "Assassin, here is your punishment." The dictator sank to the ground, tried to rise, was felled by three more bullets and died in the street. Schwartzbart then addressed the crowd: "Petlura is a murderer. He tortured my people. He outraged Jewish women. He organized pogroms. Eleven years ago I vowed to kill him. Several times I had the chance but he was accompanied by his wife or children. Now I am satisfied. Justice is done." The French courts thought so too. The executioner of the dictator was set free amidst acclamation.

In Greece, Admiral Kondylis upset the dictatorship. Pangalos was quietly arrested, placed aboard the destroyer *Pergamos,* taken prisoner towards Athens. For a moment the old demagogue spoke in him. The crew of the *Pergamos* cheered. Kondylis sent airplanes to bomb the *Pergamos*. It surrendered. Some time later the forlorn dictator sued Mrs. Pangalos for all his misfortune, blaming feminine intrigues for his downfall. She, Josephine Papaioannou, an heiress, had married the young officer and bought his way to a colonelcy and then the war ministry. She ran a magnificent salon in Athens, spent all her money surrounding Pangalos and herself with the most capable and influential minds in the nation, realizing that her husband himself was second-rate. Once he was dictator, she set about recouping her fortune by smuggling. She became the French perfume racketeer of Greece. With the Pangalos debacle, the mob in the streets shouted threats against Madame.

May 24, 1926, Pilsudski set aside the Polish constitution, not for the first or last time. "I am the man who conducted you to victories," he proclaimed to the army. A little shooting followed. Crowds of civilians got mixed up between the opposing forces; tourists came, admiring the machine guns and generally impeding "operations." Pilsudski furiously denounced the unmilitariness of the event. Twice he had to suspend his "battle" to let women and children get out of the war zone. Some were killed.

Kemal Pasha weathered the conventional counter-revolution. On July 14, at two in the morning, when Smyrna was asleep, he had the entire Opposition Party's fourteen deputies hanged in various squares of the city, each politician's neck adorned with a placard, "Caught at the moment of attempting to murder the beloved President of the Republic, the savior of Turkey and of Turkish honor, and of attempting to overthrow the government."

In Persia, Reza Khan Pahlavi mounted not the peacock throne of the Khazar dynasty but a more simple chair; he did not use the pearl crown but a plain gold one set with precious stones, and he himself placed it on his own head. He announced not a dictatorship but a liberal government. To prove this, he placed the financial affairs of the nation in the hands of Mr. A. C. Millspaugh, his American adviser.

Comic relief among the dictators was furnished by Carol of Rumania. He opened the year 1926 by abdicating again and arrived in Paris with Magda Lupescu. Before indulging in his new extra-matrimonial affairs he took a political fling at Queen Marie and Dictator Bratianu, denouncing them and incidentally praising Mussolini as the type of ruler he admired. At the same moment came news of a new addition to the scores of Rumanian government scandals. This time Vintila, the premier's brother, was involved in a forgery case, several hundred poor peasants, longing for America, having been fleeced by high officials. Clarence Streit of the New York *Times*, reporting various intrigues and the corruption which attended the elections, was expelled by Bratianu.

Zizi Lambrino Hohenzollern sued Carol in Paris. The court heard Carol's letters read. To Queen Marie he wrote, "Dear Mama, I cannot have Zizi left in this ridiculous and equivocal position and never could I admit that the child to be born out of our marriage should be considered illegitimate." To Zizi he wrote, "I always remember our luminous days together. But the chain is broken. Love of country has forced my hand. Yes, my poor little dear, I am betrothed — to a Princess." Said Zizi to the court, "I was married to Prince Carol by a priest of the Orthodox Catholic Church and our son is legitimately entitled to bear the name of Hohenzollern."

Both sides blamed Queen Marie for their troubles. Marie announced her trip to America.

Dictatorship, Fascism, Revolution, Communism — in all of Europe there had been ferment, uprising, bloodshed, terrorism, but little in Britain. Solid British climate, solid British roast beef and solid British common sense prevailed. Fascism raised laughter. It could never succeed, thought Bolitho, because of its black shirts; no Englishman would dress up even for a counter-revolution. Revolution threatened in 1926. The long series of strikes which followed Lloyd George's promises of better times were prelude to the great general strike, which began on the third of May.

The Royal Coal Commission favored one of two things, either lower wages or longer working hours; the first meant starvation, the second was inhuman. A million men muttered.

The government did not know what to do. The coal industry was running at a loss.

Reactionary British aristocracy, fearing Red revolution, quietly defended itself. The letters O.M.S. emerged from mystery as the Organization for the Maintenance of Supplies. Constitutional Tory England determined that wages would not be increased. The O.M.S. would break the strike. Among its leaders were Lord Hardinge, Viceroy of India, Viscount Jellicoe, who lost the battle of Jutland, General Sir Francis Lloyd, who stayed in London during the war, Sir Rennel Rodd, who wrote poems of love for Fascist Italy. Winston Churchill, who wanted to be the British Mussolini, was Tory spokesman.

"You have declared war," said A. J. Cook to Premier Baldwin, refusing to accept either lower wages or longer hours. A million coal miners answered Cook's call on May first. Their wages had been eight to seventeen dollars a week, the term of the employment six months out of the year, and they had refused a scale of five to thirteen dollars a week. On May third five million men were engaged in the general strike, which was a revolution, British style. (That very same day Mussolini in Rome had declared all strikes illegal and Sinclair Lewis had refused the Pulitzer prize. Two days later the American Stock Exchange experienced a slump and American labor sent its greeting to British labor.)

The general strike was not ordered until the mine owners had notified the government that they would lock one million workmen out the day the government coal subsidy stopped. The *Daily Mail* came to the defense of the owners with an editorial saying a strike would be "a revolutionary movement" which "cannot be tolerated by any civilized government and must be dealt with by every resource at the community's disposal." The typesetters refused to set the editorial. Baldwin issued an appeal to the public: "Constitutional government is being attacked. The laws of England are the people's birthright. The laws are in your keeping. You have made Parliament your guardian. The general strike is a challenge to Parliament, and is the road to anarchy and ruin."

A battle for public opinion followed. Pressmen walked out on all newspapers except the *Herald*. Baldwin published the *British Gazette* and raided the *Herald*. British labor refused a gift of a million dollars from the Soviet Government. The O.M.S. began to function. Five lords volunteered as bus drivers. One lord collected pennies. One lord-chauffeur had passengers tell him the names of the streets and the route to follow. The Women's Auxiliary Service appeared, commanded by Mary Allen, attired in a natty blue uniform and addressed as "Sir." The Countess of Warwick and Lady Cynthia Mosley worked for the strikers. "Cricket spirit," sportsmanship, it was said, prevailed. In football, a strikers' team defeated policemen 2–1, the ninth day of May, while Byrd flew over the North Pole and returned in fifteen hours.

Meanwhile the Archbishop of Canterbury had spoken to the King, and the King had spoken to the Die-hard Tories. Sir Herbert Samuel wrote a formula. Baldwin and Ramsay MacDonald conferred. On the twelfth, after nine days, the greatest labor walkout in history ended in compromise. "A civil war has been avoided." "British stolidity, British muddling through, has won." "The gods of things as they are remain; the God of the Archbishop of Canterbury has won, not the revolutionary Jesus of the striking workmen." So read the comments of the time. Both extremists were defeated, the government was not overthrown, the strike order was unconditionally withdrawn, the government agreed to continue the coal subsidy until some indefinite time, when a new plan would be produced. Neither capital nor labor was smashed. Hatred, disillusion and desperation remained.

## Interlude 1927

"All a Vixen's Pack of Lies," Chaplin Calls Lita Grey's Suit. The court awarded Mrs. Charles Chaplin $825,000.

Leon Daudet was released from prison by a ruse and fled to Belgium amidst international laughter.

May 12: Lindbergh flies from St. Louis to New York.
Zinovieff accuses Opposition of Bolshevik failure in China.
Mussolini cuts wages.
Coolidge let third term quiz go unanswered.
British raid London Soviet Headquarters.

Asked for statement on the tenth anniversary of America's war entry, Ludendorff said: "The people of the United States did not 'enter the war', as they themselves did not act. It was by their President Wilson, on order of the Jews, Freemasons and Jesuits, that they were lured, through the sufficiently well-known lying propaganda, like insects on to birdlime, and led into war like animals to the slaughtering bench."

Clara Bow, creator of the flapper type, at height of popularity.

When Isadora Duncan died, September 14, the world forgave her her communism and her fat.

The new talking pictures are timed perfectly.

Death of Bohemianism in Montparnasse recorded. About 1907 the gay night life and high rents had driven the real French and foreign artists and writers to the neighborhood of the Montparnasse cemetery. Between 1919 and 1922, the inhabitants of Greenwich Village invaded Montparnasse. They were followed by tourists and charlatans. Likewise the lower-priced franc brought not only Bohemians from all Europe but people seeking cheap living. Montparnasse became overcrowded.

*Underwood and Underwood*

THREE RUSSIAN LEADERS

Left to right: — Yenekidsky, Stalin and Maxim Gorky photographed during the parade of Physical Culturists in the Red Square of Moscow on the occasion of the 10th anniversary of the Red Sport and International Red Day.

The first American bar, the Strix, was opened in 1922. Now the ex-lumber yards become the swellest cafés.

"Old inhabitants": Joyce, Ford Madox Ford, Hemingway, Huddleston, Foujita, Sherwood Anderson, Sinclair Lewis.

Ruth Snyder, who murdered her husband, wrote before her electrocution:

> God gives us what in His sight is best
> My future in Him rests
> For in every trial God's sweet will is best.

Katherine Mayo's book "Mother India" is a sensation on both continents. "The whole pyramid of the Indians' woes rests upon a rock-bottom physical base, simply his manner of getting into the world and his sex-life thenceforward." The Soviet's famed woman diplomat, Kollontay, wrote a novel, "Red Love", in which she said:

> The modern woman, the self-supporting professional woman, cannot allow love to take first place in her life.
>
> The modern woman is learning to subdue her emotions to reason, to master her tenderer feelings and put business and work before sentiment.
>
> No, there will be no flappers — because flappers are drones.
>
> There will be no Don Juans and Lord Byrons, for the simple reason that women will not have time for them.

When Judge Gary died, Coolidge issued his eulogy: "He upheld the best ideals of commerce and industry. . . . His going is a great loss to the nation."

United States land fifteen hundred marines after Shanghai falls.

Ford's attack on Jews as race barred by court.

"Hands off China" meeting in Union Square.

Josephine Baker announces wedding with Count Pepito Albertini.

Mussolini orders thousands of Italian titles abolished.

Three, on trial, confess getting Legion of Honor for anybody at price.

The tabloids reach the nadir of smut.

Mayor Walker in Berlin: "Fellow refugees of the Eighteenth Amendment!"

Mayor Walker in Paris: "As Julius Cæsar said to Cleopatra, I didn't come here to talk."

Mayor Walker in Ireland was referred to as "The *late* Mayor of New York."

Mayor Walker in Rome: Bragaglia, artist and cabaret operator, said: "Mayor Walker, seeing two dark men dancing here, told me he was surprised that I allowed them to dance with white women. . . . I replied that the reason was that I am a Catholic and the Catholic Church not only recognized black people as brethren in Christ but the Pope creates Negro bishops. But since Mayor Walker was my distinguished guest, I asked the Brazilians in question not to dance. They were very indignant and explained they were not Negroes but Creoles, and moreover French citizens, although Brazilian born, and artists. I told this to Mayor Walker and he accepted the explanation."

Senator Norris (Republican, Nebraska) addressed Coolidge and Kellogg:

Once't there was a Bolshevik, who wouldn't say his prayers,
So Kellogg sent him off to bed, away upstairs,
An' Kellogg heerd him holler, an' Coolidge heerd him bawl,
But when they turn't the kivvers down, he wasn't there at all.
They seeked him down in Mexico, they cussed him in the press;
They seeked him round the Capitol, an' ever' wheres, I guess;
But all they ever found of him was whiskers, hair and clout —
An' the Bolsheviks 'll get you, ef you don't watch out.

# CHAPTER THIRTEEN

## ANTI-AMERICA: WAR DEBTS, SACCO-VANZETTI, ETC.

JUST as 1925, the Locarno Year, definitely marks the turn to good will among European nations, so 1926 records the climax in ill will towards America, and 1927 beholds a strange dénouement.

In Europe, France led the Anti-American Movement; in the Western Hemisphere it was Mexico, which had become a sort of spokesman for Central and South America. But hate was not a monopoly; the American interventionists consciously encouraged it against the southern neighbors, and our soldiers brought it to Europe.

As the great march of prosperity began in the United States and the nations were called one after another to settle their debts, while we in turn gained their export markets, the pride of economic progress and the fear of economic debacle intensified anti-Americanism. The Sacco-Vanzetti case was exploited everywhere; few considered the question of justice; radical mobs and the conservative press of fifty countries made of the two convicted Italians a means for demonstrating their own anger and fear.

Troubles first began when our Occupation forces moved into a clean and tidy Rhineland to live in comparative luxury, while the main army billeted in France found life unbearably dirty. There were dunghills beneath peasant windows; on them the pigs and children roamed, and the cows were housed with the family. "They call us '*sales Americains*'," commented the doughboys; "but look how filthy they themselves are." And how they hated French inefficiency.

"The most disheartening surprise which awaits the American landing in France," reported Ralph Pulitzer, who was one of the American editors accompanying President Wilson to the Peace Conference, "is the disappearance of the cordial sentiments of admiration on the one hand and of gratitude on the other, which originally flourished between the American Expeditionary Force and the French, and the substitution of mutual resentment and even antipathy." In France the American military police were busy keeping the Doughboys from fighting the Poilus, while in Germany they were keeping the soldiers from marrying the late enemy.

"We were stung," "soaked," "robbed," "cheated"; "we had to pay forty dollars for a wheel on a farmer's oxcart which one of our army trucks broke." "Why, it's a fact, we even paid rent for the trenches in which we were fighting," the American army complained, and many of their complaints were true. We did not pay rent for the trenches but we certainly had to pay for fields taken from peasants for American air bases. German propaganda was blamed for many of our protests.

The French said the Americans were an economically demoralizing force. They threw their money away, raised prices and the cost of living. Everywhere they boasted they had won the war. Some said the Germans were a fine, clean, efficient, good people; some regretted America had come in on the wrong side. In the Rhineland American soldiers courted German maidens and found affection which was not measured by the standard French price of two dollars. Foch gave interviews favoring French occupation of the left bank of the Rhine; Clemenceau thundered for more spoils of war; the rumor reached American civilians and soldiers that Wilson was being treated like a child and made a fool of in Paris and that the talk of war for democracy was bunkum, so far as the European statesmen were concerned. On the wave of general disillusion appeared the fine spray of mutual international hatred.

Between the Armistice and 1926, all Europe, except the

neutral nations and Czechoslovakia and Poland, and with the possible exception of Germany, which still hoped our dollars would save her, went anti-American. Although the prime ministers and the great heroes of the war made trips to the United States, signed peace treaties, concluded debt negotiations and pledged the undying friendship of their countries, the peoples back home suppressed their fear and their jealousy. In 1926, America was supreme among nations. The world was our oyster. The oyster was furious.

"A terrible wave of mortal hatred of Americans is sweeping over old and exhausted Europe," rightfully reported the Fascist organ, *Il Tevere,* "but the Americans do not perceive it. The Americans have their eyes full of figures, their ears are absorbed with the clicking of adding machines. They have a knife up their sleeves, namely, their most powerful dollar, which can crush twenty Europeans. They live in a state of superb obliviousness, which is astonishing and offensive. No. Things cannot go on thus. The Americans are sowing to the right and left hatred and a desire for vengeance. The right to enslave a whole continent is not to be secured even on the battlefield."

Lord Rothermere in the London *Daily Mail* attacked the United States with excessive passion. As the franc fell in Paris, the summer of 1926, Americans were hooted in the streets; mobs vented their hate on innocent tourists and shouted, "Down with Mellon" and "Down with the debts" when the Secretary of the Treasury arrived at the Gare du Nord. And in Mexico, government officials and crowds were angry at what they called the unwarranted interference of the United States in their dispute with the Church.

The French press was bitter. When Admiral Latimer landed marines in Nicaragua, ordering the liberal leader Sacasa to disarm and quit, and the State Department recognized Diaz, the friend of the international bankers, there was no unanimity of opinion in the United States, some papers even daring to inform Mr. Kellogg that "no one in the world believes we are neutral, because Nicaragua has for fifteen years been an American protectorate and Kellogg should stop pretending." But *Le Temps* declared that under guise of the Monroe Doctrine, the United States was using Dollar Diplomacy to annex all of Central America down to Panama, and establish its imperialism throughout South America.

Encouraged by the press, ten thousand wounded French soldiers marched to protest the Mellon-Bérenger debt arrangement. It was a pitiful tragic procession of broken men, a funeral procession of the living-dead. In wheeled chairs the legless propelled themselves with their hands and the blind tried to keep step, each man guided by a wife or child. Then came the men without faces. . . .

The marble memorial to Alan Seeger, American, poet, Legionnaire, one of the first to fall, was attacked by hoodlums and partly destroyed.

Mr. Kipling contributed a small hymn of hate. It created an international sensation. The title "The Vineyard", came from the twelfth verse, twentieth chapter of St. Matthew, in which the late arrival drew the same wage, a parallel to America in the war and the demand for debt payments:

"At the eleventh hour he came,
But his wages were the same
As ours who all day long had trod
The winepress of the wrath of God.

"Since his back had felt no load,
Virtue in him still abode;
So he swiftly made his own
Those lost spoils he had not won. . . ."

Senator Caraway told his colleagues, "You will find ribald and insulting remarks chalked or pencilled on the little white crosses that mark the graves of some American soldiers, such as for instance 'To hell with America' and other inscriptions." France denied and became still angrier. Senator Reed, and in a milder degree, the President himself, suggested a tourist boycott of the French Republic. Reed favored one of six months. Mr. Coolidge's view, as summed up in the press, was that if Americans did not care for the way they were being treated abroad, they should come home and spend their money seeing America first. The President did suggest to tourists that a few "bumptious" ones could create a general dislike for all; he had heard reports of misrepresentative American behavior in France at a time when there was great economic fear and general instability, and he thought tourists should be more thoughtful.

Economic federations were in preparation against the United States, notably the Steel Kartel, which was to divide up the world in exploitable zones, leaving out America but undercutting and destroying our business everywhere.

Money, of course, was the cause of most international hatred of America. But the masses, the mobs, the deformed soldiers who marched, the poets who wrote, the hoodlums who mutilated American statues, did not realize it, and continued to let their emotions sway with the headlines of the paid press. "*Ces sales Americains*" was added by the French to their terms "*meteques*" for foreigners in general, *Boches* for the Germans and *Angliches* for the British. In London "Shylock" and "usurer" were the words written across cartoons of Uncle Sam in the *Daily Mail*. "Twenty theaters and thirty weeklies earn a living by hating the Americans." A writer to the *Times* suggested that "before long, America will be obliged to pay millions of pounds sterling yearly to British companies for the oil she needs and which she will no longer be able to draw from her own resources", and the rubber monopolists raised the price to a dollar a pound. Churchill hinted in his argument with the State Department that America "had fallen on the backer of the Allies' bills" and the makers of British foreign diplomacy thought "that America is bent on crushing England out of existence."

In Belgium, the nationalist press repeated the phrase, "America ruins France and France ruins Belgium," because the Belgian franc had fallen with that of her large neighbor. Americans who rushed to Bruxelles to buy cheaply were insulted, the Belgians forgetting their own hordes who descended upon Cologne and bought up all they could of Germany when the mark collapsed. In Italy the new Fascist official textbook for children concluded the history of the World War with the words, "Then the treacherous Serbs, aided by the hypocritical Wilson and faithless Allies, joined in robbing Italy of the fruits of victory."

Xenophobia spread to China; Chang Tso-lin had seized the Chinese Eastern Railway, built by the Tsar. Feng, in the north, rallied the nationalists after he was driven out of Pekin by Chang, the protégé of Japan, and Wu Pei-fu, the upholder of British interests on the Yangtze. The students of China, many of them educated in American universities with the remitted Boxer indemnity, rallied around the nationalist Feng. The Kuomintang, the modern Nationalist Party, became a movement for freedom and self-respect, differing vastly from the blind, bitter, unenlightened nationalist Boxer movement of 1900, which had been pure xenophobia. But the American and British press promptly named the Kuomintang a Bolshevik organization and the long-lasting American sentimental attachment for China was forgotten.

The year closed with a statement from Mr. Mellon. Every agreement with a debtor nation, he said, save only that with Great Britain, did, either *de facto,* or, as with Belgium, *de jure,* amount to the cancellation of the advances made before the Armistice of November 11, 1918.

To this day Europe generally has not heard of it. If this fact could have been published prominently in every European newspaper, broadcast from every radio station, appear on every movie screen, the anti-American spirit of 1926 and of to-day would be changed. Not one Frenchman in a thousand has heard the statement. The French press has never displayed it. Yet it is probably the one most vital fact in the debt relations between America and Europe, and the debt relations are the great cause

# Un pour tous - Tous pour un

Le projet de tarif douanier américain prévoit pour les produits horlogers une augmentation **moyenne** de

**300 %** environ, sans justification.

Un tel projet constitue un **acte inamical** à l'égard de la Suisse; il **compromet** une partie de **son économie nationale.**

Pour réagir contre le danger qui nous menace et par esprit de **solidarité,** nous demandons à tous les

**Industriels,**
**Artisans,**
**Commerçants,**
**Consommateurs**

de bannir de leurs

**Bureaux, Fabriques**
**Ateliers, Garages**
**Magasins et Habitations**

toutes marchandises provenant des Etats-Unis.

L'Industrie horlogère suisse.

The Swiss watch industry has posted notices in all parts of Switzerland denouncing the proposed American tariff on watches and watch parts and appealing to the people of the country to discontinue the use of American products.

Under a headline, "One for All—All for One," the poster states that "the proposed new American tariff provides for an average increase in duty on watch products of about 300 per cent. without justification.

"Such a proposal," the poster says, "constitutes an unfriendly act to Switzerland. It endangers a part of her national economics. In order to counteract tne danger, we appeal to the spirit of solidarity and ask that all manufacturers, craftsmen, merchants and consumers banish from their offices, factories, workshops, garages, stores and residences all merchandise of United States origin."

of international hatred. The super-patriots, the makers of diplomacy and the makers of war, have succeeded in fooling all the people all the time — up to now.

### ANTI-AMERICANISM AND THE SACCO-VANZETTI CASE

The atmosphere of fear, jealousy, hatred, distrust, suspicion which since 1918 marked the world's reaction to America became supercharged in 1926 and 1927, when two Italians made their last pleas for liberty in Massachusetts and were sent to their death, despite protests from scores of nations and millions of foreigners. In fact, the names Sacco and Vanzetti were unknown outside the town of Dedham until cables from Paris told of an extraordinary event.

A small, oblong package marked perfume had arrived for Ambassador Herrick, October 19, 1921. It was sent to his residence. A valet, undoing the wrappings, was reminded by a clicking sound of his days as a grenadier in Flanders. He hurled the package into a bathroom and fled. There was an explosion.

Its sound echoed throughout the world. At first the Herrick bomb was reported sent by French communists "as a protest against the conviction of two fellow communists in the United States, charged with murder." Who these two were was not known. But the next day a mob paraded before our embassy in Bruxelles with placards "Pardon Sacco and Vanzetti." But who were Sacco and Vanzetti? On the twenty-first eight thousand attended a protest meeting in Paris; a small grenade was thrown against the police, which was clubbing the mob which might have marched on the American embassy; several persons were injured. Anatole France, Henri Barbusse, Romain Rolland and other Frenchmen asked President Harding for a pardon, while several American journalists cabled that "swarming nests of foreign anarchists and communists imbued with terrorist doctrines and pledged to embark on a merciless war against organized society" were the backers of the two convicted Italians.

Bombs were thrown in Lisbon and threats of violence were heard from Cuba to Peru; boycott of the United States and talk of a general strike resounded in South America; there were demonstrations against the ambassadors, ministers and consuls from Rome to Stockholm, from London to China. Italy was agitated deeply.

It was just one month from the day the Herrick bomb exploded that the first story of Nicola Sacco and Bartolomeo Vanzetti was published generally in America. The brief facts were: On April 15, 1920, Frederick A. Parmenter, a paymaster, and Alessandro Berardelli, a guard, were attacked in South Braintree, Massachusetts, by a hold-up gang, shot and robbed of $15,776.51. Sacco and Vanzetti, two radicals, already in bad odor for their trip to Mexico to avoid the draft, and their connection with Andrea Salseda, a man supposed to be a dangerous radical (but actually a stool pigeon for the Department of Justice), were arrested.

In due time the men were tried and sentenced to death. It was nothing but a local crime, the usual hold-up, the usual incidental murder, the usual gangsters. But a Defense Committee had been formed which began sending out propaganda to all parts of the world, charging that the men were persecuted because they were Italians, foreigners, radicals; because they were intelligent workmen active in the radical movement; because they opposed the Department of Justice at a time when the Department was hysterically leading the anti-Red campaign, etc., etc. Frank Lopez, a Spanish carpenter, flooded Mexico, Spain and South America with propaganda; Aldihno Felicani, Italy, and Eugene Lyons, a former Columbia School of Journalism student, addressed the liberal and radical publications of America and England. Several labor unions pledged their aid. Mrs. Willard Straight and Mrs. Glendower Evans, both unimpeachable Americans, had given their support and money to a "Save Sacco and Vanzetti" fund.

In May, 1922, the State Department provided its ambassadors and consuls throughout the world with ammunition for the attacks made on American justice; in its résumé of the Sacco-Vanzetti case the statement is made that the facts are given impartially. All the Commonwealth's claims of their guilt are substantiated. But by now it was no longer a question of facts. The anti-American storms were gathering in Europe. The few radicals of 1921 who had sent a bomb and staged a demonstration were being joined by millions of persons who were reading the papers about Uncle Shylock and American usury and debt extortions and our "betrayal" of the noble Allies. The Sacco-Vanzetti case, like the debt settlements, served to unite huge masses in Europe and South America and elsewhere against a common object of disdain and hate.

In 1926, when, as we have seen, anti-America was a world movement, an appeal was taken to the Superior Criminal Court in Dedham.

There on September 12, the argument was heard.

On October 23, the day Trotsky was ousted from the Politburo, the innermost circle of Russia's dictatorship, Queen Marie had reviewed the 106th Infantry in Brooklyn and John Masefield had come to New York to find Luke O'Connor's saloon, where he had once scrubbed floors, the court refused the appeal, stating, "It is not now a question of the guilt or innocence of the defendants, for that question has been determined by the jury in accordance with the law."

Governor Fuller received a threatening letter from Chicago signed "The French-American Bankers and Unions Coöperation and Ku-Klux Klan", which he gave to the press. Within the week the American Federation of Labor left its conservative position and asked a new trial for the arch-radicals; a petition with half a million names was delivered to Governor Fuller; the Episcopal bishops of America appealed to him for a new trial, and Captain Dreyfus, whose trial had once been a world affair and who had become a figure of speech, offered to come to America to aid, saying, "I am heart and soul involved in this case."

While the United States was asking what Yankee subtlety might lurk in the word "choose" used in a phrase by its President, Governor Fuller, August 3, refused a new trial.

Opinion in the United States was divided; in Europe, however, having become part of a political and economic movement, it was almost unanimous; almost every American embassy, legation and consulate was guarded by police in three continents that day.

The Vatican denied that the Pope had intervened with the American Government but admitted the matter had been called to the Pontiff's attention by the American cardinals. Charles A. Beard, Bruce Bliven, John Dewey and Jane Addams appealed to Governor Fuller. Justice Oliver Wendell Holmes said it was a matter for the State, not the Supreme Court.

Twenty members of the British Parliament, seven million members of the Labor and Socialist Internationale, Doctor Einstein, Mme. Curie, Nansen, President Masaryk of Czechoslovakia, M. Caillaux and the grandson of Lafayette sent protests.

A new trial was denied even after the defense unearthed new evidence.

As the day for the execution approached, the American press, which had been divided in its opinion, largely returned to Governor Fuller's camp, when all the correspondents abroad reported "new fires of anti-American feeling are sweeping over Europe, refueled by the Sacco-Vanzetti case." Men in the street began to say, "We won't let damned foreigners interfere with us", and "They're Reds, anyway, so let them burn." Senator Borah said, "Foreign interference is an impudent and willful challenge to our sense of decency and dignity, and ought to be dealt with accordingly." William Green, president of the American Federation of Labor, asked Coolidge to stop the execution: "I appeal for executive clemency in the name of millions."

A few minutes after midnight, August 23, in the State Prison at Charlestown, the two Italians were electrocuted.

There was rioting in twenty countries. In Paris crowds went up and down the Grands Boulevards, shouting, "*A bas les Americains*" and insulting foreigners, while in certain radical zones battles occurred with the police resulting in no less than two hundred casualties. Throughout Europe people and press spoke bitterly about America and "a great miscarriage of justice."

One fact is apparent: anti-Americanism throughout the world had produced considerable resentment, and the execution of the two men was considered by millions of Americans a fine answer to Europe. The evidence and the question of justice were smothered in emotion and hysteria. One world leader who believed the governor had done right by answering European antagonism with electrocution was the dictator of Italy. Finding himself faced with American protests over the abolition of the native language, newspapers, and civil rights in the Austrian Tyrol, Mussolini replied, "A State respecting itself cannot tolerate foreign interference. Mr. Fuller, the governor of Massachusetts, has supplied us with a striking example on that subject."

### MEXICO, PRE-LINDBERGH ERA

Mexico City was the capital of anti-Americanism of the Western Hemisphere. Frequently the tension between the two countries led to talk of war, and how close we came to marching across the Rio Grande in 1927 was not revealed until Congressmen became indiscreet two years later.

Back in 1919, Mexican editors united in an appeal to American editors to keep the nation out of war. An American consul named Jenkins had been kidnaped by bandits, then released on payment of one hundred and fifty thousand dollars; he was arrested by Mexican authorities, charged with "conniving with the outlaws who carried him off." Bail was fixed at five hundred dollars. The State Department demanded release without bail. Immediately the interventionists began a campaign for the long-awaited war with Mexico. Senator Fall asked that recognition of the Carranza Government be withdrawn. He claimed he had evidence of a grand conspiracy, and in December announced that Carranza and the International Workers of the World had plotted to restore Texas to Mexico. In 1920, Senator Fall openly preached war.

Elias Plutarco Calles was elected president in 1924. He went on a trip to Europe (which the interventionists, who charged him with being a Bolshevik, said was a trip to Moscow), and returning from Berlin and Paris, was given a dinner by Lamont, Gary, Otto Kahn and other bankers, whom he addressed as "Gentlemen Capitalists of North America." He told them Mexico had seen its last revolution and days of peace and prosperity were in sight. Calles took his oath in November.

In 1926, trouble arose between Mexico and the United States when President Calles began putting into operation the 1917 Carranza constitutional decree that the subsoil belonged to the government and public, not to private corporations. The subsoil contained all the oil and mineral wealth of the republic. In February the Spanish priests were ordered deported. At this moment the religious and the oil interests in the United States joined in another movement for military intervention.

In July, four hundred years after stout Cortez brought Christianity by the sword into Mexico, Christianity was driven from the churches by the bayonet.

On November 16, Assistant Secretary of State Olds prevailed upon the Associated Press to flood the newspapers of America with a "mischievous, sensational and altogether irresponsible report, for which Mr. Olds himself admitted privately he had no proof, to the effect that Mexican Bolshevism was reaching down through Nicaragua to threaten American defenses of the Panama Canal." The Associated Press spoke of "the specter of Bolshevism fostered by Mexico . . . a picture of Bolshevism rampant in

Latin America, menacing the safety of the key to American national defense." The United Press and the Hearst Service, the latter always favorable to intervention, refused to oblige Mr. Olds unless he gave them proofs and was willing to assume responsibility. The *World* commented, "The State Department is stooping to deception and intrigue; the Associated Press has permitted itself to be used as a semi-official news agency, with all of the loss of independence and integrity which that policy involves." Paul Anderson of the St. Louis *Post Dispatch* exposed Mr. Olds.

In December, although the State Department's propaganda had been discounted, a state of mind for war existed on both sides. Mexico insisted that all Americans owning oil and mineral leases exchange them before January 1, 1927, for a fifty-year concession; American corporations insisted on intervention to protect their properties.

The Catholic Revolt broke out with the New Year. Archbishop Ruiz y Flores was arrested. General Arteaga became military revolt leader in Oaxaca. Five States rebelled and six more prepared to follow. Secretary of State Kellogg returned to the attack, issuing a pamphlet "Bolshevist Aims in Mexico and Latin America." Mme. Kollontay, Soviet Ambassador to Mexico, denied the charges, cabling, "There exist no official documents of any of the state bodies of the Soviet Union which prove Bolshevist activities of the Soviet Union in Mexico or Latin America as stated by Mr. Kellogg. Mr. Kellogg's quotations were taken from speeches or resolutions adopted by the Comintern or the Red Trade Unions' congress. . . . Holding so high and venerable a position as Secretary of Foreign Affairs, Mr. Kellogg must know the difference."

What was behind all these notes, pamphlets, charges of Bolshevism and the stirring up of religious questions? In 1927, certain powerful interests in the United States decided upon the invasion of Mexico. Powerful newspapers prepared the campaign. Many factors favored the moment. This was to be no idle repetition of the Pershing chase after Pancho Villa in 1914, but a more serious march than General Scott's in 1847. With this difference: the United States was not to annex territory, but it was to secure the political and economic power in the southern republic and administer it.

Oil interests, mining interests, banking interests, were united with numerous politicians, numerous church interests, influential newspapers, to prepare the American people for a righteous war. This surely was to be a justifiable shedding of blood. Certainly every young American whose body was torn and smashed and left to rot in the tropical sun would be honored as a useful sacrifice. We had the strongest battalions and we were justified in using them in crushing people who represented all that was wrong. The interventionist press howled for bloody justice.

The American embassy, as in almost all the years following the death of Diaz until the advent of Dwight W. Morrow, was an imposing center of hatred. Whenever American preachers, journalists, investigators expressed themselves for friendship and reconciliation, they were denounced by our undiplomatic diplomats as "liars", "skunks" and "traitors", and the term "good-willers", until the day Morrow used it with sincerity, was a term of superior contempt.

Nor were the Mexicans inclined to be friendly. For almost two decades they had been taught to distrust the concession-seeking "Yanqui" and they never could forgive the assassination of President Madero nor forget that the conspirators met in the American embassy and discussed the *coup d'état* with the ambassadorial family. Diaz, liberator and idealist, in the years of his "*científico*" rule, had robbed the Mexican people of a great part of the natural wealth of the nation; oil, copper, silver, rich plantations, had been stolen and sold to exploiters who had fomented revolutions, organized small private armies at times, intrigued throughout the country and kept up an insistent propaganda for American intervention. Years of hatred, distrust, violence and the fear of an inevitable war, were the result.

Into these tense days of 1927 stepped a slick, short, sly little man named Miquel Avila, who carried credentials from an officer in the intelligence (*i.e.*, espionage) department of one of the Texas wartime training camps. He had any number of documents for sale which would help on the conflict. Would any prospective buyer care to see a sample?

But, most important of all, he, Avila, had documents to prove that Calles had in his pay a number of American Senators (need one explain they were practically all the liberals and progressives?) who were receiving large sums and selling out to Mexico. And if any one doubted the authenticity of his documents, let them accompany Signor Avila to the American embassy or the American consulate where, he claimed, the diplomatic officials would vouch for him and where, he said, the documents were kept in the diplomatic safes. (These documents were eventually sold to the representative of William Randolph Hearst, who, in presenting them at a Congressional investigation, declared they were not for the purpose of besmirching the Senators named, but for the purpose of cleaning up, once and for all, a very ugly secret situation.)

April 29, the United States mobilized the largest concentration of aircraft since the World War for "maneuvers" in Texas.

Canny American editors, informed that war was imminent, sent their trained war correspondents to the border.

But forces began working against intervention. Representative Huddleston of Alabama defied the Administration, saying it was "deliberately and consciously driving toward war in Mexico to protect American business interests. I am not willing a single American boy shall be sent to Mexico to lose his life in order that the oil interests may pay dividends." American labor protested war or intervention. The liberal press tried to summon public opinion against uesless bloodshed. Carleton Beals in the *New Republic* asked "Whose property is Kellogg protecting" and answered, that of H. L. Doheny, "the one, one hundred per cent. lawless operator in Mexico", the only man whose titles are under fire. "Hands off Mexico" demonstrations were held in large cities.

It soon became apparent we were still too close to the 1918 bloodshed to engage in war in 1927; instead, Morrow of the House of Morgan, "depository of half a billion dollars of Mexican bonds", was named ambassador with a mandate to restore peace and if possible replace the accumulated hatred of generations with a little friendship. Mr. Morrow was able to bring peace. Friendship was brought by Lindbergh.

### THE ANGEL OF GOOD WILL

On the eighth of May, 1927, Nungesser and Coli took off for America and two days later were given up as lost. France was in national mourning. From New York came reports that Byrd, Chamberlin and a lone lad known as "Slim" or "Lucky" Lindbergh, also as "the flying fool", were preparing to fly to Paris. A few months earlier Paris had witnessed the hooting and stoning of Americans. Ambassador Herrick asked the State Department to see that no American flyer try crossing the Atlantic at this inauspicious time.

"Well, here we are," said Lindbergh, arriving at Le Bourget flying field at 10.21 the evening of May 21. The next day it could be said that the poison of hatred of many years had been counteracted by an antidote which was almost a miracle.

There followed "the greatest one-man-hero-week in history."

"The crowning event in aviation since the invention of the airplane," said cautious Mr. Coolidge. "The greatest sporting event in history of the world," said one newspaper. "The greatest feat of a solitary man in the records of the human race"; "Truly a miracle performed by a mere boy, with the simplicity of action that amounts to genius and takes the imagination of millions by storm"; "Lindbergh has reached the utmost pinnacle of fame"; "A billion lips moved in prayer for him, the heart of the world throbbed"; "Nothing in years has brought world thought and world hope to such unity"; "He has exalted the race of men"; editors wrote. "There was more brotherhood in being than I have ever seen here since the first morning of the Armistice," concluded Heywood Broun.

In the time of the Lindbergh tumult, no one paid any attention to other world events: Europe was in a high state of tension; the soviet ambassador in Warsaw had been assassinated; Hankow was barely saved by fresh troops; overproduction sent oil prices toppling; the Italians backed the Albanians and France backed the Yugoslavs, who almost came to blows; Harry Sinclair was sent to a common jail; United States Marines killed a liberal Nicaraguan general; the House of Commons voted to break diplomatic relations with Russia; the Pope launched his second crusade against immodest dress, and Canada barred booze for casual visitors.

Mr. Lindbergh went to Bruxelles, where King Albert called him "envoy to our hearts" and to London, then back to Paris, and by ship to America. It took one hundred and ten trucks and two thousand "white wings" at a cost of sixteen thousand dollars to clear the streets of the eighteen hundred tons of paper which marked Broadway's frenzied welcome, "the greatest spontaneous outburst of a nation for a returning hero."

Mr. Lindbergh had pacified Europe. Now Mr. Morrow had had considerable success in Mexico. In presenting his credentials he made a simple two hundred word speech, by which he put the United States and Mexico on an equal status, saying he hoped the nations would adjust their difficulties as "two sovereign and independent States." President Calles replied by expelling all communist agitators. The soviet embassy was invaded and Mme. Kollontay detained. To her protest, Calles had a diplomatic official charge her with aligning European public opinion against Mexico!

December 10, the Mexican Supreme Court sustained an American oil company against the government. That day American editors declared that "the spectre of war has been laid." On the sixteenth Lindbergh won the heart of Mexico.

Ambassador Morrow, Will Rogers and Colonel Lindbergh were called the ambassadors of good will; Lindbergh was called an angel of peace. It was just eleven months from the day Secretary Kellogg, before a committee of the Senate, charged Bolshevist Mexico with threatening the peace of the United States. Lindbergh continued his flight to Central America and came home again. He made nations into friends. In Europe and America he had done more for international good will than any one could imagine possible by a human being.

## Interlude 1928

January 16, Trotsky exiled.

The world reform wave hit Afghanistan. Amanullah and Souriya went visiting Europe, saw parliaments functioning, women without veils, munitions makers growing rich and other benefits of civilization. The British built a tent village resembling an Afghanistan village and smashed it with airplane bombardment. Amanullah ordered a dozen airplanes. The French showed him the light tank in action. Amanullah ordered tanks. The Russians gave Souriya an emerald necklace from the Tsar's old stock. Amanullah told the Russians he was on their side.

Returning to Kabul, the Emir ordered up a parliament; the deputies at the gates were forced to shed turbans, beautiful embroidered flowing robes, magnificent colored sashes, gay curved scimitars, and buy top hats, striped pants, frock coats, — all made by the new factory, operated by Amanullah. Revolution impended.

"Our country," stated Mr. Hoover, "has deliberately undertaken a great social and economic experiment, noble in motive and far-reaching in purpose." He meant prohibition.

Dreiser, returning from Russia: "It is known that I am an incorrigible individualist, therefore opposed to Communism."

A foretaste of the next war. Leaky phosgene tank, destined for Russia, exploded in Hamburg factory. Colorless, odorless, heavier than air, the gas clung to the floor and ground, blighting plants, animals and men and killing them. Faint breezes lifted the unseen terror into the streets and fields. Crops shriveled. Men fell down panting for breath and died in convulsions.

Bruce Lockwood reported Peru felt libeled by Thornton

Wilder's "Bridge of San Luis Rey"; the book went into its second hundred thousand.

Gustav Hartmann, "Iron Gustav," the German Lindbergh, in his one-horse cab, rode into Paris from Berlin and Parisians shouted, "The war is over, the ambassador of good will is here."

Citroën put his advertisement on the Eiffel Tower. Blindfold tests for American smokers.

Gandhi thought "Mother India" "without doubt untruthful, be the facts stated ever so truthful."

Eight lawyers in Paris accused of bribery to obtain American divorces.

The *English Review* sums up America as "Puritanism, Provincialism and Pruriency." Publisher Cape withdraws "The Well of Loneliness." Lord Birkenhead rules "Morality is still based on family life; trial marriage is a disgusting perversion of human emotions, suitable only for a monkey house supervised by eugenists."

"To conform to a desire expressed by Signor Mussolini, all Italian male adults must wear straw hats from April 1 to September 30", and thereby save the straw-hat industry.

November 4: Rothstein, gangster, gambler, narcotic dealer, shot in hotel.

"The rumbles of revolution are shaking the foundations of Red Russia", dispatches reaching here (Paris) from Moscow clearly disclose. Rebellion impends in the Ukraine. Stalin is reported overthrown.

Armistice Day. Tenth Anniversary:

Liner *Vestris* lost at sea.
Etna eruption abating.
Wall Street's biggest day; 5,917,000 shares.
M. Poincaré at helm again.
President-elect Hoover to visit Argentina.
Sigrid Undset wins Nobel Prize.
Dorothy Thompson accuses Dreiser of plagiarism.

In December, civil war broke out in Afghanistan and the Soviets blamed busy Colonel Lawrence. Emilio Portes Gil elected president of Mexico, a unique post for a civilian. Under the new Fascist morality campaign, two couples were arrested for kissing in the moonlight.

## CHAPTER FOURTEEN

## The Golden Age

If the war-time promises of the politicians had been so much bunkum, if the world's great age did not begin in 1919, the golden years did return in the second half of the Decade of the Twenties, and heaven smiled while men grew rich.

France stabilized her franc suddenly on the morning of June 24, 1928, and began quietly accumulating some eighty billion francs in gold, while her statesmen and her press told the people at home she was so miserably poor she hadn't a cent in the world with which to keep up her army of security, let alone pay any pre-war, pendent-war or post-war debts. France became in almost incredible time the richest nation in the world, probably the richest nation in the history of the world, measuring the amount of gold to population.

Germany paid her Dawes installments, whining and protesting, but although this time the tears were real, no one believed her.

Italy, where the master showman of the world, Mussolini, juggled the budget of State and municipalities so that every economist was puzzled — although not one believed the budget was balanced — was able to borrow so many billions of lire from the too-rich American international bankers that she too made the world think her prosperous. South American dictators did likewise. Mexico dropped most of her radico-socialistic adventures and did big business.

The machine age rushed forward on greased wheels — forward to the salvation of mankind or its destruction. No one knew, questioned, or cared. And culture? Culture, said Mæcenas Otto

Kahn, subsidizer of operas and playwrights, flowers from American prosperity.

The fiscal year 1925–1926, according to the annual report of Secretary of Commerce Hoover, "has been one never surpassed in our history in the volume of production and consumption, in the physical quantity of exports and imports, and in the rate of wages. There has been practically no unemployment. . . . The country was able to maintain the highest standard of living in its history, a standard far above that in most other countries of the world at this or any other time. This represents a remarkable recovery from the great losses incurred by the Nation in the World War."

America boasted 11,000 millionaires, one for every 10,450 citizens. Seventy-four persons acknowledged a net income above a million dollars for 1924; fifteen admitted between two and three million dollars and three persons divided $27,955,319 between them, according to research by Joseph McCoy of the Treasury Department.

The barometer of Europe was the Dawes Plan. Dictator Gilbert reported his annual optimism. Germany had fulfilled. The second annuity year payment of $290,500,000 had been made, said Gilbert, out of export surplus. He deplored the fact Germany had borrowed a greater sum. The Germans did not agree with Gilbert. Unemployment was increasing in 1926, doles were increasing, the steel output was diminishing. The great recovery previously noted had proved false. Coal, it is true, was booming, but that was on account of the British strike. German views expressed at the time were: "the roseate expectation of Germany's quick economic recovery has proved to be utterly groundless and fantastic. . . . Germany's surplus of two and a half billion gold marks of exports over imports annually cannot be attained in the coming years . . . since May the trade balance has been a deficit . . . the only way to meet the payments will be through foreign credits . . . the Allies are continuing a policy of prohibitive customs duties, making exportation more difficult. . . . England and America are asking Germany to sell abroad and resenting Germany's progress in foreign markets." The socialist paper *Vorwaerts* declared that only a complete collapse of Germany would convince the Allies that the Dawes Plan is impracticable.

But all such German statements were received with suspicion. Germany had grown accustomed to self-pity; her propaganda had ceased and she was in large measure being freed in the minds of the public if not in legal phrases of governments, of the war guilt; but when it came to money matters, no one could as yet trust the ancient enemy.

In 1927, Gilbert reported that Germany must check its extravagance, its overspending, its overborrowing abroad. Americans had already invested three billion dollars in Germany. In 1924, she had made thirty loans, totaling between five and seven billion dollars, mostly from the United States, Britain and Holland. Money borrowed abroad was paid abroad under the Dawes Plan when surplus from export trade failed. The Germans who said the thing could not be done, that tariffs were making exports more difficult, and that borrowing to meet payments meant complete ruin eventually, were absolutely in the right. Mr. Gilbert could not say that plainly. Mr. Keynes did. "The Dawes Plan will break down according to schedule," he wrote in 1927. No one had listened to him in 1919; now his prediction was accepted by many.

At the time Lindbergh was oiling up his machine, the greatest stock crash since the war occurred in Germany, — "Black Friday", comparable only to a similar day in Wall Street in 1869.

In Latin-American countries the banner of boycott for American goods was raised and resolutions passed against accepting more loans from the United States, which would be protected later by the marines. Secretary Hoover proposed cessation of loans abroad except for productive purposes. Thomas Lamont, who had floated Italian and other loans for years, made the statement, "A warning needs to be given against indiscriminate lending." The first sour note was sounded by Colonel Leonard P. Ayres: "Our prosperity is showing signs of fatigue." There was a sharp slump on the American market after Mr. Coolidge, in Rapid City, South Dakota, on August 2, handed out the little typewritten slips of eleven words, "I do not choose to run for President in Nineteen Twenty-eight", but a recovery followed almost immediately, and in November Henry Ford produced his new car. "Prosperity's Harbinger." "It has set the revolution back twenty-five years."

Mr. Ford was rated a billionaire. The treasury reports showed one — it must be Ford; there were ten $1,000,000,000 corporations; the number of million-dollar incomes which were 60 in 1914 increased to 207 in 1925; American loans abroad totaled $11,000,000,000 and debts due us $11,763,000,000. In December, President Coolidge issued his glorious:

"Prosperity is here to stay.

"The tariff must be left alone.

"Make any peace pacts that are constitutional."

America was fabulously wealthy. Europe was alarmed, puzzled, enraged.

1928: American prosperity, "far transcending anything we have yet enjoyed", was Schwab's prediction to the American Iron and Steel Institute. Trumpeting through the press were "Durant, Raskob, Baruch, Brush . . . noted financiers, see nation surging forward in great industrial renaissance for long time to come." March was the record month in the history of the Stock Exchange. There were sixteen days of three million shares or more in March and four days of four millions. Seeing by radio, sound by film, the adoption of airplanes by big business, helped thrill the land. The Hoover Bull Market was following the Coolidge Bull Market triumphantly.

Reports of four million unemployed at this gorgeous time were unheeded if believed. Evans Clark, analyzing the situation, said machinery was throwing men out of work. "American prosperity has become an international sensation. American efficiency has become the eighth wonder of the world." President Green of the American Federation of Labor thought "one of the most important problems affecting labor to-day is the displacement of workmen by machines and by the devices which automatically do the work once done by trained men. Organized labor will oppose the turning adrift of men replaced by industry." June 12 was a five million share day — a debacle. But that too was overcome. July 4, Alfred Loewenstein, Belgian international financier, jumped from one of his fleet of airplanes into the English Channel; the stock markets of Europe echoed the fall, but that too was forgotten. The Hoover market became an "orgy of speculation."

Nineteen Twenty-nine dawned with a world war against the new American tariff. Nation after nation protested. Senator Smoot indignantly reported that only twenty-five, not thirty-eight countries had declared their opposition. Most Congressmen were so angry with this interference from foreigners they proposed making duties even higher. Europe had no more business interfering with our legislation than with our law courts.

Fear and hate produced, in many minds, an American peril, as it had in other times a Yellow Peril, the danger of German Imperialism, the Bolshevik Terror. Wall Street was buying up the world!

Germany, which had paid $416,500,000 and was now paying $595,000,000 a year (until Judgment Day, if the French had their way) was declared sound and fit by the Gilbert report. "There can be no reasonable doubt of the capacity of the German to pay its part of the normal contributions laid down by the (Dawes) Plan." The Germans thought they were "again betrayed by the Americans."

On March 19, Sir George Paish of the National Free Trade Conference issued a warning: "We are threatened with the gravest financial crisis that the world has ever known. Because the governments of the world have followed a policy of trade restrictions, thus preventing debtors from paying their debts, we are face to face with this crisis. Nothing can be done now to prevent a financial crash. Those who have loaned money cannot recover it. The question we now have to face is how to get out of the crisis when it comes."

The week of March 25 brought foretaste of panic. A sensational squeeze in the money market caused the Federal Reserve to warn the country to go slow. Washington correspondents wrote, "members of the Federal Reserve Bank declare they can see no ground for the Paish declaration; they do not expect a crash in this country, at any rate."

March 26, 8,246,740 shares were traded.

May 27, stocks crashed to the year's lowest; losses were two billion dollars. That day Lindbergh and Anne Morrow were reported in a "surprise" wedding; Rosika Schwimmer was barred from American citizenship; King Victor Emmanuel signed the Vatican pact; Germany offered a new plan for paying old debts and the *Dial,* for almost a decade the brightest flower of the American Intelligentsia, suspended publication.

The world which hooted Sir George Paish might have listened to an American Cassandra. Early in September Roger W. Babson said, "Sooner or later a crash is coming and it may be terrific", but the same day Professor Fisher expressed himself, "Stock prices are not too high and Wall Street will not experience anything in the nature of a crash"; every one was a Bull and every one preferred Fisher.

On September 20, one Clarence C. Hatry was suspended from the Stock Exchange in London and was arrested. He was a fairly important promotor, his failure involving thirty million dollars, not an extravagant sum, but his case was like the call of "Fire" in a crowded theater — it scared the mob. The next day a serious panic occurred in Berlin. Bear raids in New York resulted in a loss of two billion dollars, which rose to five billion by October 3. On the fourth the street was swamped by frenzied selling but on the fifth the bears were routed and the entire loss of five billions made up.

The press obtained on the twenty-second and published the next morning the opinion of Charles E. Mitchell, Chairman of the National City Bank, and other financiers, that the market was sound.

Wednesday the twenty-third the worst crash in history occurred. In a few hours the gains of the year 1929 were gone. One stock (Adams Express) broke ninety-six points. Thousands of small traders were left penniless.

It was a hysterical cyclone which had hit the market, a psychological riot, not an economic reaction.

At 1.30 P.M. that Thursday, Richard Whitney, a Morgan broker, walked dignifiedly to the United States Steel post and shouted, "205 for 25,000 Steel." The previous bids had been 190. It was an act of heroism comparable to Lindbergh's. For the day it saved the market.

On the twenty-fifth President Hoover issued a famous statement saying the country was fundamentally sound. The press announced "Bankers' Pool Halts Panic." The same day Thomas Wolfe published one of the most important contributions to literature of the American century, a novel called "Look Homeward, Angel"; Fall was finally convicted for taking a hundred thousand dollar bribe; one-year conscription began in France; the Fascisti celebrated their seventh anniversary; the American Federation of Labor was in difficulties, trying to organize the South; sympathizers with the Gastonia strikers rioted at the American embassy in London.

On the twenty-ninth the extent of the panic was measured by the world's record in selling: 16,388,700 shares changed hands, resulting in a total loss since the first serious bear raids of September 3 of no less than fifty billion dollars, or five times the amount the Allies still owed us for debts incurred in the World War.

Radio rallied the market. Julius Klein, Assistant Secretary of Commerce, broadcasted, "Regardless of regrettable speculative uncertainties, the industrial and commercial structure of the nation is sound." John D. Rockefeller the next day issued the consoling statement, "Believing that the fundamental conditions of the country are sound, and that there is nothing in the business situation to warrant the destruction of values that has taken place on the Exchange during the past week, my son and I have for some days been purchasing sound common stocks. We are continuing. . . ."

The small fry rushed back to the market. Europe cabled one word to New York: "BUY."

America called it a Prosperity Panic. Past panics had been due to something fundamentally wrong with finance, business, crops, or to earthquakes, international relations, wars, money rates, inflated inventories — but, the country being sound, this prosperity panic of 1929 was "purely speculative, all authorities agree."

It was the "greatest deflation in the world's history", "a psychological break rather than a disaster." Bankers, economists, business executives, and politicians rushed in to mend the break. The press agreed, "There is nothing in the general situation to suggest more than a slight retardation of activity." The President soon realized that something was fundamentally wrong. In November he enlisted the forty-eight governors of the United States in an eight billion dollar prosperity restoration plan.

Between twelve and fifteen million Americans had speculated and most of them had lost; at least one million persons were ruined either financially or romantically; those who had not lost their shirts had lost their dreams. The Golden Age had been and gone and would never come again. It was a great awakening. America was chastened as by a national disaster, such as defeat in a great war. Europeans decided to speculate at home. But a tremendous amount of optimism still remained. The country, the world, the economic system, were fundamentally sound. The millions of unemployed were dismissed as seasonal or far away. There were no bread lines in the big cities. Good Times would come again. There was no pessimism. America faced the Nineteen Thirties with all confidence.

### THE AGE OF GOLDEN BUNKUM

The Nineteen Twenties saw advertising become one of the great industries of America. In the opinion of President Coolidge (addressing the American Association of Advertising Agencies in October, 1926) our country had become supreme industrially largely because of advertising.

With advertising came bunkum and propaganda. Everything was a "racket", from rum-running and professional, paid murdering to fake psychoanalysis. Bunkum and propaganda made heroes out of Ivar Kreuger, and Queen Marie and Mussolini and prize fighters; they also helped destroy the work of the League of Nations and increased the orders of the munitions makers and the super-patriotic ardor for new wars.

In 1929 it was disclosed, by Congressional investigation, that a munitions makers' lobby had been active during the disarmament conference in Geneva in 1927 — one of the many conferences which had failed. William B. Shearer, who called himself "American, Christian, Protestant, Nationalist", modestly claimed that he had defeated pacifism and disarmament by publicity and propaganda.

He had brought suit against the Bethlehem Shipbuilding Corporation, the Newport News Shipbuilding Company and the American Brown Boveri Corporation, claiming he had been paid $51,230 for Big Navy propaganda work and claiming $255,655 due to him.

President Hoover, calling an investigation on September 6, 1929, said, "I do not believe that the responsible directors of these shipbuilding corporations have been a part of these transactions as represented in this lawsuit, but their statement of the case is needed. . . ."

Lord Robert Cecil confirmed the view that the munitions lobby, which had British, French and German agents at

Geneva, had helped to wreck the 1927 conference. "The United States," he said, "is not the only country to have its Shearers, its armament interests, and its professional patriots. I am acquainted with the activities of Shearer and can testify that he exerted himself to the utmost to make the agreements difficult."

The investigation proved that at least a hundred propaganda agents and lobbies existed in Washington, some favoring more wars, some favoring peace; some were religious, others anti-religious, some foreign, others native. The American Legion went on record with a demand that the National Council for the Prevention of War, the Federal Council of the Churches in Christ, the American Civil Liberties Union, the League for Industrial Democracy, the National Students' Forum and other organizations opposed to new wars be investigated.

Propaganda, bunkum and ballyhoo also featured the royal visit to America in 1926 of Marie, the Queen of Rumania. She had a reputation as a great beauty; she was faded. She had published books. One, a novel, was tenth-rate and had been published at the author's expense; another, a volume of poems, contained not only a dozen plagiarized ones but several stolen and left unchanged. Her reign had been marked by complete defeat in war followed by the seizure of Hungarian and Russian territory now held by terrorism. She had intrigued in every royal family on the Continent. The only brave thing she had ever done in her life had been to defy the conventions of the world and seek love outside the marital bonds, and children born of love. But this was the one thing the world did not honor her for. It honored her for everything that was false.

Strong, silent, honorable President Coolidge did not stoop to kiss the royal fingers, but gave her a cautious Vermont handshake instead. The trip from the Battery to California was noisy with the undying firing of motion-picture cameras. Marie asked for American soap. "I want to use everything American while I am in America," she said to fifty million newspaper readers, who were given a day or two later the name of the soap she preferred. She was paid well for preferring.

To the first report that King Ferdinand had recalled the Queen for ridiculous actions which were injuring the dynasty, the Rumanian Chargé d'Affaires, Radu Djuvara, affirmed Marie had laughed and said "It is ridiculous, Bolshevik propaganda." But her visit was shortened and she soon returned to Bucharest.

Marie's activities in America as paid endorser of cosmetics had served to call attention to that remunerative racket. America was spending annually thirty-four million dollars for creams and rouges, twenty-five million dollars for dentifrices, twenty-one million dollars for talcum and other powders, twenty million dollars for perfumes and nine million dollars for hair tonics. The beauty business had grown to one billion, eight hundred million annually, thanks to bunkum and advertising. And the good old days of 1906, when *Collier's* showed up the fraud in patent medicines, were gone.

The advertisers raided the storehouse of psychology. They capitalized fear to the extent of a hundred million dollars. They intimidated millions of Americans, telling them they probably suffered from body odors, pyorrhea, athlete's foot, bad manners, halitosis, mispronunciation, abysmal ignorance and loss of memory.

The world capital of bunkum, advertising and snobbery was in Hollywood, that "Mecca for every sort of faker, near artist, spellbinder, downright charlatan and self-advertising nobody." "Hollywood," wrote Robert Nichols in the London *Times*, "hotbed of press agents and boosters, well aware that most of them are paid out of her own pocket, guilelessly takes their utterances at face value, attributes to herself and her tastes, crazes, fashions, frenzies, disappointments, illusions, disillusions, fretfulness, tantrums, movements, an importance which would cease to be laughable and become exasperating were these manifestations not obviously the product of a temperament almost entirely superficial and a mind patently not only devoid of standards but ignorant of the existence of any such standards in the world (and particularly the artistic world) at large."

### MORALS OF THE GOLDEN AGE

From the Vatican, which surveyed the morals of the whole world, came the report in 1927 of Conte Della Torre, sometimes spokesman for the Pope, and the semi-official press, that the Jazz Age had passed, that waves of immorality were receding everywhere, that more decent clothing was being worn by women (although American dresses that year were at the knee); that indecent dancing was being stopped everywhere, including Turkey; that even Japan had passed laws curbing the social evil; that so-called modern ideas were in retreat; that Belgium and Czechoslovakia had legislated against "immorality posing as art"; that stage censorship had gained in the United States, England and Canada, and that the advocates of easy divorce and birth control were losing ground everywhere.

"The sight was terrifying when the people whose eyes had gradually returned to normal focus saw the moral pit into which they had fallen after the war," concluded the report.

In June anti-evolution laws were defeated in six States in America.

The Russian censorship turned amazing handsprings. It proscribed Plato and Kant as "idealistic philosophers", banned William James' psychology, threw out Carlyle, Ruskin, Tolstoy and Kropotkin's ethical works from all small libraries, tolerating them only in Moscow and Leningrad as outmoded reflections of a dead past; removed all copies of the Gospels, Koran and Talmud, declared Nietzsche not for the generality, excluded Dostoievski as too "mystical."

The new marriage laws came into force in January after six thousand debates, lectures and disputes in towns and villages. There had been approximately eleven divorces per ten thousand population previously and a great number of unregistered marriages. The new law established registration "in the interests of the state and public, with the object of facilitating the protection of the personal and property rights and interests of the spouses and children." Recognition was extended common-law wives who could claim support and property. The marriage age of women was raised to that of men, eighteen. Persons registering a marriage were obliged to sign a declaration of good health "especially with regard to venereal, mental and tuberculous disease."

Two battles over intolerance in 1928 were fought in Louvain and Washington. Whitney Warren had replaced on the restored balustrade of the university, "Destroyed by German fury; restored by American generosity." The Belgians, however, were not nursing Mr. Warren's anti-German hatred, and Monsignor Ladeuze thought the words might be changed to "*in bella reducta, in pace restituta*." Hoover cabled support to the priest, who consulted the Vatican and apparently received a favorable reply. Warren declared Cardinal Mercier years before had approved his motto and accordingly had "*furore teutonica diruta*" reinserted.

In April the Daughters of the American Revolution were accused of maintaining a black list and a policy "striking at the roots of American freedom and contrary to the first amendment of the Constitution."

William Allen White, credited with laughing the Ku-Klux Klan out of Kansas, confirmed the Daughters of the American Revolution black list of the following organizations: The Young Men's Christian Association, Young Women's Christian Association, National Catholic Welfare Council, National Association for the Advancement of the Colored People, Council of Jewish Women.

In 1929 the Pope affirmed that Protestantism was "getting more and more exhausted . . . its own sterility is inspiring many souls with a nostalgia for Catholicism. . . . Protestantism goes from denial to denial." Scribner's advertised that there is a "campaign of intimidation and threatened boycott against booksellers" dealing in Edwin Dakin's "Mrs. Eddy: The Biography of a Virginal Mind." The June issue of *Scribner's Magazine*, containing a chapter of Hemingway's "Farewell to Arms", was banned in Boston.

The American Civil Liberties Union summed up the year as disclosing more police interference in labor meetings as unemployment and discontent increased, less lynchings than any period in fifty years.

In April, "An American Tragedy", Theodore Dreiser's popular success, which crowned thirty-five years of economic uncertainty, was found guilty of obscenity in Boston, and the Soviet Government banned the manufacture of "matzos", the unleavened bread of Passover.

Mrs. Hoover had Mrs. Oscar De Priest, Negro wife of a Chicago Negro Republican representative in for tea, just as she was having white wives in for tea. "The first Negress to enter the White House by the front door," caused international comment. In La Coupole, on the complaint of American drinkers, the garçons threw a Negro gentleman and his party out. They proved to be Stephane Alexis, Chargé D'Affaires of Haiti and Princess Mansour Daoud, wife of the Crown Prince of Egypt. They protested to the Quai d'Orsay.

In August a religious war between the Jews and Arabs in Jerusalem resulted in one thousand dead. Trouble began at the Wailing Wall and although charged to intolerance, the rioting was proved due largely to economic causes following the buying up of land by the newcomers to Palestine.

In September labor troubles in Gastonia, North Carolina, came to national attention through the murder of Mrs. Ella May Wiggins, mother of five children, who had offended by joining a union. The MacDonald Labor Government, leaning backwards, refused Trotsky asylum or medical aid. The tabloid press attacked Lindbergh for having a private wedding and honeymoon, also attacked Tunney for going to Rome to escape reporters and photographers.

Europe, as a psychological escape for artistic souls, began to attract popular writers. Frank Ward O'Malley, one hundred per cent. American, gave his reasons for going abroad to live: prohibition and barbarous drinking; crime, racketeering, futile efforts; Rotary, pep, progress, and no parking places; reformers and general snoopery; imbecility of public officials; Philistinism in the beaux arts; money-grabbing; the insane hurry over nothing; servant problem; climate.

The language, which has been becoming tougher each year, was enriched by all the words of the underworld.

Europe looked for a word to describe the age. The Romantic Age, the Symbolists, the Parnassians, were dead. This is the age of "biographies in the romantic style, jazz, psychoanalysis, the European spirit and the confusion of the sexes." "Confusionism" was suggested. Mme. Catulle-Mendes proposed "Mondialism."

The editor of the *Revue Mondial* thought ours should be called the Nameless Epoch — "doubtless a tumultuous age in which all forces clash before gaining their equilibrium — an age of disorder, in which every one makes a show of his violence — an age, on the whole, of transition, without doctrines or rules, an uncertain foreshadowing of a dawn which will soon be lost in the full light of the day."

## Interlude 1929

February 13: Lindbergh engaged to Anne Morrow.
Rome hails Pope and King over Vatican accord.
Young opposes plea Germany cannot pay.
Van Ryn smashes Bill Tilden, 6–1, 6–4, 6–2.
Lily Langtry dead.
Two judicial reform bills result Sacco-Vanzetti case.
Calf's liver found anæmia cure.
Flagpole-sitter's mania.

"Glad to see you," said the warden, shaking hands with prisoner Number 10,520, Mr. Harry F. Sinclair, who will visit for ninety days.

Washington debated the seating of Mrs. Gann, sister of the Vice President, of semi-Indian ancestry.

"Zur Einheitlichen Feldtheorie", or "On a United Field Theory", by Einstein, would prove that the forces of electricity and magnetism are the same as those of gravitation, "to give uniform significance to the field of gravitation and the electromagnetic field."

Lynching results: 1926, 30; 1927, 16; 1928, 10.

Foch, dying, said "*Allons-y*" in reply to the question, "Are you ready to go back to bed?" "Let's go," Foch's Last Words, American headlines.

Valentine Day. Two men dressed in civilian clothes lined up seven of Al Capone's enemies, the O'Banions, and shot them to death with a machine gun. Three gangsters dressed as policemen "arrested" the two civilians and all five disappeared.

Ernest Lissauer, who wrote the only great war song of hate,

"We have one foe, and one alone, ENGLAND", pleads he was and is a pacifist; his motto is "*Nie Wieder Krieg*"; he wrote the hate poem when he read that Britain had stopped hospital supplies for Germany; he left it in a café; he did not want it published, but it went around the world and helped all nations capitalize hatred.

June 7: Pope becomes ruler of world's smallest State.
Young plan signed by delegates in Paris.
Mail-order houses offer plane for $975.

Progress: Distilling apparatus seized in 1920: 15,416; 1927, 208,073. Liquor seized, spirits, gallons, 1920: 109,370; 1927, 1,462,532.

Amanullah fled from Kabul in January, after tying up all the gold pieces of the palace in bags. Inyatullah, his elder brother, reigned three days. Habibullah, the water boy, bandit, jailbird, general, king, ruled ten months. Nadir Kahn used a hidden radio while his brother Shah Wali marched with his tribesmen into Kabul.

First notice of the five-year-plan in Russia:
Stalin fights Kulaks under five-year-plan.
*Kolkhoz* or collective farms established.
*Sovkoz* or soviet farms for poorer peasants.
*Kulaki* riot, murder, burn grain, rather than pay taxes.

Anti-soviet press reports seventy-five executions taking place daily of rich peasants, or *kulaki,* most of whom are accused of organizing an anti-soviet movement.

Professor Harmon O. De Graff was dismissed and Professor Max F. Meyer suspended for sending a sex-questionnaire to students of University of Missouri. It asked students to give their views about sexual relations, pre-marital and extra-marital and to state whether sex desires are curbed by religious belief, fears, pride, or other inhibitions. They were also told to speak out on alimony, divorce, compatibility. A startling question was, "If after marriage you were to find that your wife was unfaithful to you, would you terminate your relations with her?"

and "Would you break your engagement if you suddenly learned that the man had indulged in illicit sexual relations?"

The professors were charged with circulating a questionnaire which tended to make the students sexually immoral, which shocked the students, especially women, etc.

The committee of investigation reported that the students were neither shocked nor insulted. "There is no evidence that the questionnaire led to sexual immorality or to decreased self-control in the matter of sex behavior." Times had changed.

Armistice Day 1929: Reverend Doctor Harry Emerson Fosdick:

The militarists have long had a monopoly on patriotism. They can hold it no longer. *The peacemakers are now the Patriots* and that change is one of the most crucial in history.

# PART FOUR: OUR TERRIBLE THIRTIES

## CHAPTER FIFTEEN

### A Chronicle of World Disaster

EVENTS in Wall Street which removed fifty billion dollars' worth of castles in Spain, and bread and butter in America, were at first applauded as a sign of financial health, retributive economic justice, a good lesson for lambs and idlers. The word depression was hardly mentioned, no one thought of panic, and to question the soundness of the economic-capitalist system was absurd. To the presidential dictum of December, 1929, on the reëstablishment of confidence, came the March 7, 1930, announcement that "all evidence indicates that the worst effects of the crash and unemployment will have passed away during the next thirty days", and the December sequel, "We have already weathered the worst of the storm."

One of the few men who did question the basis, the fundamental groundwork and the structure of the system, was not a radical enemy but a foundation stone or pillar or wall of capitalism itself. At a luncheon which Mr. Lamont gave to America's leading financiers, Owen D. Young expressed doubt and issued a warning. Mr. Lamont having enforced his rule of "no direct quotations", the views of Mr. Young must be summed up as follows:

The nations of the world must coöperate if the capitalist basis is to survive.

If the capitalist machine is good, it has a right to continue; if it meets the needs of the world, its existence is justified.

But to-day the world's capitalist system is inadequate in international relations; it lacks coöperation; the world's business machinery is faulty.

If the machinery is improved, it will bring happiness to the world and end the fear of Moscow.

You can't make a turbine engine in a blacksmith's shop; the present system of international business is hopelessly bad and nothing is so bad as a bad machine.

A good machine for international banking on a big scale is necessary. It would carry out the reparations payments without upsetting world economy.

Owing to competition, nations are fighting one another instead of working together for the advancement of civilization.

When the panic came, there were of course others besides Sir George Paish who could and did say "I told you so." Some of them had been saying so for two or three, perhaps four years, and one can well understand their being regarded as infantile Cassandras when in the teeth of their dire predictions the stock rose, in a day, three to ten points.

In 1925, the very day Ford, predicting a century of prosperity, said, "Times are good and will be even better", the French industrialist Loucheur proposed that the League of Nations call an economic conference to discuss the world pooling its resources, its raw materials, and coöperate in their manufacture, "so as to bring a certain equilibrium between the great activities of production and consumption", the present inequality being a menace for the future. But the most remarkable prediction was made by Red Trotsky. He proclaimed the "slow economic strangulation of Europe" and a social, economic revolution along orthodox Marxian lines. . . . American finance and industry, he thought, would collapse "before forces of their own creation . . . overproduction of oil and steel particularly", which would be fighting for world supremacy. In 1928, Trotsky elaborated:

"We cannot help but believe that a crisis will follow the present world swing of American capitalism, and that this crisis may be both deep and acute. But to assume that this approaching crisis will result in a weakening of the North American hegemony would be altogether foolish and could lead only to the grossest errors in political strategy. Exactly the opposite will occur; in a time of crisis, the hegemony of the United States will prove more complete, more brutal, more merciless than in a time of upward swing. The United States will conquer her difficulties at the expense of Europe."

The second half of the prophecy has yet to be fulfilled. In 1931, the question of the success or failure of the capitalist system was posed by Otto H. Kahn who, "far from thinking that capitalist society can afford to indulge in complacent self-satisfaction", believed that "the world economic collapse was not traceable to capitalism."

Early in the spring of 1931 the governor of the Bank of England (Montagu Norman) wrote to M. Moret, governor of the Bank of France: "Unless drastic measures are taken to save it, the capitalist system throughout the civilized world will be wrecked within a year. I should like this prediction to be filed for future reference." (The year has passed, no drastic measures have been taken, the reference is still on file.)

Hjalmar Schacht, president of the German Reichsbank during the crisis which led to the Young Plan, published in 1931 "The End of Reparations", in which he said pessimistically: "World trade has been receding ever since the Young conference. Some fifteen million unemployed are feeding on the financial and economic reserves of the industrial countries. . . . Never was the incapacity of the economic leaders of the capitalist world so glaringly demonstrated as to-day. . . . A capitalism which cannot feed the workers of the world has no right to exist. The guilt of the capitalist system lies in its alliance with the violent policies of imperialism and militarism. . . . The ruling classes of the world to-day have as completely failed in political leadership as in economic."

If the President of the United States had any doubts or even thoughts on the subject worrying Messrs. Young, Trotsky, Norman, Kahn and Schacht, he did not express them publicly, but went on with his own plans of overcoming great troubles.

He allowed it to be known indirectly he was against high

tariff, but he did not stop the sponsors who were drawing up a prohibitive measure. June 17, 1930, he signed the Smoot-Hawley Bill with a flourish of six gold fountain pens. "The worst example of fiscal folly the world has ever seen," said Britons; the Swiss proclaimed a boycott because their third greatest industry (tourists first, cheese second), watchmaking, would be ruined; in Paris, the howl over the certain loss in the lace trade was heard in the boulevard insults to Americans in tourist wagons; in Italy, German drummers picked up American trade; the French Minister of Commerce, Flandin, called the tariff bill stupid, injurious, beyond the limit of endurance, and proposed a European economic union against the United States. Briand proposed Pan-Europa. Mussolini raised the duty on automobiles one hundred per cent. so that the cheapest Ford cost eight hundred dollars.

"Business," said Mr. Ford, "will get better but we won't know it when it does. A sick man either dies or gets well. . . . The country's business . . . is in fundamentally healthier condition than it was a year ago." President Hoover thought in May, "While the crash took place only six months ago, I am convinced we have now passed the worst and with continued unity of effort we shall rapidly recover." "PROSPERITY IS AROUND THE CORNER" became a headline; later it was to be a joke in a popular song. Towards the end of the year, words of optimistic assurances came from Messrs. Hoover, Schwab, Farrell, Raskob, William Green, Colonel Woods and Will Hays.

The reaction to the Smoot-Hawley tariff was beginning to make itself felt but the politicians refused to notice it. The economists alone were alarmed. The old "to-hell-with-Europe" policy could not be maintained; we could not force the world to buy our goods while we drove theirs back from our tariff-barricaded shores. And we had not apparently found the economic formula for everlasting prosperity. An era of questioning began. What was to blame for the failure of the return of prosperity in its cyclical order? Overproduction? Underconsumption? Gold hoarding by France and America? Accelerated machine industry? Continued wars in Europe and Asia, and the boycotts in China, India, Russia? Was it due to the upsetting of the world's natural industrial equilibrium since the war, to nationalism which was causing every nation to produce its own goods even when economically unprofitable? All these early questions indicated an economic disillusion.

A conservative estimate of Stock Exchange values showed:

| | | Average |
|---|---|---|
| October 1, 1929, listed securities, | $87,073,630,423 | $83.06 |
| October 1, 1930, listed securities, | $60,143,183,105 | $46.84 |

and with the European markets added, there was a total decline of more than one hundred billion dollars.

But there was still humor in America. Al Smith said, "Under a Republican administration it is called a business depression. In a Democratic administration they call it a panic. Somebody the other day called it a cycle. They ought to call it a bicycle, because both Democrats and Republicans are being taken for a ride."

Both Mr. Smith and Mr. Coolidge were writing little pieces for the papers every day. Mr. Smith wrote, "The American people never carry an umbrella. They prepare to walk into eternal sunshine." Mr. Coolidge was more ponderous. Wrote the journalist about the Chief Executive: "The credit for a policy of economy that produces taxes and increased prosperity belongs to the President." Also: "People are out of work because the things they could produce are not being bought."

John D. Rockefeller gave out nickels that year instead of the bright shiny dimes.

But the greatest international joker of all was Dictator Mussolini. Beginning about 1925, the Fascist régime began borrowing huge sums from J. P. Morgan and Company, Dillon, Reed and Company and other American bankers, until it had obtained between three and six hundred million dollars. In all those years Mussolini had announced in the great newspapers that his budget had balanced. Astute economists had proved in little weeklies or in monthly magazines that "the greatest financial jugglery in the history of any nation in modern times" was going on in Italy, that the budgets were far from balanced, that the Fascist régime was facing bankruptcy. In 1927, two years before the American panic, all statistics officially issued in Italy proved that there were nothing but carefully concealed deficits. These grew into billions. But Mussolini did not dare admit financial failure. To him the Wall Street crash came as a political godsend. "Mussolini," wrote American editors, "has calmed growling Italians with the information that Wall Street is responsible for their lower salaries, their unemployment, their low returns on farm products. About the only crimes not attributed to Wall Street were the earthquakes of last July."

December 18, 1930, the world's most successful and paragon dictator delivered himself thus: "The situation in Italy was satisfactory until the fall of 1929, when the American market crash exploded suddenly like a bomb. For us poor European provincials it was a great surprise. We remained astonished, like the world at the announcement of the death of Napoleon, because we had been given to understand that America was the country of prosperity, of endless and absolute prosperity, without eclipses. Every one was rich there.

"Suddenly the beautiful scene collapsed and we had a series of black days. Stocks lost, thirty, forty, and fifty per cent. of their value. The crisis grew deeper. Black days followed black days and prosperity was replaced by long lines of unemployed, waiting for soup and bread in the Great American cities. From that day we also were again pushed into the high seas, and from that day navigation has become extremely difficult for us."

The full sweep of the economic tornado was not felt in Europe until 1931. In 1930 the adoption of the Young Plan, on May 9, in fact, had put reparations and war debts on a sound business basis, removing considerable hatred and distrust and opening the way to European recovery. But in May, 1931, the Wiener Kreditanstalt, the main bank of Austria, operated by the Rothschilds and other great financiers, collapsed; although the government took it over to save the nation, it did not prevent the panic from spreading. In the next two months, every German and Austrian who possibly could withdraw his marks and schillings, converted them into Swiss francs, dollars and pounds, hoarding them abroad.

Austria and Germany had tried, in March, to make a settlement which would perhaps solve the economic question for both; they proposed a customs union or the abolition of duties between the two countries, in place of the Anschluss or political union which France and Italy had forbidden. France now howled that the sacred Treaty of Versailles, the treaty of St. Germain, and the League of Nations protocols would be violated. The Vienna press called France "a political blackmailer"; Britain sympathized with Austria, even though it was understood that a customs union would lead to a Teutonic demand for a revision of all treaties. But France won. Moreover, France retaliated by a financial boycott.

The Darmstaedter National Bank, with branches in every big city in Germany, closed its doors and bankruptcy threatened the entire German banking system as a result of French pressure, the flight of capital, and the refusal of foreign capital to extend further credit, after the American stock-market crash. The Reich has been unable to balance its budget since 1925. Heavy reparations obligations had depleted liquid capital. On June 6, Chancellor Bruening and Foreign Minister Curtius visited Premier MacDonald at Chequers. Mr. Mellon happened to be in England at the time. The United States had sunk an enormous sum in Germany since the war and Britain's holdings were second, while France had only one eighth the American investment and most of that in reparations. On June 20, Hoover announced his famous one-year moratorium, explaining: "This course of action is entirely consistent with the policy which we have hitherto pursued. We are not involved in the discussion of strictly European problems, of which the payment of German reparations is one. It represents our willingness to make a contribution to the early restoration of world prosperity in which our own people have so deep an interest."

The United States gave up $246,000,000 and Europe $400,000,000. It was the beginning of the end of reparations. Naturally the French objected. This time they said it violated the Young Plan. The negotiations were prolonged in Paris until July 6, during which time Washington made notable use of the transatlantic telephone. Germany was saved from bankruptcy, the gold standard was saved, America had taken a deep step into foreign affairs.

During the summer the French quietly began withdrawing their gold from England. The $650,000,000 credits extended the Bank of England by American and French banks was near exhaustion. There was a cabinet crisis August, 1931, from which Ramsay MacDonald emerged discredited by labor but head of a nationalist government. The pound sterling went off the gold standard. It dropped to $4.40 from $4.86, went down to $3.45 and recovered in October to $3.92. Reactionary *La Liberté* thought, "A pillar of civilization has fallen and it is Socialism that has brought it down."

The same French financial attacks which brought down the pound turned, in autumn of the year, against the American dollar. Europe became distrustful and Switzerland discounted the dollar as money now carrying a risk. Every French ship began carrying back gold from New York, until eventually France piled up some eighty-three billion francs' worth in Paris, or more than one hundred per cent. coverage for the paper money in circulation. All this while the French press was telling the French public how poor the nation was and how it could not pay its debts unless Germany was forced to pay every sou under the Young Plan.

In October, Norway, Sweden and Denmark followed Britain in dropping the gold standard and Americans began hoarding gold in vaults, while Europeans, fearful that American credit, almost the last to remain at par, would follow the way of all currency, also hoarded metal money of all kinds, paying a premium for gold. Finland, Spain, Portugal, Greece, Egypt, China, Japan and South American republics, a total of twenty-two countries, followed Britain in turn, and in 1933, South Africa, producer of gold, also dropped it as the basis of world economy.

Hunger, rioting, marching men, bread lines, police clubs, charity and governmental action and panaceas began to replace optimism and watchful waiting for the "turn" in 1931. The "we-have-touched-bottom" prophets were deserted. As masses began to starve, economists ironically called it The Age of Plenty. There was more than plenty, there was undreamed-of superabundance — of everything except liquid money.

Wheat rotted in the sheds of Canada and meat rotted in the storehouses of Argentine, while in Hungary, in the poor villages, not water but wine was used to put out fires. In Brazil, the sea swallowed up the surplus coffee or it was used for stoking furnaces, while in New York long lines of bedraggled men waited for coffee in tin cups and begged nickels in the streets. Modern science and a century of invention had brought about an age in which every food that could be grown and every article that could be manufactured, everything that human beings needed for life and luxury, were available in unlimited amounts and for the smallest effort. Never in recorded history had this happened. Yet the statistics for the world showed thirty million men out of jobs and a large number of them facing starvation. The world, said Lord Revelstoke to the bankers of London, is "writhing in a purgatory of its own making."

In 1932, half of all Europe's industrial equipment was idle. Millions of men in many countries were living on social insurances and doles while machinery crumbled and governments raised tariffs and encouraged campaigns of "Buy British", "*Kaufft nur deutsche Waren*", "*Achetez Français.*" Japan was described as worse off than any other large nation, although there were no war debts to pay and none to receive. Her foreign trade in 1931 had decreased thirty-one per cent., compared to Germany's nine per cent. and America's sixteen per cent. and domestic trade even more. The younger generation was adopting the revolutionary ideas of the restless Western world, while the rich class refused to look at the situation seriously. The economic crisis urged on the war in China. As the yen fell, bonds declined, budget balancing became impossible, hunger increased, the Japanese army was sent to Shanghai, Nanking and Harbin, winning victories over a foe equipped with modern patriotism but medieval guns. Japanese drums beat and the poverty-stricken land turned to thoughts of war.

England fought desperately to save her financial, naval and imperial power by increasing taxes and issuing doles to the unemployed, a system which many thought would lead to national suicide.

Among the various palliatives appearing in America was block-aiding in which each city street became a little independent unit to care for its own distress. John Pierpont Morgan helped. He broadcasted: "We have reached a point where the aid of government or the gifts of individuals, no matter how generous, are insufficient to meet the conditions which have come upon us. So we must all do our bit. . . ." The former dictator of Poland, the pianist Paderewski, thought the depression due to "the vanity of the rich, the envy of the poor, and the greed of merchants in encouraging the poor to live beyond their means through the installment system of buying." Mr. Mellon, arriving as ambassador to London in 1931, announced "there is nothing fundamentally wrong with the existing social system; it has shown that it can produce an abundance of food and clothing with all the necessities of life."

To the Third Internationale, Dictator Stalin, the first day of

1932, announced, "We will try to erect more blast furnaces than the United States will close down."

In America, communists in Detroit and New York and other cities started whispering campaigns and wrote letters saying certain banks were unsound; bank runs followed disastrously.

On the twelfth of March, 1932, one of the ten "uncrowned" rulers of the world, Ivar Kreuger, the Swedish financial and industrial genius, shot himself in Paris, thereby accentuating the international economic and financial debacle. Ironically enough, Kreuger appeared in America as a "success story" almost coincidentally. Isaac F. Marcosson, who through the *Saturday Evening Post* had already sung the praises of such heroes as Hugo Stinnes, one of the men who ruined Germany, and Benito Mussolini (in 1926, retracted in 1930), now introduced his new idol: "Kreuger is more than an industrial Titan," he wrote; "Kreuger's industrial empire" was described, and his conclusion given that, "All factors considered, I feel hopeful regarding the immediate future." The day the weekly was in the press, the Titan of the hopeful future was in his coffin.

It was testified before the Federal referee in bankruptcy that Kreuger, head of the International Match Corporation, through his American bankers, had sold a quarter of a billion dollars' worth of stocks and bonds without informing the bankers or public whether assets to secure his loans actually existed. Within a few weeks it became apparent that Kreuger was the greatest crook of the century. The King of Matches had forged forty-two treasury bonds of half a million pounds sterling each of the Italian Government, also five treaties of £1,533,700 each, a total of £28,668,500. To the man who helped him print the forgeries, Kreuger said, "I have never succeeded in a more noble enterprise; my Italian affair has contributed more towards an accord among the great powers than the conference of Geneva." But to a few intimates he whispered, "It is an absolute secret: I have advanced the money to Italy to build new cruisers."

In the books of his consortium, he carried the fraudulent Italian titles at one fifth their "value."

The American international bankers were censured by Senator Hiram Johnson, who introduced three bills to regulate loans in the future. "If ever there was a racket imposed on the American people," said the Senator, "that racket was the one imposed by the bankers on American investors." He showed that $1,600,000,000 worth of bonds of sixteen European countries had fallen to $742,000,000; that South American bonds had depreciated $1,175,000,000 and $815,468,000 was in default. "The money madness of our people," continued the Senator, "the greed and even worse of international bankers, and the smug complacency and supine indifference of government have contributed to the unhappy result. The bankers simply did not heed the facts. . . . They acted only for profits. They were perfectly willing to contribute their loans to maintain dictators in power. . . . Indeed they contributed the money in some instances for the destruction of liberty itself." In South America "the loans were made to go hand in hand with concessions", the Senator continued, assailing "the Mellon interests." He cited the bribes paid Juan Leguia, one of the former dictators of Peru, to help arrange a loan of one hundred million dollars, and charged the State Department with issuing reports it had no objection to South American loans. The public had been "infamously exploited by the bankers."

The scandal grew greater as one European nation after another followed South America dictatorships in defaulting, and reached its worst with the French refusal to pay the installment of the war debts in December, 1932. In that month, France, the leader of the world in every move to punish Russia, committed the one unforgivable crime of the Bolsheviki. The new régime in Moscow had said, "No" to the debts the Tsar incurred; the French Republic said "No" to the repayment of money which won her the war. But no one flew to arms.

In Russia, all this time, the thunder of the world crisis was

AMMINISTRAZIONE AUTONOMA
DEI
MONOPOLI DI STATO

6% SIX PERCENT 6%

Treasury Bill due 15 August 1935

£ 500.000:—
*Fivehundred thousand Pounds Sterling*

Interest payable 15 February and 15 August every year first time 15 August 1931 against stamping of this certificate. Principal and interest payable at Barclays Bank Ltd London

Rome 15 August 1930

Boselli
*General Director*

Guaranteed as to principal and interest by the Kingdom of Italy

*Minister of Finance*

AMMINISTRAZIONE AUTONOMA
DEI MONOPOLI DI STATO

*We promise to pay against this bill*
*at Barclays Bank Ltd London*

*£ 1.533.700:—*

*on 15 November 1932*

*Rome 20 Nov. 1930*

Boselli
IL DIRETTORE GENERALE

KREUGER'S FORGED TREASURY BONDS OF ITALY (1932)

not heard. Russia had fallen into such economic depths in 1921 that there was nothing left but to die there or to climb out. The climbing began in 1926 with the contract to Hugh L. Cooper to build a sixty million dollar hydroelectric plant on the Dnieper. In October, 1928, not a word was heard in Europe or America about Stalin's five-year reconstruction plan, called in Russia "Piatiletka." In 1930, the second anniversary, the Red dictator said, "We are doing something in Soviet Russia, the success of which will turn the world upside down." At about the same time a series of leisurely articles on Russian conditions written by the Berlin correspondent of the Philadelphia *Ledger* and New York *Evening Post,* H. R. Knickerbocker, was headlined "The Russian Trade Menace", and from then on the soviet idea of ordered economy became a rival to the American and European system of *laissez faire* individualistic capitalism in the public mind.

The five-year-plan of October 1, 1928–1933, to produce the means and communications for war, provided:

An investment of $33,000,000,000.
Reconstruction of industrial plants.
Purchase of foreign equipment and machinery.
Imports of $3,200,000,000.
Two tractor factories with an output of 40,000 units each per year.
An automobile factory producing 100,000 cars annually.
Steel mills to produce 5,000,000 tons yearly.
Oil production 22,000,000 tons, and
Cast iron production of 10,000,000 tons annually.

The oil production was raised to thirty-eight million in 1930 and the iron figure set at seventeen million tons. The investment of thirty-three billion dollars, having been figured in rubles, is a much lesser sum, owing to the depreciation abroad (although not officially at home) of the new soviet currency.

In 1931 the official organ *Pravda* reported successful progress of the Piatiletka: The oil industry had increased three hundred per cent. since 1913, had completed its goal, and had started its second program; steel production had doubled since 1913; likewise electric power; coal had gone up to eighty-three million tons a year from a previous twenty-nine million tons. In 1927, eighty-five per cent. of the grain had come from the poor peasants, thirteen per cent. from the rich or *kulaki,* two per cent. from collective farms. In 1931, fifty per cent. came from collective farms, forty-six and eight tenths per cent. from the poor peasants. The figures were generally believed exaggerated, but showed startling progress in the face of continued disaster in all other countries.

Of the "retreats" which Trotsky envisaged, the first occurred in March, 1930, when Stalin changed the plan, halted the collectivization of the villages, reformed the agricultural program and stopped crushing the *kulaki,* who, with the poorer peasants, up in arms against Moscow, had slaughtered millions of horses and cows rather than add them to any collective scheme, and at times murdered the agents of the government. But the great retreat, similar to Lenin's New Economic Policy but in this case an abandonment of the very principles of communism itself, occurred June 23, 1931. The five-day week was abandoned, unequal wages sanctioned as well as piecework, and individual responsibility in production. The new policy as summed up by George Counts:

Reorganization of the industrial labor system.
Mechanization of the more onerous processes of labor.
Abolition of the level wage scale.
Creation of labor classes, skilled and unskilled; promotions, higher wages, competitive impulses, pay according to production.
Non-communists invited to key positions.
Attitude towards old intelligentsia, engineering and technical forces changed.
System of cost accounting introduced.
Lack of responsibility in production "must come to an end."

When the outside world emphasized this apparent abandonment of communism, Stalin defended himself with the simple statement that at no time during the soviet experiment has there been pure communism and that any step is justified in an emergency to reach the strict theoretical goal. Land, tools, production, foreign trade remained in the hands of the government.

Some time later in the year, Stalin began to make of the Piatiletka a challenge to the world.

The following figures of progress under the plan were compiled by a French economist, Réné Depuis, in September, 1932:

| | 1913 | 1927 | 1928 | 1929 | 1930 | 1931 |
|---|---|---|---|---|---|---|
| *In millions of tons:* | | | | | | |
| Coal | 28.9 | 32.3 | 35.8 | 41.7 | 47 | 56.6 |
| Oil | 9.3 | 11.9 | 12.3 | 14.5 | 18.6 | 22.9 |
| Iron, etc. | 4.2 | 3 | 3.3 | 4.3 | 5 | 4.9 |
| *In thousands of units:* | | | | | | |
| Tractors | | 0.874 | 1.4 | 4.6 | 12.6 | 41.3 |
| *In millions of hectares:* | | | | | | |
| Wheat | 27 | 31.2 | 27.7 | 29.7 | 32.6 | 37.3 |
| *In thousands of hectares:* | | | | | | |
| Cotton | 537 | 802 | 971 | 1056 | 1583 | 2100 |
| *In millions of kilowatts:* | | | | | | |
| Electric energy | | | | 2343 | 2894 | 3968 |

Finally we have the report Stalin delivered to the plenary session of the central commission of control of the Communist Party, January 7, 1933, in which he began by saying that "History has shown that the Five-Year-Plan is not a private affair of the Soviet Union but a matter for the entire international proletariat. . . . The principal task of the first plan was to place our country, with its retarded technical development, partly of the Middle Ages, on the road of modern technique. The principal task of the first plan was to transform the Soviet Union from an agrarian country, a country weak and dependent on capitalist countries, into an industrial nation, powerful and completely independent of the caprices of world capital. . . . Finally, the task of the first plan consisted of the creation in our country of indispensable premises, technical as well as economic, to push to the maximum the capacity of defense of the nation, capable of inflicting decisive check to each and all attempt at armed intervention from abroad, to each and every warlike attack.

"Heavy industry and its vital nerve, mechanical industry, were the principal links in the plan. . . . What are its results? Have we won victory in this field? Yes. . . . Our country has become an industrial country out of an agrarian country; the industrial production had increased, in comparison with agricultural production, by forty-eight per cent. at the beginning of the plan in 1928, has reached seventy per cent. at the end of the fourth year." In agriculture, the fourth part of the report, Stalin claimed the plan realized three hundred per cent. increase, while farm collectivization embraced sixty per cent. of the land. Part Five, materialistic amelioration of living conditions, concludes with this summary:

"Increase of number of workers and employees in the large industries, double 1928; augmentation of national revenue, that is to say, augmentation in the revenues of workers and peasants of 45 billion rubles, 1932, which gives an augmentation of eighty-five per cent. in comparison with 1928; augmentation in the social insurance funds of two hundred and ninety-two per cent. compared to 1928, four billion rubles compared to one and a half in 1928, or one hundred and eleven per cent. over the plan. . . ."

In Part Six, soviet commerce, Stalin reports augmentation in the light industries of one hundred and eighty-seven per cent. augmentation in government retail coöperative store sales, thirty-nine billion rubles or one hundred and seventy-five per cent. In conclusion: "The results of the Piatiletka have shown finally that the Communist Party is invincible so long as it knows where it is going and has no fears of difficulties." The congress arose and applauded.

While the world questioned success or failure, Stalin, January 9, 1933, announced the second Piatiletka. Russia would be permitted to catch her breath. Instead of a tempo of twenty-two per cent. increase per year, Stalin would be content with thirteen or fourteen, although 1933 would be driven through at sixteen. With Russia facing a food shortage and a general lack of goods and a new agriculture crisis, Stalin proposed the abolition of the system of grain collection, a fixed grain tax, greater attention to local industries, and completion of the heavy industries now building. A hundred per cent. increase in housing, fifty per cent. increase in cultural and social services, thirty per cent. in manufacturing for household use, unlimited increases in domestic food and thirty-three per cent. increase in wages were proposed.

A challenge to Stalin was made by Don Levine, who in "Red Smoke" claimed that Russian official reports proved the nation had neither the natural resources nor the communications "to catch up with America in our day or at any future date."

In celebrating the birth of 1933, many nations believed that the worst had been left behind. Britain was more optimistic. The new taxes were paid in January, 1933, by crowds in queues like bread lines; the government converted the war and victory loans, reducing the interest from five to three and one half per cent., which almost every holder voluntarily accepted. The debt installment was paid to America. Financially, Britons felt they had come through and that they had saved not only their country but Western civilization from chaos. Football, cricket, hunting and greyhound races were as popular as ever. If the people lacked bread, there was no want of circuses.

The Pope decreed a holy year between Easter, 1933, and Easter, 1934, calling on the world to forget its worry and cares of the depression; "men should turn their thoughts for an instant at least from the earthly and transitory things in which they are struggling so unhappily, towards eternal, celestial things, abandoning the sadness of present conditions."

The American bankers grew most optimistic, although their

words were no longer so impressive. Charles E. Mitchell said hoarded currency was coming back to the banks and the large body of short-term foreign investments had been liquidated; the country was in a stronger position, bank deposits were rising and reserves have regained the losses of the early part of the year. (Mr. Mitchell was indicted for evasion of his 1929 income tax payments.)

Just before Inauguration Day a series of bank moratoria was begun by the State of Michigan. On March 4, Mr. Roosevelt did two things: he took the oath of office as President of the United States and he declared a bank holiday for the nation and the closing of its stock exchanges.

It was a strong and brave action and it had the coöperation of a puzzled and disheartened but ever hopeful nation. The President proposed legislation, assumed what have been loosely termed "dictatorial" powers, and kept the public informed by radio. He let no day pass without action. Within a fortnight, the banks were reopened — all but the weak or dangerous ones — and again there was a feeling of returned confidence in the Government and the present structure of society.

J. M. Keynes, the prophet of doom, was optimistic. Had the world economic system lost resiliency? "Yet to judge from previous cases," answered the economist in his predictions for 1933, "we moved past the lowest point in the second half of 1932. . . . In 1929, some Americans persuaded themselves that the boom was permanent. To-day they are beginning to believe the same thing about the slump. But slumps, like booms, do come to an end; at least they always have. It is true that this slump has been more violent than usual, but it has not yet been more prolonged. Slumps carry within themselves the seeds of a reaction — just as booms do."

Britain's escape from the gold standard (September, 1931) and the loss of fear in using cheap money, Keynes considered paramount; next to that the settlement "in the negative" of the war debt problem at Lausanne; India, China, South Africa have almost solved their economic problems and even Germany has shown economic stability and "faint signs of improvement which it would have been rash to forecast a year ago." "If only one could forget about the United States! Yet even in that helpless conglomeration the indications suggest that the tide has fitfully turned, and that the low points of last summer will not be repeated. America is not built to turn easily in traffic; but she is a new model (in parts), and does not lack horse power or petrol."

Finally, having begun with predictions of debacle by one of the arch-enemies of the capitalist system, we can close this chronicle of disaster with a later prediction of the same prophet. "To-day," believes Leon Trotsky, "dominant America has not extricated herself from the perplexing situation caused by the crisis, but this state of affairs will pass. It will be followed by an effort on her part to safeguard in every corner of the world positions that will act as safety valves against a new crisis. In the third quarter of the fifteenth century, Europe discovered America; in the second quarter of the twentieth century, America will discover the world. Her policy will be that of the open door, which, as is well known, opens not inward but only outward in America."

## INTERLUDE 1930

The Bambergers and the Watkins of Chicago got their babies mixed up in a hospital. Every mother in the world was touched.

Fish found: twelve thousand dues-paying members Communist Party in America; eighty-two thousand voters, five hundred thousand sympathizers. "The best defense against the red shirt of the Communist and the black shirt of the Fascist," said Congressman Nelson, "is the blue shirt of the American workingmen." Wall Street reports an additional million speculators lost their shirts in last crash. Congressman O'Connor declared the best way to fight communist propaganda "is to put something in the soup besides statistics." Mrs. Hearst opened a soup kitchen in Times Square.

Robert Tyre Jones won the United States Amateur Golf Championship, making four major titles in a year.

Weitzenkorn's play "Five Star Final" bludgeoned the tabloid press and the New York *Daily News* became less tabloid.

Al Capone came out of jail after nine months for carrying a gun. Gandhi went into jail for six months.

Tree-sitting. Bicycle-riding. Rocking-chair rocking. The youngest generation went in for publicity.

"The Strange Death of President Harding" replaced "The Specialist" on the best-seller list.

The German Catholic newspapers, *Germania,* etc., accused the Oberammergau Passion Players of doctoring up the show with theatrical trimmings which they call "dollar effects" to please American audiences.

Miniature golf craze. Backgammon. Humanism again.

King George announced the succession of the Throne of Great

Britain: Prince of Wales, Duke of York, Princess Elizabeth. The lady most admired by the Prince of Wales, Mrs. Dudley Ward, applied for a divorce.

"Why, I married her for her money, of course," said George Bernard Shaw on his seventy-fourth birthday. Mr. Mencken married and the critics quoted his "Prejudices": "No normal man ever fell in love, within the ordinary meaning of the term, after the age of thirty." On June 22 a son was born to the Lindberghs. In August, Heywood Broun ran for Congress. In July, "Calvin Coolidge Says" appeared on Page 1.

The *Digest* poll showed forty per cent. wet, twenty-nine per cent. for modification, thirty-one per cent. dry.

Freud discoursed on civilization and its discontents: "If the evolution of civilization has such a far-reaching similarity with the development of the individual, and if the same methods are employed in both, would not the diagnosis be justified that many systems of civilizations — or epochs of it — possibly even the whole of humanity — have become 'neurotic' under the pressure of the civilizing trend?"

"What are the prospects of world revolution?" Eugene Lyons of the United Press asked Stalin. "Prospects good," replied the ruler of the Kremlin. "You look every inch a dictator," added Lyons. "It is just very funny," replied Tavarish Stalin. "Why does the press of the world countenance so many lies?" broke in War Commissar Voroshiloff, without waiting for Mr. Lyons to disappear. "Why do you refuse to see correspondents?" continued Mr. Lyons. "Because interviews do not fit in very well with my personal five-year-plan," replied Stalin. Mr. Lyons wrote Stalin looked and acted like (Theodore) Roosevelt.

The five-year-plan of Broadway's leading crooner of blues, a girl of twenty-four named Libby Holman: "When a girl's young and voluptuous she can't help but be adored. Old age is the problem. Here's my program. Five more years of the theater, I hope to have enough money to give me a sure income of $15,000 a year. I'll go to France and get a villa. Then I'll concentrate on the development of my mind. But no millionaires. A man who has achieved something in the arts . . . I haven't met a soul who qualifies. I'll have a child — that's a necessary part of experience. I'll write stories, novels, poetry. There'll be a salon like Mme. Sévigné's. . . . I want the sensitivity and understanding of Katherine Mansfield and the penetration of George Sand. . . . I'll never be crying my heart out over a guy that loves and leaves me."

The author of "Lady Chatterley's Lover" lay dying in his little villa on the Vence hillside. The doctors had told Frieda, his wife, he had not three days to live. D. H. Lawrence was not told. He said, "Read me some Persian philosophy." Frieda read, "When a man is in the best of health and has no fear of death, he should make his testament." "Perhaps I should make mine," said Lawrence, laughing. "No," said Frieda, "you've got years and years yet." The next day he died. Virginia Hersch led three or four American writers up hill for the dismal funeral. Aldous Huxley stood by, as the friend of the family. On the gravestone was carved the phœnix and flames which was Lawrence's symbol.

Election Day: fifty million Americans hear returns via radio. Election day, 1920, KDKA broadcasted elections for one hundred persons with earphones, who also heard phonograph records between bulletins.

In his Christmas message to the Cardinals, the Pope said: "It is difficult, if not impossible, for peace to become permanent so long as selfishness and hard nationalism prevail in place of true and genuine love of country, so long as we find hatred and jealousy in place of good will, suspicion in place of brotherly confidence, ambitions of hegemony and domination in place of respect for the rights of the weak and small."

## CHAPTER SIXTEEN

### MONEY, DICTATORSHIPS, WAR AND PEACE

THE course of empire, no less than an average mortal's daily activity, was affected by the empty pocketbook, the international symbol under which the Decade of the Thirties was born. The crisis at times brought on revolutions. It made democracies of dictatorships, dictatorships of democracies; it carried disillusion to many millions in one land but gave fighting ideals to many millions in another.

Reactions to world poverty were as varied as the rise of Hitlerism in Germany and the repudiation of the Republican Administration of President Hoover in the United States. The crisis exposed the falsity of the heralded economic revival through Fascism in Italy and Spain and brought the international attention, if not secret admiration, of ordered and planned economy through Communism in Russia.

It made for peace and for war. Bankrupt Japan was driven into new Chinese adventures, warlike France was forced to reduce its army, while sword-rattling Mussolini played the pipes of peace for the first time and with many a sour grimace.

Pacifism through poverty became almost as much an axiom as foreign wars to cure internal disorders.

At the beginning of the Decade of the Thirties, Hoover spoke with despair of the more than thirty million men under arms, ten million more than in 1914. Six million soldiers were on active service, of whom three and a half million were in Europe. The war expenditures of all nations had grown and the pension system was eating up almost half the national budgets of Europe.

No big war was being fought but preparations were being

made. The new menace to the world, by consensus of opinion, was Italy. Frankly the dictator admitted in 1930, "We are obliged to fight on our soil, too small for our overpopulation, for the smallest grain of nutritive substance. Italy cannot nourish its people. I do not feel myself authorized to believe in the humanitarian idealism of pacifists. We must expand or explode." France was preparing for the explosion.

Russia and China were threatening war when on December 2, 1929, the United States took a unique step in diplomatic history and invited fifty-three nations to put pressure on public opinion in both nations to halt hostilities. In 1930, conflicts continued over Manchuria but there was no official war. Japan in the East and France in the West led in militarism, both pleading self-defense or national security.

Four South American governments stricken by financial panic went down in revolution; none of the ten escaped disorder and Central America could not withstand the military tumult. In 1930 and 1931, eleven uprisings were successful, one in Cuba failed, and every new government was recognized by the United States.

In 1933 the thought uppermost in the minds of the budget-makers of the world was reduction of armaments. Mussolini openly admitted the armament race could not go on because there was no money for it anywhere.

The military budgets of the seven great powers at three distinct periods, the pre-war, the first disarmament years culminating in 1927, and the new armament race, as compiled by the League of Nations, showed:

| | 1913–1914 | 1920–1927 | 1930–1931 |
|---|---|---|---|
| | (In millions of dollars) | | |
| Great Britain | 375.1 | 564 | 535 |
| France | 348.7 | 210.5 | 455.3 |
| Italy | 179.1 | 207.8 | 258.9 |
| Japan | 95.5 | 212 | 232.1 |
| Russia | 447.7 | 362.9 | 579.4 |
| United States | 244.6 | 591.5 | 727.7 |
| Germany | 463.3 | 156.6 | 170.4 |

The total expenditure in 1930 was four and one half billion dollars. In the air France was first, the United States second.

Nineteen Twenty-nine was not a decisive year among the dictators. On the sixth of January, the proclamation "I, King Alexander . . . have decided that the constitution of the Serb-Croat-Slovene Kingdom of June 28, 1921, ceases to be in force", made General Peter Zivkovitch dictator of Yugoslavia. Parliament was abolished on the twenty-first; Zivkovitch ruled by decrees. He ordered school authorities to refuse admission to girls using lipsticks and powder, wearing short skirts or silk stockings.

The peasants took over the Rumanian Government. Julius Maniu, a believer in Abraham Lincoln, ousted the three Bratianus who had given the Balkans one of the most corrupt reigns in modern history. Among the items of graft discovered was the disappearance of a $4,000,000 railroad, with its cars, its locomotives, rails and danger signals. Maniu's first program provided: restoration of the liberties of the people, elimination of the army from politics, restoration of the standing of the judiciary and economic and agrarian reforms.

In March, the students of Spain rioted against De Rivera, demanding the restoration of their liberal professors and the freedom of political prisoners. The dictator had no difficulty in suppressing the lads.

Graft and corruption in Spain had been covered by foreign loans and budget jugglery. No one knew this as well as De Rivera. He opened the new year with the declaration: "The year 1929 has been a disastrous one. Let it go to the devil. I hope 1930 will be easier and enable me to retire and rest in peace. I hope God will take Spain under His blessing and protection." He resigned on the twenty-eighth, leaving General Berenguer the task of restoring the constitution and finding money.

In July, Waldemaras, dictator of Lithuania, was banished for a year as a danger to public safety. With his old humor, the dictator insisted on signing the order himself. His newspaper, the *People's Pathway*, was suppressed, and his Fascisti, the twenty thousand Iron Wolves, ordered disbanded. Lithuania honored him for one great act. In December, 1927, he had gone to Geneva, asking help against Poland. Pilsudski arrived with clashing swords, Polish eagle flying, his car decorated as for a pageant or parade. He walked blustering and clattering into the council chamber.

"I have come all the way from Warsaw," he declaimed oratorically, "to hear pronounced here at the League of Nations, the word 'Peace.' I have not heard that word."

M. Briand assured the Polish president-dictator in his usual suave French voice that he would soon be able to hear a lengthy report on that subject.

Pilsudski was not satisfied. He arose. He pointed his long finger at the Lithuanian little professor-dictator-prime minister and fixed him with an ancient mariner's eye. "I have an explicit question to put to the Honorable Representative of Lithuania — Is it Peace or War?"

The little professor arose but did not get dramatic. "It is Peace," he said quietly. He had come there to make peace, had never dreamed to attack the dread White Eagle.

"I shall order a Te Deum to be sung in all the churches of Poland," replied Pilsudski with a flourish.

"I also will have a Te Deum sung," replied Waldemaras quietly, adding with an irony which was not lost on Briand and the others at the secret council, "but may these Te Deums be for peace among men of good will."

June 7, 1930, taking advantage of Queen Marie's trip to the Passion Play at Oberammergau, Prince Carol flew from Paris to Rumania and sent Magda Lupescu by train via Interlaken. Four hundred and eighty-six delegates voted Carol king; one, the last Bratianu, Vintila, opposed. People danced in the streets. It was something new in dynastic history, a man who succeeded both his father and his son as king. Marie, the most foiled woman in Europe, said wryly, "As a mother, I can only rejoice." Carol's first work was to tear out the secret telephone system between the apartments of the Queen and Prince Stirbey.

In Budapest food riots broke out, shops and restaurants were looted, and Bolshevism raised its head again, despite Dictator Horthy, the hungry crowds crying, "Long live Kun Bela." The police killed two and wounded two hundred.

In September, Pilsudski called on Poland to legalize his dictatorship by popular vote. He began the campaign by putting his boyhood friend, ex-Premier Witos, into prison with seventeen other members of parliament and holding an election with bayonets. He obtained a majority. In November, the Austrian socialists carried the country, breaking the Fascist plan of dictatorship. In December, a revolt broke out at Jaca, Spain, and Alcala Zamora, in jail, was called provisional president. The government advanced ruthlessly. Firman Falan, hero of Jaca, was executed by a firing squad. Major Franco, who had flown the Atlantic, escaped by airplane.

In August, 1931, the International Committee for Political Prisoners, reported:

> The world is burdened with dictatorships — more than ever before in history. A dictatorship means a government by one group or party to the exclusion of all other groups or parties, accompanied by suppression of all opposition, either by imprisonment, exile or censorship. . . .
>
> Repression is most severe in the following countries: Europe, Italy, Russia, Poland, Hungary and the Balkan States, particularly Yugoslavia; Latin America, Venezuela and Cuba; Asia and the Orient, Turkey, India, Burma, China, Japan, Korea, French Indo-China, Dutch East Indies and the Philippines; Africa, Egypt and the French, English and Belgian colonies.

This report could have been changed considerably before the year was out. Spain, Turkey, Yugoslavia and a dozen South and Central American countries abolished or ameliorated their dictatorships and the prisons were opened.

The march of industrialism, a new national conscience and the failure of American bankers to continue loans contributed to the Latin-American uprisings. A fairly free press and fairly free parliaments awoke national emotions against graft, waste, inefficiency and suppressive measures of dictators, the egotism of ruling cliques. They had made no provision for economic distress. At its first signs they collapsed.

The case of Leguia of Peru is typical. Here was a dictator credited with a program and economic forethought, "a Roosevelt", "a South American Mussolini", according to certain journalists. What Leguia actually did was to borrow big amounts from the United States for the purpose largely of supporting himself in power. As in Italy, concessions were given away, graft was rampant, and the budget was tricked out in gold trimmings. The manifesto of the revolutionary Colonel Sanchez-Cerro accused the dictator of raising the foreign debt from eighty million, to six hundred million soles, placing the country "at the mercy of foreign lenders and imperiling national sovereignty." The national sanctions court fined Leguia and his three sons twenty-five million soles (about $7,625,000) for graft in eleven years, a large part of the sum being the "rake-off" from American bankers for floating unneeded loans.

The autocrat and hero of the Argentine, Hipólito Irigoyen, fell amidst charges of unparalleled graft. President Uriburu claimed that a deficit of seven hundred and twenty million pesos in the last two years of the second administration and one billion, one hundred million pesos in the first administration, was due to dictatorial mismanagement. In Brazil, President Vargas found that the dictatorship of Washington Luiz was rotten with political corruption: seventy thousand dollars had been spent to bribe the newspapers of São Paulo, the total graft in the State amounted to twelve million dollars and the State of Rio had got into debt thirty-six million dollars. The students of Chile began a revolution in July, forcing President Carãlos Ibáñez to resign. Dominica, Bolivia, Ecuador, had their revolutions and more dictators disappeared. In Cuba, Dictator Machado suppressed all liberal publications and reaped weeks of bomb-throwing. He offered to restore constitutional rights and free the political prisoners if bombing ended.

Finally the most important revolution occurred in Spain. On April 12, four million men voted, the majority for a republic, and Zamora, coming out of jail, called on Alfonso to resign. The King issued a proclamation beginning with the words, "The elections which took place Sunday have clearly shown me that I have lost the affection of my people. . . . A king can make mistakes, and doubtless I have erred," but ending with, "I do not renounce any of my rights."

Ten days that shook the world — with laughter — followed. A bloodless revolution occurred in Madrid. Crowds chopped the imperial crowns off buildings. Firemen posted a sign on the royal palace, "Workmen, respect this building, it is now yours." It was like Armistice Day in New York. Thousands of persons danced in the streets and threw confetti. Dawn found the gutters full of drunken, happy men.

On the fourteenth, Alfonso in a racing car was escorted to the gates of Madrid by provisional President Zamora. Colonel Macia, who had been arrested in France through the intrigue of the Fascist agent Garibaldi, now was proclaimed president of the Catalonian Republic. Zamora cancelled the Morgan loan.

King Alfonso came to Paris to receive the condolences of Elizabeth, Queen of the Belgians, Zita, deposed Queen of Hungary, Prince Nicholas, who had lost the throne of Greece, Grand Duke Dmitri of Russia and Marie of Rumania. The Republican Party announced that the banking houses Morgan; Chase; National City; Kuhn Loeb; Guaranty Trust; Dillon, Read; Lee, Higginson, had offered thirty-eight million dollars and the Banque de Paris et des Pays Bas the balance of a sixty million dollar loan a few days before the overthrow. This money would have saved the dictatorship. The house of Morgan in 1928 had rescued De Rivera by a loan of twenty-five million when the peseta was slumping.

Financial scandals came to light throughout Spain. Primo's

gang had made millions. As taught him by his idol, Mussolini, Primo had falsified the budget for years. Four billion pesetas had been spent, there was a deficit of a quarter of a billion, and the treasury had only sixty-eight million pesetas on hand instead of the three hundred and twenty million which appeared in the official figures. The Duke of Tetuan held the dictatorship responsible for the flight of capital, the loss of confidence, a financial crisis, the censorship of the press, dishonest elections, general distrust and the waste which accompanies dictatorship.

The coming of the republic did not end Spain's troubles. The liberals, socialists, syndicalists and monarchists continued sporadic warfare. The labor unions and socialists who, with the students, were responsible for Alfonso's flight, began to incorporate their program. The communists and syndicalists proposed extremist measures.

The inevitable monarchist reaction occurred at 2 A.M. August 10, 1932, when General Sanjurjo arrived in Seville from Madrid and occupied the telegraph office, property of an American corporation. Sanjurjo was trying to capture the keys of industry and movement, according to the rules of the modern *coup d'état* first proved effective by Trotsky and best described by Malaparte. In the pre-machine age one stormed a symbol, a Bastille; in enlightened times one occupied the gas works or the telegraph offices. To seize power, one seized power plants.

But Seville refused to revolt and within a few hours Sanjurjo was fleeing by automobile to Portugal. He did not get there.

In January, 1933, the awaited radical reaction, an anarcho-syndicalist revolutionary plot, proved abortive.

In the Nineteen Thirties a leader, about whom little was known or said, made a great experiment in government. Mustapha Kemal, Dictator of Turkey, super-patriot, master-hand of the technique of revolutions and counter-revolutions, military genius, fanatic believer in New Turkey, and Turkey for the Turks, had said: "I am Turkey. To destroy me is to destroy Turkey." In 1926, after he had thoroughly ruined the Opposition by brutal hangings and exile, he, the People's Party, had entire control of the State down to the most routine and insignificant detail. Kemal understood that his people must be driven and wheedled into becoming the great nation he willed. They were like children and he was their teacher. He must lead them away from their past with the Ottoman Empire, and to do that he must change their ideas and customs and sweep away the débris of religion and sultanism.

His first order was to abolish the fez for the hat. If he could succeed in doing this, other changes would come easily for the Turk, to whom a hat was the symbol of uncleanliness that all Christian pigs wore. Kemal started cautiously by replacing the fezzes of his guard and when they did not protest against the advantages of the European brim, he toured Turkey, shocking his subjects by appearing at public meetings in a Panama hat. "The fez is the sign of ignorance," preached Kemal, and the Turks were shocked and refused to remove their signs of ignorance. A law was passed making the wearing of the fez illegal, and those who refused to obey and assaulted officials who tore their national pride from their heads, were beaten and shot and hanged, hundreds of them, until they ceased to riot and resist, and the fez disappeared in a wild scramble for hats.

But there were not many in Turkey since the Christians had been driven out by Kemal, and in desperation, padlocked shops formerly run by accursed foreigners, Greeks and Armenians, were raided and pillaged of all the brims they had to offer. The fez indeed disappeared and from one end of the country to the other Turkish men appeared in derbies, bowlers and ladies' straw hats with flowers, feathers and ribbons.

Religion was the next to go. The Church had weakened the nation and confiscated its wealth. Monasteries were closed and Church property taken over by the State.

With the destruction of religion went the rest of the social structure which for centuries had been based on it. Kemal proceeded to adopt the Swiss, German and Italian Civil and Legal codes. The Swiss Code abolished the harem, made polygamy illegal, and women ceased to be men's property and were able to have jurisdiction and rights of their own. They were encouraged to shed their veils and take an active part in the running of the state.

"Turkey for the Turks." Arabic and Persian words must go and never reappear to smirch the pure Tartar of the language. Speeches, laws passed, Koran and New Testament translated, were all to be in Turkish, which few of this almost illiterate nation understood. Latin must take the place of the complicated Arabic characters in the language and the people must all go to school, young and old, illiterate and scholarly, and learn the new letters. So Kemal enthusiastically set out as a teacher, this time with a box of chalk and a blackboard, and from platform to platform he explained and chalked the new letters and was patient and brilliant and witty, and men who had never before been able to write their names now wrote them laboriously and eagerly. The new alphabet became a fad and a game, and prizes were offered by Professor Kemal Pasha for the most proficient. This time force had not been necessary. The country was spontaneous in its approval and enthusiasm. The new alphabet became the touchstone for wealth and prosperity. Almost simultaneously beggars were forbidden the streets, it became punishable to laugh at the maimed and crippled and eccentric, and bills of health had to be presented by both parties contracting a marriage. The nation must learn to dance, and dance it did to American Negro jazz and Viennese waltzes, with Kemal leading the steps. He ruled against the Charleston and Black Bottom.

In 1930, opposition headed by Ismet Pasha threatened the dictatorial power of Mustapha. Ismet was assuming the executive head of the State and strutting that fact. An outlet was needed and it was time to try out the Turkish people. Kemal established the "Republican Liberal Party" in opposition to his own and waited to see what would happen to the experiment. He gave orders and trained both parties to attack each other in and out of the Assembly. Censorship of speech and press was lifted, the People's Party was attacked in the streets, in cafés and in the Assembly. Riots resulted, indignation and general suspicion of a government that actually sanctioned a rival party! The country was on the verge of financial ruin, credit and trade destroyed through Mustapha's bitterness for the foreigner. The ousted priests and dervishes now encouraged the people and communist outbreaks spread, Mustapha Kemal was threatened, therefore Turkey was threatened. Kemal had not expected such an outcome to his great experiment. What to do? The Kurds settled it by revolting and destroying and burning. The soldier Kemal Pasha was needed once more to save Turkey. The press and speech were censored again and those who had led the cries against Kemal were jailed and martial law declared. The Kurdish revolts on the Persian frontier were quelled and the people could again look to their savior, Gazi the Victorious.

The Great Experiment had failed. Turkey still needed a wise and good dictator. He, Mustapha Kemal, and the People's Party must educate the people until they were ready. There must be no Opposition. Said Mustapha Kemal in 1932: "But, let the people leave politics alone for the present. Let them interest themselves in agriculture and commerce. For ten or fifteen years more I must rule. After that, perhaps I may be able to let them speak openly."

The great contrasting figure in the world's strife between parliamentary liberalism and dictatorship was the Indian Gandhi. India produced a prophet and a "General" in the Mahatma, whose battle cry was "Nonresistance." A general who was not five feet high, weighed under one hundred pounds, with a shaved head, huge ears and a long nose. He was Britain's public enemy Number 1. In April, 1930, Gandhi and eighty-two followers walked to Jalapur in India, where they dipped their buckets in the sea, evaporated the water, and made salt — thereby breaking British monopoly. In Bombay half a million ardent followers went on a picnic and made salt. Gandhi was arrested and put in jail. British officers with flashlights came into his tent one morning at Surat, province Bombay, and read him the riot act or Bombay anti-sedition ordinance of 1827. After washing his teeth with the salt he himself had made, he had a Hindu hymn sung, but not loud enough to waken his official staff, put on his loin cloth, threw a cotton sheet he himself had woven over his shoulders, lifted his own spinning wheel, and went with the officers quietly. They drove five hours in an American automobile, a "bridal car with pink curtains", stopping at the roadside once to milk somebody's goat, so he could have his usual breakfast before arriving at the jail in Poona. At the Indian Round Table Conference in London, Indian princes now asked for Gandhi's release from prison; ten years before they had agreed with the conservatives that Gandhi was a nuisance at best, a traitor at worst, and much better off, so far as Britain and they were concerned, in prison.

September 12, 1931, Gandhi himself arrived in London for the India Round Table Conference, to demand complete independence for India. He was armed with:

3 spinning wheels
3 looms
1 can of goat's milk
1 package dried raisins
1 copy of Thoreau's "Civil Disobedience"
1 set false teeth
6 fresh diapers

From the time the Mahatma, clad in his loin cloth, landed at Marseilles until he reached London, he was the object of an incredulous, smirking and shocked multitude.

At the Conference he talked simply and forcefully on what he wanted for India, repeated his pleas for coöperation over the radio for twenty minutes, and talked for two hours to the formidable and heckling House of Commons.

"The tests by which Indians will know whether they are free are whether they have been granted control of Indian defense, the Indian Civil Service, and Indian finance. . . . I will not accept the husks of independence. Rather would I declare myself a rebel. We know what that means, but thousands of Indian nationalists have rid themselves of the fear of death."

During this time the new Indian Constitution was being drafted and the British were granting an independence to India that excluded the very things Gandhi had asked for.

Charlie Chaplin, in London at the time, had a talk with "the half-naked seditious fakir", as Chaplin's week-end host, Winston Churchill, called Gandhi, and told the press "Gandhi is a tremendous personality, tremendous! He is a great international figure! More, he is *a great dramatic figure.*" Gandhi had explained his loin cloth. Ten years earlier, in Madura, natives had complained they were too poor to buy *khadder,* native cloth. Gandhi realized how much richer he was than the common people. He divested himself. "Millions of Indians," he continued, "own nothing in the world but that little strip of cloth which preserves them from disgrace. I am not leading a back-to-the-loin-cloth movement. We have been in these straits ever since the British ruled India. In London, if I am invited to visit His Majesty, the King Emperor, I will wear nothing more than that which is the symbol of India's distress — the loin cloth." He visited Buckingham Palace but wore a handmade shawl to supplement the symbol of India's distress.

September 20, 1932, Gandhi, again in the Yeravda Prison at Poona for non-violent aggression against the British, declared a "fast unto death" as a protest against the British granting of separate electorates for the untouchables or depressed class of India. Millions of his faithful followers stopped work, the stock markets in Bombay and Rangoon closed at noon, and a crowd gathered around the prison where Gandhi continued to stay and fast after a last meal of tomatoes, oranges, dates, goat's milk curds, whole wheat bread and lemon juice. The leader of the "untouchables", Doctor Ambedkar, called the fast a "political stunt." But the "political stunt" attracted the headlines, and daily medical bulletins were flashed to England, where the Indian Committee were made responsible for a life and the freedom of the "untouchables." The British Government gave up its electoral project on the twenty-sixth and Gandhi ate.

Finding human nature slow and his desired goal of permitting the untouchables to enter Hindu temples still unsanctioned by the Viceroy, Gandhi declared again on January 24, 1933, that he would fast. "When my usefulness is over, I shall starve myself to death," he had said on one occasion, and his last two fasts were "until death" or victory for his principles. By passive resistance and fasting he had won as much or more for his people than any dictator in Europe and shown the power of non-violence to the world.

In 1932, outside of Hitler, there was but one dictatorial interlude. Vintori Kozola organized the Finnish Fascisti, Lapuans, who raided, destroyed, burned and looted socialist clubs, homes and coöperatives in the approved Fascist style. The pretender to power was called "Kozollini" until March of that year, when he was defeated by government forces and public antipathy.

Hitler alone triumphed. He came out of his beer-hall adventure a hero instead of a "has-been"; he emerged from his trial for treason a leader instead of a laughingstock. Americans wondered if Germany had lost her sense of humor, if whining and self-pity, all the "*armes Deutschland*" propaganda, the weight of injustices of peace treaties and plebiscites, and the poverty forced upon the nation by its Stinneses and Hugenbergs and the Dawes Plan, had completely undermined the national good common sense. Instead of resuming the honest labor of house-painting, Hitler, with the financial aid of the Vereinigte Stahlwerke (Fritz Thyssen), Alfred Hugenberg, Emil

*Keystone View Co.*

RAMSAY MACDONALD, BRITISH PREMIER, AND
M. BRIAND, FRENCH FOREIGN MINISTER,
AT SEVEN POWER CONFERENCE IN LONDON

Kirdorf, Doctor Voegeler and other owners of the largest part of Germany's coal and iron and steel wealth, built up the National Socialist (Nazi) Party and fought his way to the chancellorship, as the parliamentary election figures through the years clearly show:.

| | 1920 | 1924 | 1930 | July 1932 | Nov. 1932 | March 1933 |
|---|---|---|---|---|---|---|
| Social Democrats | 112 | 100 | 143 | 133 | 121 | 120 |
| Independent Socialists | 81 | | | | | |
| Centrists (Catholic) | 68 | 65 | 68 | 75 | 69 | 73 |
| Nationalists | 66 | 95 | 43 | 40 | 51 | 52 |
| People's | 62 | 45 | 29 | 7 | 11 | 4 |
| Democrats | 45 | 28 | | | | |
| Communists | 2 | 62 | 77 | 89 | 100 | 81 |
| Hitlerites | .. | 32 | 107 | 230 | 195 | 288 |

Hitler, who once had said, "If Germany could be given a Mussolini, the people would kneel down and worship him," demanded the chancellorship on August 13, 1932. Hindenburg said, "Are you willing to enter a government headed by the present chancellor?"

Hitler: "I am not willing, nor are my associates. We wish to request the president to entrust us with leadership. . . ."

Hindenburg: "What power do you imply in that request?"

Hitler: "The same power that Mussolini exercised after the March on Rome."

Hindenburg: "Before my own conscience and in the light of my duty to the Fatherland, I will not entrust such power to a party which intends to use it so one-sidedly."

In January, 1933, Hindenburg named Hitler to form a government.

For a few weeks the world commented on the mildness of the Fascist reign. The Treaty of Versailles was not torn up and heads did not roll in the dust, as Hitler had promised; neither were the twenty-six billion marks in foreign loans repudiated nor were the Jews expropriated.

Then, taking his lesson from Mussolini, the German chancellor began to condense ten years of Italian Fascist progress into so many weeks. First of all he suppressed the freedom of the press — and from then on the road to absolute power became easy. The Prussian authorities were ordered to supply arms to the Nazi army; the armed Fascists began to terrorize all opposition elements, socialists as well as communists, Catholics as well as Jews. Riots and street fights occurred in a hundred cities. As in Italy, the Fascisti were armed by the government, the Opposition almost defenseless. The Fascisti won.

At the end of February, with the new general election near, there was a great sensation in the burning of the Reichstag. A Dutch youth was arrested. Hitler said it was a communist plot. Proof was found by the foreign press that the incendiary Van Der Lubbe was a Fascist *agent provocateur,* had been expelled from the Dutch Communist Party two years earlier, had arrived on a forged passport supplied by Germans, and had probably entered the Reichstag with numerous assistants through the palace of the Reichstag president, the Fascist Goering. Hitler, furious that foreign nations called the Reichstag destruction a plot, blamed the radicals and Jews, the chancellor of Germany using phrases such as, "We will exterminate these dogs with a fist of iron."

On the 28th of February, Hitler persuaded the so-called savior of the Republic, Hindenburg, to abolish the constitutional guarantees. Articles Number 114, 115, 117, 118, and 153 were decreed ineffective and the terror began. Liberty of press and person went the way of Russia and Italy. The government in its official statement to the press actually declared, "The parliamentary and democratic government has disappeared." Goering ordered the mass arrest of communist members of parliament. Workers who went on strike could be tried for treason. Stegerwald, the Catholic leader, was slugged by Fascists. Jews by the hundreds were beaten and robbed. Hundreds of newspapers were suppressed. The one hundred and thirty members of the foreign press corps were warned that attempts to smuggle news unfavorable to Fascism abroad would not be tolerated. Several were arrested for holding the Hitlerites responsible for the Reichstag fire.

On March 5, with the Opposition press muzzled, with five thousand Opposition leaders in prison, and with Opposition meetings suppressed, Hitler obtained a great victory in the general election. It was a mandate to dictatorship. The Third Empire came into life. The Republic was dead.

The Hitlerite celebration of victory was marked with attacks upon the Jews, news of which was suppressed for many days. American Jews protested to the embassy in Berlin. The Hitler Government apologized. On the tenth, Goering issued a statement that there would be no police protection for Jews. Atrocities increased throughout March. The New York *Post's* correspondent, Knickerbocker, reporting "an indeterminate number of Jews killed, hundreds beaten and tortured, thousands deprived of their livelihood." Captain Goering, according to the smuggled reports of the same journalist, told the press the atrocities "never happened; they will be investigated; they will never happen again."

Claiming that the Jewish protests were untrue, the Fascisti on the first day of April began a national boycott of the six hundred thousand Jews of the Empire. Nazi braves stood at every Jewish store, using violence when necessary to prevent persons entering; Jewish judges, lawyers, doctors and other professional men were barred from practice. Bank accounts, including that of Professor Einstein, were seized. In almost every instance of violence, the victims were robbed as well as beaten or tortured in Fascist barracks.

Emulating his great Italian teacher, Hitler began meddling with the Church. A noted Lutheran preacher declared Christ was a Nazi and the Fascisti proclaimed their Swastika of equal value with the original Christian cross. Ludendorff's "return to Wotan" was revived. It was said the German Fascists were going back to sagas and fairies.

What meanwhile was happening to Fascism itself? "The epoch of reprisals, devastations and violences is finished. Illegalism in all form must end," the Duce ordered and sold an article to the *Cosmopolitan*, "Why I Am Closing Italy's Cabarets."

Mont Blanc was renamed Monte Mussolini by Secretary General Turati, despite the fact the peak is in France.

A treaty and concordat were announced by Cardinal Gasparri on February 11, 1929, peace ending the fifty-nine-year struggle between the Vatican and the State, Mussolini succeeding where Cavour, Crispi and Nitti had failed. Four days later the Pope said to the Catholic students of the University of Milan, "We believe that, thanks to the concordat, we have given back God to Italy and Italy to God", but early in May the first rift occurred when Mussolini said publicly, "We are Fascists and Catholics, but Fascists first. No pact, no concordat, can modify our moral character. The Church is not sovereign in the State."

The question whether the Church or the State educate the young was raised immediately.

In America, Marcus Duffield, in *Harper's,* published "Mussolini's Empire: The Fascist Invasion of the United States", bringing to the attention of the State Department and the Senate the charges that Mussolini "has set up a political organization in the United States . . . provides Fascist schools and courts, even imposes taxes" and that "neither in this country nor in Italy does American citizenship safeguard the Italo-American from Fascist domination or terrorism." The Senate heard that Italian consuls endeavored to influence the American school curriculum, tried to collect the bachelor taxes, discouraged Italians from becoming citizens; that returning naturalized citizens had their passports torn up by Fascists and were forced into the army, and that the Fascist organization in America takes an oath of allegiance to the Duce and Italy. Count Thaon di Revel ordered the Fascist League of North America dissolved and it reappeared immediately under the name Federation of the Lictor.

*Underwood and Underwood*

ADOLF HITLER EMERGING FROM THE HEADQUARTERS OF THE NAZIS AT MUNICH

HITLERITE CAMPAIGN PROPAGANDA, 1932

"German girls, repulse the Jews; send them back to their dark Sarahs and Rebeccas!"

In November all Italian youths between the ages of eighteen and twenty were ordered into military training. Inasmuch as the army claims them at twenty and the Balilla, Avanguardia and other children's organizations give military training up to eighteen, a complete militarization of youth was achieved.

D'Annunzio, refusing to join the Fascist Academy, said, "A horse of pure blood should not mix with asses," explaining it was not meant as an insult but was an "eugenic-artistic fact."

Nineteen Thirty-one again brought the United States into an imbroglio with Fascism when Major General Smedley D. Butler, commander of the Marine base at Quantico, Virginia, made a speech to the Contemporary Club which was not kept confidential. He portrayed Mussolini as "a mad dog about to break loose in Europe" and quoted a friend who claimed to have made an inspection tour by automobile with Mussolini in the course of which the dictator struck a child and let it die, saying, "What is one life in the affairs of State?"

Cornelius Vanderbilt claimed he was the journalist who accompanied the Duce. "I was riding with Mussolini, who drove. A small child ran in front of the machine . . . and was hit. I looked back to see if the child was hurt. Mussolini placed his hand on my knee and said, 'Never look back, Vanderbilt, always look ahead in life'."

General Butler was up for court-martial but apologized to Secretary Adams and closed the incident.

In summer, 1931, came the long-awaited battle between Church and State. In April, the Pope had written Cardinal Schuster of Milan a complaint that the Fascisti were exposing the youth of Italy "to inspirations of hate and irreverence, making difficult and almost impossible the practice of religious duties", and all the newsboys of Rome were arrested for shouting "Pope's letter" and their copies of the Vatican organ, *Osservatore Romano,* confiscated. (May 28 a naturalized American, Michele Schirru, who had left the banana business in the Bronx for a voyage to Rome, was charged with conspiring to blow up the dictator with a bomb, and executed.) May 30, Mussolini dissolved the Azione Cattolica, an organization of half a million young Catholics (the only rival of the Fascist Youth organizations) which the official Fascist press accused of political plotting, aiming to supplant the régime with a Catholic dictatorship under the guidance of Monsignor Pizzardo, the undersecretary of the Vatican State.

*Osservatore Romano* reported that young Fascists attacked Catholics, that students shouted "Death to the Pope", that Fascisti smashed all the windows to the fifth floor of the Catholic Students' Association, raided a Catholic publishing house and threw copies of a book, "The Pope", into the street with shouts of "traitor", trampled underfoot a painting of the Pope, and other acts of violence totaling thirty-five. The Roman police raided and closed three hundred Catholic clubs and the Knights of Columbus playground. Edward L. Hearn, its representative, went to the American embassy, saying, "I demand simple Yankee justice", but no action of the ambassador is recorded. Mussolini ordered the prefects of Italy to use discretionary power, with the result that fifteen thousand Catholic centers were closed.

To break the Fascist censorship, the Pope smuggled to Paris on the twenty-ninth of June an encyclical in which Fascism was declared incompatible with Catholicism: "A conception of the State which makes the rising generations belong to it entirely, without any exception, from the tenderest years up to adult life, cannot be reconciled by a Catholic either with Catholic doctrine or with the natural rights of the family."

The dictator replied, making Catholicism incompatible with Fascism: "From to-day membership of the Fascist Party and membership of the organizations of the Catholic Action Party is irreconcilable. These orders have been issued by the Government and the Duce."

In February, 1929, Mussolini had given up everything the Pope demanded, in exchange for the prestige his régime would get by making peace with the Vatican; now he was trying to win everything back. In September, a compromise was reached, by which the Azione Cattolica became diocesan, under the bishops, promised to refrain from political activity, banned former members of the Catholic Party, barred professional associations and trade unions, made Catholics promise to "refrain from pursuing any activity whatever of an athletic and sporting nature", and to restrict themselves to religious and spiritual purposes. Thus the hope of anti-Fascists that a liberal reform might come through the Catholic Church was shattered. The year closed with the arrest of all university professors who refused to take an oath of allegiance to the Fascist régime. Oxford, Cambridge, Harvard and a hundred other universities protested in the name of academic freedom.

In 1932, through Ambassador di Martino, the Duce warned Paramount that unless the film made from Hemingway's "Farewell to Arms" was cut so that the Caporetto disaster became anything but a disaster, all Paramount movies would be banned in Italy. The film was cut!

In August, owing to the economic crisis, the marriage and birth rates, despite repeated orders from the dictator to the contrary, declined to the lowest point in ten years.

January 1, 1933, the preliminary estimate given the Cabinet for the 1933–1934 budget showed a deficit of two billion, nine hundred million lire, which with the losses due to the movement of capital, would amount to double the deficit of the past fiscal year.

The outstanding armed conflict of the Thirties was Japan's undeclared war in China. When in January, 1933, Count Uchida, Japanese Foreign Minister, proclaimed the Asiatic Monroe Doctrine, Asia for the Asiatics, it was interpreted to mean Asia for the Japanese, and partly confirmed the secret survey and report, often denied by Japan but declared official by China, made by Premier Tanaka in 1927. The Tanaka document, published by the Progressive-Republican Party of

China, was stolen by a Chinese translator in the Japanese Foreign Office. It details for the emperor the possible ways and means of imperialistic expansion in China, Manchuria, French Indo-China, India, the Philippines and Siberia. Events have proved the plan is being carried out methodically.

China, unable to contend with Japan on the battle field, originated a policy of "prolonged resistance." It involved, economically, a complete boycott of Japanese goods, active societies being formed everywhere, unlike the half-hearted disorganized boycotting of past years. The center of resistance was Shanghai.

Japan protested that a boycott equals an open declaration of war. September 18, 1931, the destruction of a railroad bridge near Mukden was used by the Japanese as a Sarajevo excuse to occupy important towns in Manchuria and Mukden itself. China protested to the League of Nations in October. Japan denied territorial ambitions in Manchuria but protested the boycott and the anti-Japanese campaign. In November, Japan occupied Tsitsihar. The United States sent a note. The League called a meeting in Paris. Japan ignored them all and extended her occupation of Manchuria. It was the viewpoint of the whole world, outside Japan, that this nation had violated the Nine Power Treaty.

Universal opinion against Japan was broken when the French press turned color. During the first months of the Sino-Japanese "war" the big Paris newspapers sent their special correspondents, whose dispatches accused Japan of the entire guilt. There were even Japanese atrocity stories. China won the sympathy of France. Soon, however, huge orders for ammunitions were received, important diplomatic conferences were held, loans were issued by French banks. The Banque Franco-Nippone came under the control of the great French munitions firm of Schneider. The munitions makers and bankers told the French press to change its tune. Cablegrams were sent the correspondents in the Far East. Soon news dispatches began

*International News Photos.*

DICTATOR ADOLF HITLER AND THE FORMER CROWN PRINCE WILHELM OF GERMANY

appearing in France which, instead of lionizing the brave, outnumbered and outgunned Chinese, referred to them as bandits, called their campaign guerilla warfare, declared their country in a state of anarchy. France soon stood on the side of Japan.

Japan opened the year 1932 by attacking Shanghai, imperiling the European and American settlements. China appealed to the League. In February Manchuria was declared independent.

Czechoslovakia, Esthonia, Greece, with her memories of Corfu, and twelve more nations accused Japan of forcing the war, of being morally wrong, of violating the League's various peace treaties; they demanded removal of Japanese troops. But the great powers refused to take sides. Not only was France supplying loans and ammunitions, but other countries were apparently earning a little easy money the same way. Hugh Gibson, the representative of the United States, gave the League the impression that Hoover was against the proposed economic sanctions, let alone military sanctions which might be warranted in this situation. The League could do no more than pass a resolution.

New Year's Day, 1933, the Japanese propaganda bureau in Geneva reported, two bombs were thrown by Chinese soldiers at a Japanese outpost at Shanhaikwan, the junction of the Great Wall of the Peiping-Mukden Railway; the propaganda does not state whether the bombs exploded, whether any one was killed or injured, whether property or chickens were damaged. Within a few days the Japanese army was on the march. Japanese airplanes were dropping bombs on soldiers and civilians alike, and not only was Shanhaikwan captured but the road opened for the control of the province of Jehol. Japan entered the Great Wall. There was a rumor that Pu-yi, the puppet president of Manchuria, or Manchukuo as Japan named the country, would within the year be Japan's president of a United Japanese China.

However, in 1933, the League of Nations, which somehow had survived Mussolini's attack in 1923 and regained its prestige by stopping the Bulgar war of 1925, now faced its own problem, frankly called life or death. China again called for aid. A committee of nineteen was named, but, unable to accomplish anything, resigned at the end of January and threw the Manchurian war into the lap of the Assembly of the League. Lord Rothermere's press went over to Japan. "No European Power is deeply interested in the control of Manchuria," editorialized the *Daily Mail;* "whereas that control is vital to the safety of Japan. She has rights which every impartial mind must admit. . . . For her interests there she fought the war of 1904–1905 with Russia." The old dead Red bogey of 1920, given a new coat of paint, was raised in 1933 by Lord Rothermere.

The decade saw few other military movements but many peace efforts. In 1930, Venizelos and Kemal Pasha ended five hundred years of warfare by the treaty of Ankora. Liberia abolished slavery. The London Naval Treaty was signed for a building holiday to 1936 by Britain, Japan, and the United States. The French army quit the Rhineland five years ahead of treaty time. Bells tolled and bonfires burned. The French flag was hauled down in silence and the Germans sang "Deutschland über Alles" as theirs went up. A few feeble Separatists were beaten by patriots.

"Thus," said Burgomaster Ehrhard of Mainz, "ends the world War more than a decade after the Armistice was signed."

## Interlude 1931

Signor Marinetti issued Futurist-Fascist edicts against spaghetti; Italians needed dishes to make them dynamic; *pasta asciutta* produced torpor, pessimism and scepticism. Willie Seabrook ate a rib stew and a rump steak cut from a fresh Negro warrior just killed in jungle battle. It tasted like a coarse veal. Never again will the "long pork" myth dare raise its gory head in Willie's presence.

The ten-year respectful silence at the Tomb of the Unknown Soldier in France was broken by an American mayor, who had to deliver a speech. President Hoover, dedicating Harding's tomb, said, "Warren Harding had a dim realization that he had been betrayed . . . these men betrayed not alone the friendship and trust of their stanch and loyal friend, but they betrayed their country. Those crimes never touched the character of Warren Harding."

The Titanic, Homeric, epiphenomenal duel of the ages: Culbertson *v.* Lenz.

The Jazz Age is over.

The Yoshiwara, celebrated for over three hundred years as the gay night-life center of Tokio, has been closed. Public tastes have changed under the pressure of hard times.

The tabloid press was accused of killing Benita Bischoff. An underworld character, Vivian Gordon, having been found strangled to death, the three New York tabloids pounced upon the daughter, who never knew her mother was a gold-digger. Benita wrote in her diary, "What an awful mess mother got herself into. The papers are saying such terrible things. . . . I just can't live any longer." She turned on the gas.

Gavreau, first editor of the so-called porno-*Graphic*, resigned after five years of dealing in scandal, crime, sex, smut and faked pictures. "Read a fresh magazine. All our editors are cellophane wrapped," ballyhooed *Ballyhoo,* whose editor got several hundred thousand circulation by parodying the advertisements.

British electioneering went Americanese. Lady Diana Manners' husband, Duff Cooper, said, "Lord Rothermere hasn't got the guts of a louse." Lady Cynthia Mosley said, "England needs a government with guts."

The British novelist-lecturers still criticize America. Priestley was quoted as saying, "You Americans are literary snobs. . . . You spoil your women. . . . I turned in the direction of the United States and thumbed my nose."

Prince Nicholas punched King Carol in the jaw. (Prince Carol had punched Queen Marie's friend, Prince Stirbey, historically in the jaw.) Nicholas had married a plebeian, a Mme. Deletz. King Carol said it was a crime against the royal dynasty. (Prince Carol had married a plebeian, Mlle. Zambrino.) Magda Lupescu, Prince and King Carol's Jewish mistress, embraced the Orthodox Catholic religion. Rumania went tabloid again in 1931.

Prince August Wilhelm, fourth son of the august Kaiser, went Fascist. "Adolf Hitler is God's gift to Germany. Where Hitler leads, a Hohenzollern can conscientiously follow." The Kaiser was more cautious.

Paul Doumer, perpetual candidate for President of France since 1906, was elected for many reasons: he was perpetual; he had lost four sons; he opposed Briand and Briand was a pacifist.

Willy Post and Harold Gatty flew around the world in eight days fifteen hours and fifty-one minutes. Knute Rockne, coach of Notre Dame football team, one of the greatest names in the history of football, was killed with seven others, when their ice-coated plane lost a wing. Later it was said gangsters had tampered with the machine in order to kill a witness who was going to Chicago.

Owing to the increase of suicide in Monte Carlo and Nice, a Never-Say-Die club was formed with the coöperation of the managers of the casinos. All persons losing heavily are turned over to the club.

The losses in dividends from the 1929 panic to September 30, 1931, are two and one half billion dollars. New York Stock Exchange figures for September 1 indicate loss in listed stocks of more than forty-five billion dollars or more than fifty per cent. their value September, 1929, while additional depreciation in month makes total of sixty billion dollars.

Germany's birth rate, first time in history below France's, blamed on depression.

Soviet papers turned the tables on American papers, proving that fake news makes the world go round. Reported Moscow, to the delight of its anti-capitalist readers: "Thirty million are literally dying of hunger in the United States. Many farmers are literally starving to death — hundreds of thousands are ill with pellagra, the disease of famine sufferers. The fighting spirit of the masses against starvation is fast flaring up." Emma Goldman published her memoirs, "Living My Life." She described Moscow: "People raided, imprisoned and shot for their *ideas!* . . . The best human values betrayed, the very spirit of revolution daily crucified. . . . The Cheka was nothing more than a gang of cutthroats."

Many people thought the world crisis would be killed by the Empress Eugénie hat — small, but full of feathers and trickeries, requiring a loosening up of the pocketbook.

General Ludendorff was going to save Germany by manufacturing cheap gold, by a process which the alchemist Franz Tausend taught him. Franz got three years eight months in jail.

A Dutchman, who thought the nude body immoral, slashed Rembrandt's "The Anatomy Lesson" in the Rijks Museum.

New York mourned the end of the *World*.

## CHAPTER SEVENTEEN

### Our Own Chastened or Enlightened Times

Change, perhaps progress, in the world's customs, manners, thinking and actions must be recorded in the years of self-criticism, disillusion, and revaluation which followed the bursting of the Golden Age. The Nineteen Thirties were chastened or enlightened, perhaps both.

Balancing the emotional and moral budget would be a thankless task; in which column, for example, should one place the failure of prohibition in many countries, the passage of laws raising or lowering alcohol percentages, the increase of crime, the restatement of the inviolability of the marriage sacrament by one great Church, the easing of divorce by another great Church, the spread of smoking among women? Consider, for instance, the discovery that Queen Mary of England, the Paragon of Purity, the Viceroy of Virtue, the Mistress of Morality, the supremely excellent this, that and the other of all that was Right and Good and Decent in this muddled world — smoked cigarettes! Ohio and Kansas clubwomen cabled protests in 1930. Alas, the fact was confirmed. Nicotine and Barleycorn recorded many victories at this time. Was it progress, or were America and Europe going to hell again, as in the old days?

The American Child Health Association revealed the fact that flapper and jazzy mothers, despite short skirts, rouge, drinking and cigarettes, were raising healthier babies than the lavender and old lace ladies. The death rate had been one hundred and eleven per thousand pre-war, seventy-five per thousand in 1920, the flapper age, sixty-four in 1928, the jazz age, and was somewhat lower in the Thirties. Sports apparently were overcoming cocktails and cigarettes.

Sermons were preached on thousands of miscellaneous subjects and conflicting lessons drawn of progress or decay, regeneration or failure. The Reverend John Haynes Holmes named his ten greatest living women: Jane Addams, Annie Besant, Catherine Breshkovsky, the Russian revolutionist, Mme. Curie, Emma Goldman, deported anarchist, Helen Keller, Edna Millay, who wrote poems and picketed in favor of Sacco and Vanzetti, Mme. Naidu, the Indian revolutionist, Sigrid Undset and Margaret Sanger, the birth-control revolutionist. The rebel Jefferson Davis appeared at last in Washington, in bronze. Sir Edmund Ovey, British ambassador to Russia, reported, "There is no religious persecution in Russia in the strict sense of the term 'persecution', and no case has been discovered of a priest or any one being punished for the practice of religion."

Her Highness Maharani Setu Lakshmi Bayi, ruling the State of Travancore in India, abolished *devadasi* (handmaiden of the god) or temple prostitution. The Spanish Republic abolished the decree which apparently had remained in force since the inquisition of 1492, banishing the Jews and Moors. A hundred such events and expressions indicating tolerance and progress, or their opposite, could be recorded at the beginning of the decade.

In the Vatican, the old radio receiving set was now superseded by a broadcasting station, and in many other mechanical ways modernity entered, but in respect to such matters as marriage, for instance, the Roman Catholic Church remained adamant.

In 1931 the Pope issued an encyclical in which no concessions were granted to birth control, sterilization, easy divorces, loose marriage bonds or the pleasures of the flesh.

In June the Presbyterian General Assembly in Pittsburgh voted in favor of universal stringent barriers to divorce; it also took occasion to denounce the follies of Hollywood, the divorce mill of Reno, the tabloid and sensational press, and evil movies.

But in other Churches there were reforms or changes. The Episcopal Church, convened in Denver, in September, adopted a new canon whereby "any person whose former marriage has been annulled or dissolved by a civil court and pronounced null by the bishop, may be married by a minister of this church as if he had never previously been married." Restrictions which dated behind the Reformation to the Church of Rome were thus discarded.

The Religious Society of Friends, commonly known as Quakers, amended its Book of Discipline, which had ordered plain dress without frills or laces.

In 1932, a joint commission of the Methodist Episcopal and Methodist Protestant churches revised the hymnal eliminating "fountains of blood" from Watts' famous poem and other bloody references.

In September of the same year a great step in church unity was recorded in England, when the three Methodist Churches became one.

The question of birth control now became international. In 1931 the clinics of Moscow, which had flourished with signs like commonplace shops, were removed to side streets and unadvertised, the Soviet Government apparently having decided it needed more men for future industry and wars. It was announced that sixty thousand births and seventy thousand abortions were Moscow's average for a year. Physicians reported they always advised against abortion of a first child. "Soviet technique," the report added, "is so advanced that the simple operation is now performed in about three minutes." It is a government service and free.

Julian Huxley, the British biologist, lecturing in Philadelphia, predicted the world would turn towards birth control because sooner or later there would not be standing room left.

Mussolini, addressing a convention of Italian doctors, warned them against birth control "in language coarse and picturesque", which unfortunately the censorship replaced with euphemisms. To a group of important American tourists he made the statement, "Birth control is a crime", which led some vile dog of an anti-Fascist in a Paris newspaper to remark, "but it has saved the world at least one hundred little Mussolinis in the past twenty years."

The behavior of the younger generation continued to agitate the older. Mrs. Franklin D. Roosevelt, who was appearing in numerous magazines and newspaper syndicates, gave her opinion, that "To-day a girl may go out with any young man that she knows — quite regardless of whether her parents know him — and her parents must be able to trust her judgment. . . . I think I would say that I really would not bring up a daughter to-day at all — I would let her grow, in as sympathetic and understanding an atmosphere as possible, and I would encourage her to develop, having always in mind that her life was her own to lead and she must be helped to lead it satisfactorily."

Dame Beatrix Lyall, Vice Chairman of the London County Council, learned "during the last few years that quite respectable girls go away for week-ends with men to whom they are not married. Some of them are engaged to be married and some are not. In my view, it is utterly unfair to put a man in such temptation, and it is trying human nature too far."

The collapse of Coolidge-Hoover prosperity shortly after the arrival of Dry Mr. Hoover started the anti-prohibition movement of the Nineteen Thirties to its victorious goal. For the first time since the passage of the Eighteenth Amendment (January 16, 1919, effective one year later), the war-time prohibition law (November, 1918, effective June 30, 1919) and the National Prohibition Act (Volstead Act, effective January 17, 1920, after the passage over President Wilson's veto on October 28, 1919) the movement became so popular it could claim a majority of the citizenry. Again the cry was repeated that prohibition had been passed while two million men were enjoying beer and wine when not in the trenches overseas, that it was a symptom of war-time hysteria, that it was an act of small-time politicians and not a universal movement.

The country had grown tired of bad liquor and of racketeering, which had become big business. It had grown accustomed to speak-easies. For the second time in history, the sacredness of law was questioned — the first was State Rights and had led to Civil War, and the second was leading to a crime war in which the criminal element was, if not winning, at least holding its own. Referendums indicated the time had come for some change. The builders of the Republican platform who had guessed right in 1928 now in 1932 were forced to adopt an ambiguous plank which gave hope to the Wets; the Democrats, sensing the general dissatisfaction better, went wetter than ever.

The momentum for revision or/and repeal, which had been slow in the Twenties, came along with tremendous force in the Thirties.

In the 1932 election, President Hoover entered the fray a Damp and Governor Roosevelt a Dripping Wet. Prohibition, of course, was not the great issue in a time of twelve million unemployed and an economic breakdown. Just as the Wets were able to say twelve years earlier that the law which deprived them of their liquor was part of war-time hysteria, so the Drys now began to say they lost because the Democratic landslide, which was an economic protest, carried prohibition along.

November 8, 1932, millions of persons thought that by Christmas they would be drinking real stuff again publicly. They were disappointed. The best that could be done for them was modification of the Volstead Act, which defined liquor as alcohol, brandy, whisky, rum, gin, beer, ale, porter and wine or other beverages containing .005 or more of alcohol. The battle for 3.2 liquor ended successfully and the seventh of April witnessed the return of beer and light wines.

In February, 1932, the Finnish Parliament responded to the national demand for cheap liquor by setting prices such as thirty cents a bottle for vodka, seventy-five cents a quart for whisky and thirty-five cents to a dollar and a half for wine. The Drys, who had lost the prohibition referendum, succeeded in having Parliament devote a portion of the profits therefrom to teaching prohibition, and the bootleggers, who had copied American manners perfectly and had also supported prohibition, were utterly frustrated.

Switzerland, in 1933, devoted the greatest part of the liquor taxes, which are from twenty cents a quart up, for old-age pensions, providing incidentally food and shelter for gentlemen who drink themselves out of home and job in their best years. Beer and wine are not taxed. In 1931 a Dry referendum failed.

In 1927, the partial prohibition act in Norway was repealed by plebiscite. Prohibition was defeated in New Zealand in 1928. The Bratt System, which had worked well in Sweden since 1922 and by which hard liquor was apportioned by coupon books, was recommended in America by numerous persons who feared the old drunken but now highly romanticized and applauded corner saloon would replace the present unromantic, expensive speak-easy.

A Southern commission, issuing its report on lynching, showed that from 1889 to 1931 three thousand, six hundred and three persons were the victims of mobs, four hundred and sixty-five in Georgia and four hundred and sixty-four in Mississippi, although based on Negro population, Florida had been first in number. It showed that in fifty per cent. of the lynchings there was real doubt of guilt, and the most remarkable of all facts, that less than twenty-five per cent. of the victims were accused of what is called "the usual crime", — attacks on white women. The report declared that mob leaders can always be identified if there is sufficient public demand. In the bad business year, 1892, there were 255 lynchings (one hundred white); in the boom time, 1929, only ten, and in 1930 the number rose to twenty-one.

In Russia, the assault of a Negro worker in a soviet factory led to the prison sentence of Lem Lewis and Bill Brown, two white American employees guilty of "racial chauvinism." They were deported "because they are persons imbued with the spirit of race prejudice and therefore dangerous, menacing persons to have in Russia." At the same time, the Third Internationale intensified its effort to stir discontent among Negro workers in America, many of whom joined the Communist Party. In 1932, it chose James W. Ford, a Negro, candidate for the Vice President.

Mrs. Mary Ware Dennett, author of a booklet, "The Sex Side of Life", written for her children and distributed by the Young Men's Christian Association, was brought into court, United States Attorney Wilkinson calling the book "pure and simple smut." It was a *cause célèbre,* fought by Attorney Morris L. Ernst to victory in the court of appeals. The postal authorities and Sumner found they could do nothing to stop the Spanish Government from reproducing Goya's Maja, nude, on its peso stamps. New York clergymen denounced Gilbert Seldes' modern translation of Aristophanes' "Lysistrata" and Earl Carroll's "Vanities", both as "unabashed pagan mockery . . . audacious assault upon public decency . . . which unfortunately cannot be reached by the police."

Judge Woolsey permitted publication of Marie Stopes' "Married Love", banned since 1918, now that America had matured, and Van Der Velde's "Ideal Marriage" was published with all its diagrams for doctors, ministers and social workers. Clarence Darrow prepared for a second Scopes trial when the New York State Board of Censors tried to stop "The Mystery of Life", made chiefly from old U.F.A. and other animal movies. Among the orders sent by Doctor Wingate were "Remove views of child at mother's breast.". . . Reason, "Indecent." Among royalty which added critical opinion to the decade was Prince George of England, who was sure "that Doctor Johnson would have quickly sickened of novels which only exist on a disproportionate interest in sex."

Gentle Professor Einstein has been the cause of battle between pacifists and militarists in Germany, France and California at least once every year of the new decade.

He arrived in New York on December 11, 1930, terrified by the boat reporters, of whom he said laughingly, "They are like wolves biting into my flesh." One shouted, "Will religion bring about world peace?" to which he replied, "Until now it has not done so. I am no prophet"; and another demanded, "Define the fourth dimension in a word." The professor didn't. Mrs. Einstein wrote a very human report on the professor and herself:

> To be the wife of a genius is not the ideal life. Far from it. Your life does not belong to you. Every minute of the day belongs to my husband, and therefore to the public.
>
> My husband has never offered to explain the Einstein theory to me. My interest in mathematics is largely confined to the grocery bill.
>
> Professor Einstein is no eccentric.
> He is not absent-minded.
> He dislikes dirt and confusion.
> Politically we are socialists.

The professor was immediately accused of being a pacifist, socialist, communist. He did not deny the first impeachment. In fact, he proposed the first militant-pacifist program, a sort of "war resisters of the world unite" idea, at a meeting of the New History Society. His three proposals were:

In time of peace, in nations which have compulsory conscription, refuse to do such service.

In time of war, refuse to do service.

To prove you are not a coward, engage in dangerous services for the cause of peace.

"In our political situation," said the professor in German, "it is the duty of man to commit crime in the name of his State or his country; it seems to me that it is more his duty to free mankind from this sort of thing. Pacifists should work actively to recruit people to the idea all over the world. And to the timid ones it is necessary to say that if you only got two per cent. of the people, the cause of peace would be saved, for that many people would be by far too many to cope with. There would not be jail room enough for them all."

All the professional patriotic societies in many countries were annoyed by the Einstein program. In Paris, the Camelots du Roi denounced it and in Berlin the students of the university shouted "Sau Jude" at the mention of Einstein's name. In Los Angeles the American Legion was urged by its organizer, Doctor A. D. Houghton, to prevent the scientist's visit to California.

A year later the first international conference of war resisters was held in Lyons, France, the home town of ex-mayor and ex-Premier Herriot. Einstein sent a message:

"Those who think that the danger of war is past are living in a fools' paradise. We have to face to-day a militarism far more powerful and destructive than the militarism which brought the disaster of the World War.

"This is the achievement of governments. But among the peoples of the world, the idea of war resistance is spreading.

"I appeal to the intellectuals of the world. I appeal to my fellow scientists to refuse to coöperate in research for war purposes. I appeal to all men and women to declare they will refuse to give any further assistance to war or to preparation for war."

Asked to express his credo, Einstein wrote in 1931: "The ideals which have always shone before me and filled me with joy of living are goodness, beauty and truth." This stamped him as an absolutely hopeless and naïve idealist and removed him from the list of dangerous persons. Except to American consuls. In December, 1932, when Einstein prepared to come to Princeton, the Woman Patriot Corporation protested and called him a communist. The professor was catechized "like a little boy", in the words of Mrs. Einstein, by the American consul in Berlin. "Are you doing this on supreme authority or for your own amusement?" Einstein finally asked. The consul continued to pump questions about socialism, anarchism, communism, pacifism.

"If ever the law was an ass," commented Walter Lippmann, "it was when Mr. Messersmith (Consul General, Berlin) undertook to administer the law. For his benefit and for bureaucrats like him all future laws of Congress should contain a clause saying, 'This law is to be administered by men in possession of at least ordinary intelligence and common sense'." The State Department closed the incident by claiming an assistant consul was responsible.

The literary sensation of 1930 was Sinclair Lewis' speech of acceptance of the Nobel prize, and the literary scandal of 1931 was the slap which Theodore Dreiser gave Mr. Lewis, a slap that was heard around the world. On the first occasion Lewis reviewed American literature and *litterateurs:*

I imagined what would have been said had you chosen some American other than myself.

Suppose you had taken Theodore Dreiser. Now to me, as to many other American writers, Dreiser, more than any other man, is marching alone. Usually unappreciated, often hounded, he has cleared the trail from Victorian, Howellsian timidity and gentility in American fiction to honesty, boldness, and passion of life.

Without his pioneering, I doubt if any of us could, unless we liked to be sent to jail, seek to express life, beauty, and terror.

There is Ernest Hemingway, a bitter youth educated by the most intense experience, disciplined by his own high standards, an authentic artist whose home is in the whole of life.

There is Thomas Wolfe, a child of, I believe, thirty or younger, whose only novel, "Look Homeward, Angel", is worthy to be compared with the best of our literary productions, a Gargantuan creature with a great gusto of life.

There is Thornton Wilder, who in an age of realism, dreams of old love and dreams of eternal romances.

There is John Dos Passos, with a hatred of the safe and sane standards of *Babbitt,* and with the splendor of revolution.

There is Stephen Benét, who, to American drabness, has restored the epic poem with his glorious memory of John Brown; and there are a dozen young poets and fictionists, most of them living in Paris, most of them a little insane in the tradition of James Joyce, who, however insane they may be, have refused to be genteel, traditional, and dull.

The Lewisian strictures found little approval in the American lay press. Critics, however, believed that fifty to one hundred years from now this writer would still stand out as the representative of his age and country, thereby justifying the choice of the Nobel committee. Mr. Shaw's view was: "Sinclair Lewis said just the right thing in the right place to the Swedish Academy. . . .

"I myself have been particularly careful never to say a civil word to the United States. I have scoffed at their inhabitants as a nation of villagers. I have defined the one hundred per cent. American as ninety-nine per cent. an idiot. And they just adore me and will go on adoring me, until in a moment of senile sentimentality I say something nice about them, when they will at once begin to suspect me of being only a cheap skate after all, and drop me like a hot potato."

In March, 1931, Ray Long invited American writers to honor Boris Pilnyak, the first soviet *litterateur* to visit America. Among those present were Messrs. Dreiser and Lewis. Called upon to say something, "Red" Lewis refused. "I do not care to speak in the presence of one man who has plagiarized three thousand words from my wife's book on Russia. Nor do I care to talk before two sage critics who have lamented the action of the Nobel committee in selecting me as America's representative writer." To Dreiser's first slap Lewis turned the other red cheek and literature became almost as important in New York as a prize fight.

Art went very patriotic. Hard times caused dealers who had been supporting young artists in Montparnasse to recall them to the American scene. A picture described "Old Houses, St. Paul, Minn." had twenty times the chance of "Vieux Maisons,

St. Paul, Alpes Maritimes." Every boat now found American painters and sculptors going home — to stay home.

Jacob Epstein, American resident of London, produced a white marble "Genesis" for Alfred Charles Bossom, designer of buildings in New York, Boston and Dallas. The Manchester *Guardian*, politically liberal, thought it fine; the London *Express*, politically reactionary, called it "white foulness."

A great Picasso retrospective show was held in London. Mrs. Chester Dale thought that Picasso, "like a God, destroys Nature itself when the impulse seizes him and re-creates it in a new and more wonderful form which he has discovered." Brisbane said, "You feel ashamed for the human race when you realize that stuff such as this is actually shown and bought by people supposed to be sane."

In 1932, American artists lost their pride or self-consciousness and held their first open-air show in Washington Square, in the manner of weekly summer happenings on the Boulevard Raspail. One picture, a nude, was turned on its back on complaint of a passer-by. There was a storm in the Art Students' League when Georg Grosz of Berlin was engaged. Jonas Lie, an American Academician, thought Grosz was not a healthy influence for the progress of American youth. Others whispered "communist." Grosz, however, was engaged.

In Paris, of all places, American artists had their nudes thrown out when they tried to hang them at the American Women's Club. The art committee explained, "There are nudes and nudes. One has to draw the line somewhere. . . . The nudes we are showing are decorative and chaste!"

The myth which had always connected foreigners with crime in America was finally laid in the Wickersham Report, which showed that, proportionately, aliens commit fewer crimes. Foreign-born residents approach the record of native-born most closely in the commission of crimes of personal violence, the report concludes, and in crimes for gain the native-born greatly exceed the foreign-born. The New York Crime Commission presented figures showing racketeering is bleeding America about twelve to eighteen billion dollars a year, or ninety-six dollars to one hundred and forty-four dollars per capita.

The criminal sensation of 1930 in America was Jack or "Legs" Diamond. That autumn there was bloody revolution in all South America, civil war in Brazil, dictators were collapsing and springing up, republicanism broke out in Spain, Hitler announced at a trial of Reichswehr officers that he would tear up the Versailles Treaty the day he took over the government, a new oil conspiracy was discovered, a new famine in Russia, a new victory by Stalin, a new menace to America by soviet dumping. In Cuba, an editor was killed for his political views. The Fall case was again delayed, there were anti-Semitic riots in Berlin, and new scandals in prohibition enforcement in twenty cities in America. But a Follies beauty, with red hair and a glorifiable figure, a child in Boston, a Broadway celebrity in 1924, known as "Marion Roberts", swept all these events into oblivion merely because she was the girl friend of Mr. Jack Diamond. Mr. Diamond had been shot.

Shortly afterwards, about mid-October, there was a plot to assassinate Dictator Pilsudski, to which he replied, with Mussolinian grandeur, "They may try but they will never succeed"; the American Federation of Labor shelved the five-hour-day proposal; the German Reichsbank was forced to sell its foreign exchange and raise its discount rate to save the mark; New York bankers planned to raise one hundred and fifty thousand a week for men in the bread line; Mr. Hoover sent a welcome to the Lutherans, which Father Burke called unfair to the Catholics; the Pope granted a dispensation to King Boris on the written promise that all his children without exception would be brought up in the Catholic faith, that is, that the Bulgarian dynasty would be Catholic in the future, and the Fascist Cabinet announced it would take over national censorship. All this was as nothing to the relapse which Mr. "Legs" Diamond suffered.

This gangster's record tells the story of bootlegging, dope-peddling, racketeering, crime, and the failure to punish crime in America in the prohibition decade. From 1914, when he was seventeen years old, Jack Diamond was arrested twenty-three times for larceny, burglary, assault, homicide, and only twice had he served time.

"Either Diamond is an innocent man," editors said, "often wrongly arrested on trumped-up charges, or he is a super-criminal, too powerful to punish. What is the truth about the strange and suggestive record of adventure with the police and in the courts?" The editors were not answered. Diamond was killed by opposition gangsters in 1931.

On March 1, 1932, occurred a crime which brought public opinion, already enraged by the Al Capone and Legs Diamond cases, to the breaking point. Kidnapers, between 8.30 and 9.15 that evening entered a house in Hopewell, New Jersey, using a ladder to the nursery, which was directly above the room in which Mrs. Lindbergh was sitting. They abducted the Lindbergh baby, Charles, Jr., and disappeared, leaving behind them the ladder, footprints, a chisel and a note.

If the criminal underworld were highly organized, and if it had wanted to declare war on the rest of the American people, it could not have begun in a more sensational way. The Lindbergh baby kidnaping and the subsequent discovery that the child had been murdered shortly afterward was considered "a challenge to our civilization", "a challenge to law and order in America", "an indictment of easy tolerance of corruption in public life"; "we have the alternative, — destroying the criminal system or being destroyed by it." The crime was attributed to the "jazzed-up hypocritical age in which we live, an age that pays racketeers for protection, that elects crooks to office, that outlaws bootleggers but buys their goods at exorbitant prices."

While five thousand Federal operatives by order of the President and the police throughout America continued their search, a Negro named William Allen, driving a truck on the Princeton-Hopewell road, and his white companion, Orville Wilson, whom he summoned, found the body of the murdered child on May 11, in the underbrush about seventy-five feet away. The sympathy of the whole world was sent to the Lindberghs. President Hoover ordered the Federal authorities to continue their war on crime, "to make the kidnaping and murder of the Lindbergh baby a live and never-to-be-forgotten case, never to be relaxed until the criminals are implacably brought to justice." The country was determined to win in its war on crime. Typical was the attitude of the New York *Daily News* editorial which said, "Christ died, according to the Bible, to atone for the sins of the world. . . . Is it possible that this little boy is destined to play some such rôle in the history of the United States? . . . If that comes to pass, this child will not have been taken in vain."

The country was almost unanimous in the view that crime, having grown greatly with prohibition, would retreat under the blessings of a 3.2 alcoholic interpretation of the Volstead Act. The Finnish experiment, which showed bootlegging successful when hard liquor alone was barred, was not heeded. Beer and light wines meant the end of liquor racketeering and its attending crime, in the popular mind.

Paraphrasing Billy Sunday's 1919 prediction for prohibition, "the rain of tears will be over", liquor optimists believed the reign of crime would end in the Nineteen Thirties.

## Interlude 1932

Crisis notes: Samuel Insull stepped out of his office — "Here I go after fifty years of work, a man without a job." He went to Athens but not to jail. In 1929 there were 513 million-dollar incomes; in 1930, 150; in 1931, 73. Incomes reported in 1931: thirteen billion dollars, or half that of 1928.

Fifty thousand of Japan's seventy thousand Buddhist temples feel agricultural crisis. Many close, others put inferior clergy to work on temple fields.

Repeatedly Paul Doumer, thirteenth President of France, joked about thirteen, his lucky number. He was the kindliest, sweetest old gentleman in France. When an assassin shot him, he exclaimed, "Oh, la, la," and "Is it possible."

"Kill me. Kill me," cried the assassin, "I am Paul Gorgulof, president of the National Fascist Party of Russia. Europe and America are favoring Bolshevism, so I decided to assassinate the President of France to cause France to declare war on the Bolsheviki. I am a follower of Hitler and Mussolini. I have no accomplices." (The Fascist ambassador protested the confession of the murderer!) The assassin of President Carnot had been an Italian. Xenophobia broke out in France. Anti-Americanism revived with debt talk. The Boulevards laughed sneeringly over the story:

A passenger liner, in the Mediterranean, ran into a school of sharks. A Frenchman bet an American five hundred dollars he could go swimming among the sharks for an hour, return safe and unscarred. The bet was made. The Frenchman put on his bathing suit, dived, swam an hour, came back. The American paid the bet. "But," he said, "I'll gladly pay another five hundred dollars if you will tell me how you did it." The Frenchman replied, "Just as I was about to dive, I chalked on my bathing suit 'America won the war', and even the sharks couldn't swallow that."

Advertisement in a Chicago newspaper:

BULLET HOLES REWOVEN PERFECTLY
in damaged clothes — low price

"More Washington Merry-Go-Round." More Washington correspondents fired.

The Federal Council of Churches was called the greatest menace to the Reserve Officers Training Camp by its executive secretary, Lieutenant Colonel Orvel Johnson. The *Reformed Church Messenger* editorialized: "Smash the R.O.T.C., it is insidiously encouraging the abominable spirit of militarism. . . . Does the commander exhibit the horrible aspects of actual war. . . . Does he show them the mangled bodies of the unfortunates who have become cannon fodder." — "Only those pictures which show the pleasant features of war can be released," ruled Major General Irving J. Carr of the United States Signal Corps. A nice pleasant war was fought by all. ("So far as America is concerned, there are no dead in this war.")

Eighteen years after the battle, a German court sentenced August Jaeger for desertion and revealing Ludendorff's gas attack to the French. General Gallieni's memoirs revealed colossal stupidity of military chiefs. General Castelnau disobeyed orders and saved Nancy in 1914; General Sarrail disobeyed orders and saved Verdun; Gallieni disobeyed orders and, taking the offensive, saved Paris. "These were actions independent of the will of the commander in chief."

William Faulkner's "Sanctuary" justifies Hal Smith's five-year plan in putting over new great American author. Faulkner called head of the "cult of cruelty." The first "Godless five-year-plan" announced by the league of young atheists of Moscow.

In *L'Esprit Français,* Shaw urged the extermination of all patriots as the best means of establishing world peace, because "patriotism is a pernicious, psychopathic form of idiocy."

Mussolini told the Italian Medical Congress to stop prescribing diets for Italian women because when Italians reduce they stop having babies.

Prussian dictator Bracht prohibited nudism ("shameless exhibitions of indecency") and beauty contests ("a sign of moral decadence") and ordered a triangular enforcement (*zwickel*) of every bathing-suit crotch in the empire.

Prince George of England favored book censorship — "many books should have been operated upon for gangrene at a point approximately two thirds way through."

The American College of Surgeons decided that cancer was curable. Henrik Willem Van Loon defined happiness: "Any person, any living creature, is happy whose circumstances allow him to play the rôle which best satisfies him in his own eyes." The *New Yorker* discovered among the doings of 1932:

Nevada, bill, legislature, limits persons to three divorces in one lifetime.

Brickville, Ontario, W.C.T.U. wants "fruit cocktail" changed to fruit appetizer.

Professor Lyman of Chicago wanted Poe eliminated because irreligious and used narcotics.

West Frankfort, Illinois, city council passed law, declaring home dances without city permits are a crime.

Baltimore man arrested selling Bibles on *Sunday*.

In 1932, the first *Literary Digest* poll favored President Hoover, the later ones Governor Roosevelt; the last gave him forty-one States.

Several thousand war veterans marched into Washington and camped at Anacostia. The B.E.F. — Bonus Expeditionary Force. Loud cries of "Reds" from the Republicans, who saw embarrassment. Eventually the troops were called out to fight the former troops. The Battle of Anacostia.

Governor Roosevelt wins the presidential nomination.

Democratic landslide carries forty-five States.

Headlines: Roosevelt will liquidate the war. — Roosevelt expected to free Mooney. — Roosevelt plans great economic reconstruction program. — Colonel House, Wilson's adviser, discusses Roosevelt policies. — William Bullitt, who went to Russia for Wilson, interviewing statesmen in Europe. — Roosevelt expected to continue Wilson's leadership of American liberalism. — Europe turns to Roosevelt in 1932 as it turned to Wilson in 1918. . . .

## CHAPTER EIGHTEEN

### LONG ARMISTICE

War is only a certain policy carried out with other weapons.

— CLAUSEWITZ

"There is little use of renouncing war as an instrument of national policy if economic weapons are substituted for those laid down by the military and naval forces of the nations."

— NICHOLAS MURRAY BUTLER

How far and over what road had the world traveled since that day in December, 1918, when the French Foreign Minister in the Chamber of Deputies, after announcing his peace terms, heard the shout, "The war is beginning anew", and the day in December, 1932, when Colonel House wrote that the aim of the new Roosevelt administration would be "to liquidate the war and liquidate it finally!"

It had traveled the road of war — war with other weapons. It had at least proved that the treaty was only a prolongation of an armistice, — an armistice now in its fifteenth year. It had brought about its own economic collapse through its refusal to solve its problems in an international coöperative way. And finally, in February, 1933, it had to listen to the Japanese delegate to the League of Nations, Yosuko Matsuoka, threaten a second world war if the nations attempted to enforce any sanctions against Japan's plan for Prussianizing the Far East.

The economic war begun Armistice Day had resulted in defeat for every one. The reparations war against Germany had resulted in defeat for every one. The armament race had drained the budgets of the world and helped on the economic debacle. The causes for war written into the Treaty of Versailles remained unchanged in the fifteen years of armistice. The situation in Europe summed up by an Allied general (Fuller, of Britain) sounds hopelessly true. "The hegemony established by France," he concludes, "is intolerable. The pre-war diplomats were *escrocs* . . . those of to-day are bandits. They speak without ceasing of peace but do nothing to permit its establishment. The present Austria is an anomaly. The Polish frontiers cannot be maintained. The Corridor is a veritable anachronism. The Baltic States cannot continue to live. The situation in Hungary is a crying injustice. The vanquished nations are disarmed; the conquerors increase their armament each year. These are the results of the French panic. . . . War itself would be preferable to the present situation."

Against the resumption of armed conflict, the League of Nations, after five years of preparation, adopted at the close of the first part of the Disarmament Conference, July 23, 1932, the Benes Plan for a substantial reduction of world armament to include naval, air and land arms. Airplane attacks against civilians were forbidden, bacteriological and chemical warfare were forbidden, the reduction of national defense budgets was recommended and an armament truce extended four months! "Wars will be able to continue, but they will be humanized." That was the progress made.

It had been written in Versailles that the world was to follow Germany in disarming but all nations had forgotten that clause. "The immense land armaments of France," Lloyd George mourned in 1932, "are a glaring and arrogant breach of the undertakings."

Yet France also had a case to present to the court of world opinion. In 1870 she had realized she would never regain her lost provinces without outside aid. She signed treaties, indulged in foreign friendships, plotted with Russia. Nineteen Eighteen taught her she would never retain her gains without outside aid. She lost America, then Britain, then Italy. She was forced to join with Poland, Yugoslavia, Rumania and other minor countries. Her one program became Security. But no great nation was willing to countersign it, surely not faraway America. Economic destruction of Germany therefore became the implement of the policy of security.

The League of Nations did not make up for the Anglo-American failure to guarantee France. But the League could be made into a weapon. So France, after deriding it, accepted it and sought to dominate it. She built up the French hegemony of the Continent, defeating all diplomatic and financial efforts of England and other nations, sabotaging the peace and disarmament conference when need be, and laughing realistically at the Utopian demand of her public enemy Number 2, Russia, that the nations of Europe cease talking disarmament and actually disarm.

The only great step towards peace was the destruction of the reparations war against Germany — at a time when the imminent German national bankruptcy threatened to bring Bolshevism to the Rhine and to the threshold of France. Like the Versailles Treaty, the end of reparations was acknowledged in the lengthening shadow of the Red Kremlin. The Lausanne conference of July 9, 1932, fixed the total amount due at seven hundred and fourteen million dollars — Germany was ordered to pay just one cent on the original dollar the victor nations had asked. Reparations history, according to the figures of Lloyd George, began with the Boulogne conference, June 20, 1920, where the total suggested was two hundred and sixty-nine billion gold marks, or from three billions a year in 1921 to seven billions in the years 1931 to 1963.

Paris conference, January 29, 1921. Total, two hundred and twenty-six billion gold marks.

German offer to President Harding, April 24, 1921, two hundred billion gold marks.

Dawes Plan, April 11, 1924, one billion gold marks in 1924, increasing to two and a half billions in 1928.

Young Plan, June 7, 1929, sixty-year payments scaled to a maximum of about two billions a year.

Lausanne, the original sixty-four billion dollars down to seven hundred and fourteen million dollars.

"We have reached, I believe, the best conclusion that could be reached for world peace," exclaimed Premier MacDonald, while the German chancellor chafed because the "war guilt lie" was not erased from the Versailles Treaty.

There was no let-up in the world tariff war. The first attack was made by the greatest of free-trade nations, Britain, in January, 1919, while the peacemakers were convening in Paris. Drastic import regulations, which had been enforced during the world conflict, were prolonged for the purpose of giving English manufacturers a breathing space in which to place their plants on a peace basis and recapture some of the world trade lost to America.

Soon all European nations began building up medieval walls against foreign trade; their frontiers took the place of ancient stones and towers and moats, keeping out not only their defeated enemy but their political allies. In 1927, France announced a new tariff, making American importation almost prohibitive. It was called "the opening gun of an economic war, Europe *versus* America." Duties were four to six times those previously existing. Under the Fordney-McCumber Tariff, the United States could retaliate by presidential decree, raising duties on French goods fifty per cent. At that time the balance of trade was heavily in our favor. European nations also began forming cartels and when M. Briand announced his United States of Europe plan in 1929 it too was taken as an economic measure against us. M. Herriot declared Europe must present a united front to the increasing economic menace of America.

Thus the whole world after the war adopted the policy of economic nationalism. Few foresaw that it might mean the end of all international trade in a not too distant future. To prevent this and incidentally make Russia's peace with the world, M. Litvinoff at Geneva in 1931, after speaking of the possibility of the co-existence of the two systems, Capitalism and Communism, uttered a thought that would have shocked the die-hard Leninists in Russia and other countries. He proposed an *economic non-aggression pact* and moved for immediate signature. Tewfik Rushdi Bey seconded. Mr. Curtius of Germany had to consult his government. M. Briand admitted that every one present was "in sympathy with M. Litvinoff's proposal", but the matter had to be studied, and so it was shelved.

In 1932, the British anti-dumping act, officially the "Abnormal Importation (customs duties) Act" having been rushed through the House of Lords, the Board of Trade the same night issued a long list of articles upon which a fifty per cent. duty was established. Typewriters, silk stockings, safety razors, vacuum cleaners and other items specified made American exporters appear particularly hit.

The next day the Treasury Department began preparing a list for President Hoover which would increase tariffs on British goods. The British heard of this and the conservatives insisted their fifty per cent. list be extended. Beaverbrook contended: "It is reported that the United States will impose duty for duty against the new British list. But how can they do that? For every five shillings' worth of goods we sell in America they sell us nearly one pound sterling's worth here. If such a course is embarked upon, we have nothing to lose, whereas America will lose a great deal."

The Germans, hard hit by the cheap textile, clothing, tool, and household article list of British tariff, found they had no means for reprisals under existing treaties. Their export trade with Britain immediately fell off.

The Hearst Press in 1932 started a Buy American movement, hoisting the battle flag "Protect American Industry", and found it had struck at the psychologically right moment. France having defaulted and Britain paid her installment with a bang which said, this is the last you'll ever get, the temper of newspaper readers was easily aroused. Patriotism and nationalism were commercialized.

Senator Kenneth McKeller of Tennessee offered a tourist boycott bill which would keep Americans out of France or other defaulting countries by making visa fees prohibitive. Soon the newspapers of America began printing hundreds of letters amply proving "*vox populi*" and "*pro bono publico*" were being won to the boycott game.

France in 1931 and 1932 passed about forty quota restrictions, most of which crippled American imports. Some of these decrees were purely retaliatory. For instance, movies. Bad as Hollywood products are, they are preferred by Frenchmen to most of the films made in France. The action of the French Government therefore was against the interests and wishes of the exhibitors, importers and audiences. Again, in setting the tonnage for radio machinery importation, the French Government permitted the Dutch to send in five times and the enemy Germans three times the amount allotted to American manufacturers. Every week the American Club in Paris and the American Chamber of Commerce would hold meetings or luncheons and pledge undying Franco-American friendship (for publication in the newspapers), while they raged over the tariff war which France seemed to be winning.

"A country which reaches a system of quotas does not denounce treaties, it destroys them," said Silas Strawn, President of the United States Chamber of Commerce, in March, 1932, summing up America's objections to the new war.

In June, 1932, the French and Belgian governments signed a commercial convention, effective in August, which further endangered twenty million dollars' worth of American trade. These nations having engaged in a tariff war which had hurt both extensively, realized the danger, quit fighting and combined against the rest of the world. They abolished the import business turnover tax of two to six per cent., which, however, they maintained against other countries. The semi-official organ of the French government, *Le Temps,* clearly stated the national viewpoint: "While fearing some future war the people are unaware that war is being fought at this very moment. It is an economic and monetary war whereby the States, without resorting to machine guns or submarines, seek, at the time that they pretend to defend themselves, to strike at one another's basic resources, at their vital forces. It is a war of tariffs, of contingents and regulations of all sorts; this really means a war of the unemployed of one nation against the unemployed of other nations. . . . For to-day — and this will be all the more clearly seen day by day — the only way of disarming a nation is to ruin it. When will there be statesmen who will understand and who will make others understand that an economic war, like a real war, in our civilized state, definitely weakens the victors as well as the vanquished?"

Apparently President Roosevelt, besides being a free trade Democrat, was statesman enough to see the danger. He immediately called Senator Cordell Hull, who was to become his Secretary of State, for a discussion on reciprocal tariff agreements linked with the stabilization of currencies as the key to the war-debt problem.

In the midst of world disaster there was also realization that the scientific perfection of machinery produced a double result. In Russia it might increase employment, goods, clothing for the body, leisure for the soul — and guns for the next war. In Europe and America it might produce unemployment and unparalleled suffering.

Albert Einstein believed the fundamental reason for the crisis is the Machine, which has caused too rapid production without need of human working power, resulting in unemployment and overproduction, due to the inability to buy by the vast majority whose earning capacity has been deprived by the machine. He suggested community control of production and distribution and some method of keeping the workers' buying power up to a certain minimum.

Spengler believed that man might at some moment arise and destroy the present artificial life, which draws its sustenance from mechanical power, and "blot the machine from his memory and his environment, and create about himself a wholly new environment in which nothing of this devil's technique is left." The philosopher Keyserling mourned the end of the individual in America, believing the nation had become standardized, its manners, customs, intellectual interests, all reduced to dead uniformity. If mechanization is continued, men will become nothing but sterile workers like ants or bees. The fault is due to considering humanity as raw material instead of as individuals. Lenin's philosophy, Keyserling thought, was typical of a criminal mentality, willing to sacrifice two thirds of humanity, to ride rough-shod over an entire class, to attain an aim he held ideal. The solution, in the mechanical age, was the development of the soul and intelligence equally with technical perfection. "Otherwise life will become so colorless and boresome as to make existence not worth while."

To his 1932 pronunciamento, Ford added in 1933 the declaration that humanity was only in the ox-cart stage of the machine age, which, when perfected, will do away with "dirt, ugliness, confusion, noise and the disregard of human rights which are all about us to-day."

Caillaux, chairman of the French Finance Commission, believed that "Science has outpaced man, who is laboring in its wake, and the great, the vast question which is far more important than any other, is how to apportion the employment of technical appliances and technique itself to the needs, capacities and conditions of man's existence — problems the existence of which neither the founders of liberal economy nor even more modern economists could scarcely have suspected."

The practical, matter-of-fact solution offered by this financier

# KRIEGSAUSRÜSTUNGEN
## ALLER ART

**VICKERS - CARDEN - LOYD**
**PATROUILLE-KAMPFWAGEN**

Der weltberühmte Vickers-Carden-Loyd Panzerkraftwagen mit verstärktem Motorbetrieb und Panzerturm mit Richtfeld von 360°.

| Allgemeine Angaben: | | |
|---|---|---|
| | Bemannung ... ... ... ... | 2 Mann. |
| | Bewaffnung | Vickers-M.G., mit 3500 Patronen. |
| | Geschwindigkeit ... ... .. | 48 km Std. |
| | Steigung ... ... ... ... | 25° |
| | Drehkreis ... ... ... ... | 4 m. |
| | Höhe ... ... ... ... | 1,65 m. |
| | Breite ... ... ... ... | 1,75 m. |
| | Länge ... ... ... ... | 2,59 m. |
| | Gewicht ... ... ... | ca. 2,000 kg. |

**VICKERS-ARMSTRONGS LIMITED**
VICKERS HOUSE, BROADWAY, LONDON, S.W.1, ENGLAND

Verantwortlich für den redaktionellen Teil: Generalleutnant a. D. von Altrock, Berlin W 15, Fasanenstraße 60, Fernruf Oliva 978.
Verantwortlich für den Anzeigenteil: Hugo Hertel, Berlin-Schöneberg, Thorwaldsenstraße 11.
Druck von Ernst Siegfried Mittler und Sohn, Buchdruckerei G. m. b. H., Berlin SW 68, Kochstraße 68—71.

MUNITION MAKERS OF GREAT BRITAIN OFFER TO SELL TANKS TO GERMANY FOR THE NEXT WAR

From a German advertisement reproduced (without charge) in a French Newspaper

and politician was coöperation between employers, financiers and merchants in their own countries, then beyond their frontiers, "to adapt production to consumption, to coördinate their forces, to unite, to rationalize, if this barbarism is preferred, their technical appliances."

M. Paul Valery, now the leading intellectual of France, described ours as "The era of the completed world."

For several weeks Howard Scott's "Technocracy" attracted widespread attention.

The energy-survey report made in August, 1932, by several engineers and experts connected with Columbia University resulted at the end of the year in a boom for the new science and salvation of mankind. The new messiah, Mr. Scott, contended that the machine age had made such progress that should the 1929 conditions of world business miraculously reappear to-day, only twenty-five per cent. of labor would find employment, inasmuch as it could produce all that is necessary in America, and that unless there was a general reconstruction of society, there would be twenty-four million unemployed by 1935.

The discussion in America came to a climax in January, 1933, with a rift among the eight Columbia experts and the departure of Howard Scott from the sacred precincts of learning, and the great Technocracy sensation came to a sudden end.

Less sensational were the plans and panaceas offered the world by numerous persons of diverse qualities. Sir Arthur Salter, the eminent economist who had been general secretary of the reparations commission and later chief of the finance and economic section of the League, hoped the nations would "reflate" and raise prices rather than seek salvation through return to gold.

Stuart Chase in "A New Deal" rejected the road to violent revolution and business dictatorship but proposed progressive revision of the economic structure with the aid of collectivism. The villain was not private profit but wasteful, reckless irresponsible economic behavior. Gerard Swope, favoring "planned industry", proposed a minimum amount of employment each year for industrial workers at adequate compensation, unemployment insurance, equal contributions by employer and employees, controlled production.

The executive council of the American Federation of Labor drew up a program favoring beer, "the spark to lift us out of the depression as the automobile did in the hard times of 1921, a national conference on labor called by the President, the five-day working week, maintenance of wages, prohibition of child labor."

Paul Boncour, Premier of France for a few weeks in 1933, made an attempt to incorporate syndicalism into the State. Although he met with failure, the idea persists not only in France but elsewhere in Europe. The Fascist Infallible announced a five-point plan to save the world: the renunciation of reparations and cancellation of war debts, the suppression of restrictions on international trade, relief for the Danubian and Balkan States, revision of the peace treaties, renunciation of too frequent international conferences, which raise vain hopes and thus create pessimism. Einstein proposed a group of the twenty-five greatest minds "to function in the best interest of mankind . . . the most potent moral and idealistic force in the world." A. R. Orage, fearing that art, religion, culture, education, sociology, world peace, internationalism, the whole future of mankind, are at stake, proposed the solution "of creating and distributing purchasing-power *pari passu* with our expanding means of production." Money is the fundamental problem since science has settled every other. President Roosevelt's friend and adviser, Professor Tugwell of Columbia, drew up a seven-point program for drastic increase in income and inheritance taxes (but no sales tax of the Hoover kind), widespread public works program, reduction of interest rates on public utility charges, balanced budget as far as current expenditures are concerned, with repeal of the Eighteenth Amendment for revenue, restoration of balance between wholesale and retail prices, especially for agricultural products, which will be helped by the domestic allotment plan, and rationalizing international debts.

Shades of the early 1920's! Scarcely had 1930 dawned when an attempt to revive the long dead but never quite completely interred Red hysteria was made in many lands.

May Day, 1930, "Red labor day", the world over, was awaited for revolution. May Day came — and not a bomb was thrown, not a revolution was recorded anywhere. There were parades in Berlin, London and New York. Some shouts.

In 1931, the Fish Report, which ten years earlier would have been taken seriously, was received coldly. A rock-bound conservative paper like the New York *Evening Post,* for example, had referred to Fish as "our most muddle-headed statesman", but the report, instead of arousing national hysteria, found the representative himself saying, "I believe in capitalism as opposed to communism but capitalism shorn of its abuses and ugly greed to exploit labor and mankind for the almighty dollar. . . . Grave abuses have crept into our industrial capitalism, such as child labor and long hours. . . . If communism is on trial, so also is capitalism." This certainly did not sound like the Nineteen Thirties.

The Pope in an encyclical very carefully drew the lines between communism and socialism: "One section of socialism has degenerated into communism. Communism teaches and pursues a twofold aim: Merciless class warfare and complete abolition of private ownership. . . . We do not think it necessary to warn upright and faithful children of the Church against the impious and nefarious character of communism.

"Whether socialism be considered as a doctrine, or as a historical fact, or as a movement, if it really remain socialism, it cannot be brought into harmony with the dogmas of the Catholic Church."

A week earlier, the Pope had said: " 'Religious Socialism', 'Christian Socialism' are expressions implying a contradiction in terms. No one can be at the same time a sincere Catholic and a true socialist."

In Karachi, the Young Indian Redshirts marched against Saint Gandhi to accuse him of treason. Gandhi spoke:

"If you say I am doing harm to India you have a right to do so, but it is my duty to turn you to the path of affection and truth. I have no weapon against you except love. . . ."

The Redshirts wept and repented.

A group of American writers, notably Dreiser and Dos Passos, went to Harlan County, Kentucky, to investigate a strike; they were indicted for criminal syndicalism to overthrow the government.

The 1932 elections proved a great disappointment to all radical parties. The official thirteen million unemployed, the unofficial twenty-five million unemployed and the official or unofficial hundred and twenty million disgruntled, disillusioned and unhappy American people showed they were just enough disgruntled, disillusioned and unhappy to turn Mr. Hoover out of the White House, but not to turn either Communist Foster or Socialist Thomas into it. In fact, the *Literary Digest's* almost infallible straw vote had shown Thomas would get two million votes and he got less than one. The dreaded communist "landslide" did not eventuate.

But even before Mr. Roosevelt took office it was said he intended to recognize Russia for purely economic purposes. After France defaulted her debt payment without a break in diplomatic relations, the Bolshevik renunciation of the Tsarist loans could no longer remain the prime reason, as heretofore, for strained relations. It was now a matter of sentiment and moral force *versus* the almighty dollar. The American Federation of Labor, various Catholic and other patriotic societies immediately protested. Big business interests began pulling the Congressional strings too.

The United Veterans of the Republic called upon the Senate to investigate "quasi-religious pacifist, radical and communist organizations attacking each and every law of the United States dealing with the vital question of National Defense. . . . Among the organizations which should be investigated are the following in the order in which it is urged they be investigated: National Council for the Prevention of War, Federal Council of Churches of Christ, Women's International League for Peace and Freedom, American Civil Liberties Union, League of Industrial Democracy, National Student Forum, War Registers' League and Young Workers' League."

In February, 1933, the Honorable George H. Tinkham of Massachusetts began war on the peace societies because they have a dangerously debilitating and seditious influence on American citizens. He wanted the Carnegie Foundation of International Peace and the Rockefeller Foundation investigated as "the largest and most formidable promoters of disloyal, seditious movements against American independence and neutrality."

The swing to the Left, which had been noticeable among writers and intellectuals throughout the world for a hundred years, became noticeable in America in the 1930's. For the first two decades there had been merely sympathy or admiration or tolerance for the Europeans who had embraced socialism and communism. Anatole France was thought to be doddering, Bernard Shaw just Shavian, Unamuno just a Spanish republican, Thomas Mann simply a pacifist.

The Sacco-Vanzetti case, however, brought a new group of radical writers to the fore, and the Kentucky miners' strike found Waldo Frank, Edmund Wilson, Malcolm Cowley, Mary Heaton Vorse, Harold Hicherson, Charles Walker and Doctor Elsie Reed Mitchell not only writing but taking action. Theodore Dreiser, the mountainous doyen of American letters, had come out of Russia saying he was too much of an individualist to embrace communism, but in 1932 he was claimed as the largest victory that party won from the intelligentsia. In 1932 "to protest against the chaos, the appalling wastefulness and the indescribable misery inherent in the present economic system", a call was sent to educators, writers, engineers, social workers, artists, architects and intellectuals in general, to support the communist presidential candidate. It was signed, alphabetically, by the following:

Sherwood Anderson, Newton Arvin, Emjo Basshe, Slater Brown, Erskine Caldwell, Robert Cantwell, Winifred L. Chapell, Lester Cohen, Louis Colman, Lewis Corey, Henry Cowell, Malcolm Cowley, Bruce Crawford, H. W. L. Dana, Adolph Dehn, Alfred Frueh, Miriam Allen De Ford, Howard N. Doughty, Jr., John Dos Passos, Theodore Dreiser, Waldo Frank, Murray Godwin, Horace Gregory, Louis Grundin, John Hermann, Granville Hicks, Sidney Hook, Sidney Howard, Langston Hughes, Orrick Johns, Matthew Josephson, Alfred Kreymborg, Louis Lozowick, Grace Lumpkin, Felix Morrow, Samuel Ornitz, James Rorty, Isidor Schneider, Edwin Seaver, Frederick L. Schuman, Norman Simpson, Lincoln Steffens, Charles R. Walker, Edmund Wilson, Ella May Winter, Robert Witaker.

The movement towards communism in America is notably different from its European corollary because it shows the liberals overleaping socialism and accepting Moscow as the radical haven, the ultimate in social ideology, the Vatican of infallible Marxism before which there was nothing but bourgeois hypocrisy and corruption, and beyond which there was nothing but a non-existent Heaven. The movement left behind such men as Villard of the *Nation*, Walter Lippmann, with his nineteenth-century theory of individual liberty, Max Eastman, one of the first radicals, now disciple of an exiled Trotsky, and many other liberal writers and critics who were apparently cursed with non-conformity.

The election of Roosevelt also brought promise that something would at last be done in the Mooney and Billings case. In the seventeen years which the two men spent in prison for the alleged bombing of a preparedness parade in San Francisco, there had been a growing feeling that justice had erred. The lives of the men had been saved by the intervention of President

Wilson in 1918; in 1919, newspaper investigations showed that the trial had been unfair and that the men were probably not guilty. The chief witness of the prosecution, Oxman, it was proved, had arrived in San Francisco after the explosion — although he swore he was there at the time — and a letter was found in which a friend was invited to come and earn a living giving false testimony.

In July, 1930, another murder witness, MacDonald, admitted he had lied and other witnesses admitted their testimony was perjured. The judge who sentenced Mooney and Billings admitted later the trial was "one of the dirtiest jobs ever put over." Nine of the ten surviving jurors who found the men guilty admitted they had changed their minds.

In 1931, the Wickersham Crime Commission report said of the judicial process in California: "Such a state of law is shocking to one's sense of justice."

It would seem that there was enough to go on for a revision in the case, but California refused to act. The explanation was given by Ernest Jerome Hopkins in his book "What Happened in the Mooney Case", published in 1932. Hopkins, a reporter of the San Francisco *Bulletin*, covered the trials in 1916 when the city was neurotic with hysteria. He at that time believed in the guilt of the accused. Now he had changed his view. The book is a record of perjured witnesses, corruption of the courts, conflicting evidence, suppression of testimony. The real issue, concludes Hopkins, is not Mooney but "easy corruptibility of government by economic interests, the gross perversion of law and justice which imprisonment for opinion implies. . . . Sixteen years of printed poison have convinced Californians that evidence or none, it is better to keep two radicals in prison than remove a nation-wide stimulus to radicalism. . . . 'We got the right men on the wrong evidence. . . . They may not be guilty of the bomb explosion but they belong where they are. . . . Any governor who pardons Mooney will be digging his own political grave' " — was the attitude of Californians.

Old Mrs. Mooney came to Albany to see Governor and President-elect Roosevelt, saying, "I wish you would do your utmost to help my boy who has been in prison, although innocent, for years. My boy is a good boy." Roosevelt replied, "I feel sure that because so many people feel he is innocent there must be some reason for believing in his innocence."

The six members of the International Workers of the World who are in jail for the riot in Centralia, Washington, in November, 1919, also hoped for presidential relief when the National Catholic Welfare Conference and the Federal Council of Churches issued their report on the case. Four paraders had been killed. Soldiers had stormed the I.W.W. hall and lynched one "Wobbly." Of the eleven tried for conspiracy to kill, six are serving terms of twenty-five to forty years. The report of the religious bodies shows that there was no conspiracy to kill, that no shots were fired on the paraders until the paraders had begun the battle by attacking the I.W.W. hall, that no crime was premeditated and therefore the sentence "seems very severe."

In 1933 it was also proved that the bombing of the cathedral of Sofia in 1925, in which one hundred and forty persons were killed and for which thousands were arrested, accused of rioting for Moscow, was the work of an individual who later committed suicide in a prison in Luxembourg.

In 1918, some fifteen million minority peoples were under Pan-German dictatorship; in 1933 of eighty million Germans, no less than fifteen million were under the rule of foreign nations.

In 1918, Lenin quoted Marx to the effect that a class war is inevitable, once a socialistic State becomes successful. In 1933, Stalin quoted Lenin to the effect a war between Communist Russia and its capitalist neighbors was inevitable.

1919 saw the Japanese defeating the treaty makers by threatening to quit the conference unless their spoils were legalized; 1933 they were defying the world on account of Manchuria.

1918 saw the Kaiser fleeing to Holland in fear and trembling;

*Underwood and Underwood*

PRESIDENT ROOSEVELT SIGNS THE BILL THAT MADE HIM THE BANK DICTATOR OF THE UNITED STATES, WITH SECRETARY OF THE TREASURY WOODIN LOOKING ON

1933 reported him packing his baggage for a return to emperorship.

1918 found the world not only fighting for peace but insisting on international disarmament as its best guaranty; 1932 heard the renewed demand of Germany for a larger army.

1919 found all the victor nations girding themselves for a great commercial recovery; 1933 found such stagnation in international trade — there had been a sixty per cent. decrease in four years due to economic nationalism and tariff barriers — that an official American observer on the preparatory committee of the 1933 world economic conference predicted that all international trade would cease by May, 1934.

1919 saw Clemenceau chopping off the political heads of generals who might want to ride into the Quai d'Orsay on horseback; in 1933 the Duc de Guise, pretender to the throne of France, issued a proclamation of monarchy to save the country from "the oppression of socialistic anarchy."

1919 saw the beginning of Fascism in Italy. Raids, riots, street fights, reprisals, burning and looting, the Fascists armed, the labor organizations and socialist clubs practically disarmed, finally victory by a private militia and a strong leader. 1933 found Fascism triumphant in Germany in the very same manner, with Hitler proclaimed dictator for four years.

In 1919 some twenty million were demobilized. 1933 found new standing armies of five million men (France with her reserves included had more than that number) — the largest known in times of "peace." Five billion dollars a year was the price of war preparations in 1931, 1932, 1933 (provisionally). "While millions are on the verge of starvation, growing restless and ugly," broadcast Senator Borah, "from eighty to eighty-five per cent. of all taxes extorted from the people go for war purposes. All this is another name for slow and inevitable suicide." His words were "magnificently and justly howled down" by the Fascist Jeunesses Patriotes at the Trocadero, Paris, peace congress.

1919 found all the world emerging from a great catastrophe

with a spirit of idealism it thought justified the slaughter of a generation. 1933 finds it hoping it will emerge from hunger and suffering, once more to enjoy radios and automobiles and the materialistic comforts of a scientific civilization.

1918 saw several hundred million men stirred by a vision of a noble world. In 1933, thirty million had their bread taken away and many times that number thought of nothing but jobs.

For fifteen years the stale phrase about making the world safe for democracy had been moldering in its grave with its creator — the reaction to the World War had been the inevitable and opposite one. Democracy appeared to be in a decline. Revolutions, it is true, had come out of the war and some people had been liberated, but almost always the victor nations plunged backward into tyranny. The movements of progress, individual liberty, public liberty, private emancipation, collectivism, international coöperation, Wells' Cosmopolitanism, the religious and political soap-box idea of the brotherhood of man, had been overwhelmed by nationalism, conservatism, super-patriotism, dictatorial egotism and the wild scramble for spoils, wheat fields, African and Asiatic mines, for naked races to exploit with calico sheets, for land and more land for surplus populations.

Was Fascism the way out? Or communism? Did the world need a Gandhi or a second Woodrow Wilson, or a second Lenin? It desperately needed some one with intelligence and power. Such a savior the great majority of Americans believed they had found in the new President. The nation seemed to enter into its second historical "era of good feeling." Sacred political alignments were forgotten in the rush to coöperate. Even Congressmen stopped hindering the intelligent executives.

The use of the word "dictator" for Roosevelt, declared Mark Sullivan, was utterly wrong: Congress existed, it still talked, it had conferred only temporary powers and could take them back. The President made the most of them. He reduced the budget a billion dollars by strong-arm methods, defying well-entrenched powerful groups such as the veterans and the government employees, cutting pensions about four hundred million dollars. April 19 he took America off the gold standard by dropping support of the dollar abroad.

Like Wilson, the new Democrat broke traditions. Like Wilson, he declared himself a liberal and surrounded himself with liberals. Harding's "noninvolvement in European affairs" which the provincial Coolidge and the internationalist Hoover had inherited, gave way to a new Wilsonian coöperation with the rest of the world. Isolated economic nationalism had helped ruin the world; Mr. Roosevelt, whose policy, termed "the new deal", had raised the greatest hopes of revival of national *morale* and prosperity, was facing the future with the eyes and mind of an enlightened international leader.

In many lands millions of persons who were afraid of bloody reactionary dictators and hesitant over radical revolution of the social system, were looking to Roosevelt, as they once looked to Wilson, for a second "charter for the liberation of mankind." They hoped he would lead not only America but Europe out of economic debacle into a brave new world — free from economic fear. The one American cold rhetorical messiah had met historically magnificent tragedy and defeat. For a moment he had won "the heart of the world", about which he spoke so well and knew so little. Would Roosevelt succeed where Wilson failed?

In 1933, as in 1918, the world is in a state of perilous confusion. It is still in a state of armistice. It still needs peace. It desperately needs leadership. Apparently it is ready for neither Utopian radicalism or medieval reactionaryism. If ever a man had the opportunity to lead a world as well as a nation, that man is Franklin Delano Roosevelt.

## PRELUDE 1933

February 6: Reign of terror in Cuba; 150 students executed.
Java mutineers seize warship.
Matsuoka sees second world war if League acts.
Hitlerites kill 4, wound 24 communists.
American arrested for pirating Paris fashions.

After a year of religious revival, a human sacrifice was made in Tomahawk, Martin County, Kentucky, the victim, Mrs. Lucinda Mills, being killed by her son after fasting and sacrificial rites.

British scientists predicting sun will live only fifteen trillion years; Sir Arthur Eddington predicting that in the course of billions of years the universe is doomed to destruction; Professor Tolman of California Tech predicting the world will last forever because gravitation winds it up every day radiation runs it down. "On my death bed," Shaw contributed to a Swedish symposium, "my thoughts would not be different from other men's. I believe I have not succeeded, but the world believes I have." Irish humor.

Rabid republicans demand Irishman replace Englishman as official hangman. Field Marshal Badoglio informed Mussolini that twenty years of slaughtering the natives of Libya had produced peace on that earth.

Ulysses W. Lyttlemore protested educational films depicting the propagation and growth of plants "in far too intimate detail."

Hollywood was described by Vicki Baum: a terrible battlefield in the field of Paradise; Garbo — what melancholy and solitude in her look, what chagrin, what suffering, what sadness;

Dietrich, how could she be happy amidst scandal which never ceased seething about her. Heart-broken. In Berlin she danced. Pola Negri told me in Hollywood a pestilential atmosphere poisons the town and people, it destroys everything; Ann Harding said she was happy only when she escaped the town in her airplane. And the jobless, the vanquished, the desperate? And the thousands of queens of beauty lured there by foolish hopes, find beauty worth less than potatoes.

World unemployment figures: United States thirteen million; Germany seven million; Britain two and three quarters million; Italy two million; . . . France two hundred and sixty-two thousand. World total: thirty-eight million.

"Hollywood needs no apology for the character of entertainment produced," dictated Tsar Hays. Thanks to the movies, two new words, "Scram" and "Screwy", were added to the popular vocabulary.

The dictator of Prussia, Bracht, ordered all the gilded youth who had been wearing women's clothes as gorgeous as the violets and pansies of the wide-open spaces to return to pants and act accordingly. Simultaneously were published letters from Hitler's boy friend Captain Ernst Roehm, chief of staff of the Brown Shirt Army and one of the leaders of the Youth Movement, complaining he had winked daily at gentlemen on the streets of La Paz but had been misunderstood.

Rumania's Fascisti, the Iron Guard, quarreled bitterly over the religion of the few bones which constitute the Unknown Soldier. The infallible Rumanian Patriarch settled the controversy by declaring the unknown a Rumanian Orthodox.

Crisis clothes for women appeared in Paris. Crisis fails to hit Sing Sing where prison revenue increased fifty thousand dollars over 1931. Weeping over tales of unemployment in America, the near-naked black Gold Coast congregation collected forty dollars for Reverend Underhill's relief fund. "Nobody Starves," by Catherine Brody hailed as first American proletarian novel. V. F. Calverton published "The Liberation of American Literature." "I want to cry aloud my sympathy with the U.R.S.S.," writes M. Gide in the *Nouvelle Revue Française,* "and I hope that my cry is heard and has some influence. I should like to live long enough to see the success of that enormous effort. I want it to succeed with all my soul and should like to contribute toward it. I want to see what can come of a State without religion and a society without barriers. Religion and the family are the two worst enemies of Progress."

Trotsky laid the suicide of his daughter, Frau Wolkov of Berlin, on Dictator Stalin, who had refused her son permission to come to Germany and the mother permission to come to Moscow. . . . "The persecution of my daughter was entirely devoid of political purpose . . . Stalin had forced death upon her."

1933: sixty-seven thousand homeless children wander streets of New York. (1923, one hundred thousand children homeless in Moscow.)

The year 1932 goes down in history as the worst since 1893, according to United States Census bureau. The villages Monte San Giacomo and Sassano refuse to pay taxes; Mussolini sends Fascist militia to collect. Stalin orders soldiers to force *kulaki* to pay grain tax. American customs suppress soviet posters addressed to Thomas Lamont by son Corliss Lamont, who went communist.

New York Irish protest Irish Players.

"We are entertaining a New Era. . . . We are emerging from the darkness of the Jungle Generation, the Jazz Age, sex and noise, destructive tendencies." So James Stephens, of "Crock of Gold" fame, returning from America. Joyce and Proust "belong to the Jazz Age . . . they wrote prose epics which summed up social orders that have disappeared."

Philosophy Professor Edman looked fifty years ahead, prophesying from present hypothesis: increasing tendency towards socialization in industry, education and personal relations. . . . "I cannot share that belief in an imminent and absolute communism now so popular among intellectuals in this country. . . . The subtle and specific alchemy of love and hate will operate as hitherto. . . . Along with economic ambition I suspect economic fear will have been removed.

"The neurosis and breakdown born of sexual maladjustment will be greatly reduced, partly because of the passing of now persisting tabus and the breakdown of the legally tight family relationships of the present. That there will be some sexual maladjustment and always a certain proportion of sexual abnormality, I have no question. But such sexual maladjustment and perversion as are due to flight, to fear, to the desire for hysterical release from monotony, strain, or insecurity in economic life, will be no longer widely current."

In the fifteen years since the signing of the Armistice, investigation showed great progress has been made in the war on illiteracy in Russia, Turkey and other countries, and the mentality of the world of adults, proved in wartime to be 47.3% — about equal to that of children of twelve — has also declined a slight fraction. Einstein announced he had "absolute information" half the armies of the world would revolt if a new war is declared in 1933. Germany celebrated Hitler's forty-fourth birthday, April 20, by parading to the Nazi song, "When Blood Flows From Our Knives." France cried "Fraud!" when Roosevelt led America gently off the gold standard. Mr. Shaw, at the Metropolitan Opera House, New York, smiled at Thomas Lamont and said, "The capitalist system has broken down." Mr. Lamont smiled back. Morgan endorsed Roosevelt. Hitlerites got a cold reception in the Vatican. The Fascist deficit increased. The Japanese, after invading Jehol, entered China proper. On all fronts, military, economic, spiritual, there was not a day of peace. The panorama changed; the world moved on, — no one could predict whither.

THE END

# INDEX